CLEANING UP

BARRY MINKOW

NELSON CURRENT

A Division of Thomas Nelson, Inc.

Published in Nashville, Tennessee, by Nelson Current, a subsidiary of Thomas Nelson, Inc.

Nelson Current books may be purchased in bulk for educational, business, fundraising, or sales promotional use. For information, please email SpecialMarkets@ThomasNelson.com.

Library of Congress Cataloging-in-Publication Data

Minkow, Barry.
  Cleaning up : one man's redemptive journey through the seductive world of corporate crime / Barry Minkow.
    p. cm.
  ISBN 1-59555-004-6
  1. Minkow, Barry. 2. Businessmen—United States—Biography. 3. Swindlers and swindling—United States—Biography. 4. Christian converts—United States—Biography. 5. Fraud—United States. I. Title.
  HC102.5.M5A3 2005
  364.16'3'092—dc22

2004025940

Printed in the United States of America

05 06 07 08 09 QW 6 5 4 3

CONTENTS

To Lisa,
my loving wife and best friend who always chose to focus on
my potential rather than my past.

And to Peanut, whose influence in my life
lives on even after he died.

SPECIAL THANKS: First, I would like to thank my two editors, Joel Miller and Erin Hattenberg, who tirelessly labored over not only the contents of this book but having to work with the likes of me! Their work and labor of love should not be overlooked. I would also like to thank my agent Joni Evans from the William Morris Agency. If there is a better agent out there and a more loving and encouraging one, I never met him/her. And finally to Ted Squires at Thomas Nelson, who has the dubious honor of being the first non family member to believe that in 1995, when I was released from prison, I really had changed. In prison, we have a saying for people like Ted: "You're the man . . ."

PROLOGUE

21 Years Old + 25 Year Sentence + 26 Million in Restitution =
1 Billion in Fraud Findings

If failure were a pair of shoes, mine would be dingy gray athletic sneakers with zero traction. My name is Barry Minkow, and I'm intimately familiar with failure. By the time I was *twenty-one* I was the renowned wiz kid of Wall Street. That same year I traded a sprawling Southern California mansion for a tiny piece of real estate on the cellblock.

I committed a white-collar crime that ultimately earned me a *twenty-five* year prison sentence handed down by Judge Dickran Tevrizian in federal court. He also ordered me to repay *twenty-six* million dollars in victim restitution. These judgments were dealt at the request of my prosecutor, James Asperger, who was at the time chief of the Major Frauds Division of the United States Attorney's Office in Los Angeles. He actually authored the restitution order that the judge signed. I refer to the obstacles that I had to overcome as the *21, 25, and 26 problem*. I never want you to forget those three numbers because it is highly probable your current situation is not nearly as bad as mine was!

I have one objective with this autobiography: encouragement. I would like to inspire anyone who has failed to realize they can overcome failure. *Any* failure. It may sound trite, maybe even too simplistic, but it's true. If God had enough grace to deliver me from the 21, 25, and 26 scenario, He can and will do the same for you.

Your failure does not necessarily have to be criminal in nature, although that is certainly my story. (Please understand I am not equating crimes with other less victim-impacting errors.) However, failing at anything seems to elicit similar emotions of devastation, rejection, and grief. Only those of us who have experienced failure know how debilitating these emotions can be.

Admittedly the journey to failure recovery is difficult and riddled with challenges. You will likely experience disappointment and temptation to return to habits that caused you to fail in the first place. My story definitely includes those battles. But I believe my story can provide one thing that all of us require: hope, joyous hope. Failure is temporary, and God's forgiveness is permanent. If I can overcome the 21, 25, and 26 problem, so can you.

Still have doubts? Consider the following facts. The judge who sentenced me to that twenty-five-year prison sentence wrote a letter to the parole board seven years and four months into my sentence demanding my release. Years later on August 2, 2002, that same judge dismissed my twenty-six-million-dollar restitution order in federal court and released me from probation three and a half years early. Why would a federal judge, who at one time said on the record that I had "no conscience," do such a thing? Because the prosecutor who demanded those harsh penalties, James Asperger, wrote a three-page letter to Judge Tevrizian asking him to do so.

Now the same prosecutor who asked Judge Tevrizian to sentence me to twenty-five years and twenty-six million in restitution asks me regularly to speak to the summer interns at his law firm. Of course I am no longer twenty-one years old, but neither do I have a twenty-five-year prison sentence hanging over my head, or a twenty-six-million-dollar restitution order to pay.

There is one more part of my story that you need to know about. You can still call me a fraud . . . investigator, that is. I remember the techniques I used to deceive people and now apply them to fraud detection. In the process I have uncovered over one billion dollars in fraud, and I am not finished. That is why *21 plus 25 plus 26 equals one billion*!

1 ONE AND DONE

Eight hundred million dollars is a lot of money. And twenty years is a long time. There is *no way* that this deal is a Ponzi scheme," Fred Kirshner challenged as he sat across from me sipping his steaming coffee. "No mutual fund on Wall Street has outperformed the Financial Advisory Consultant Funds' income and growth funds. I know one investor who has one hundred million dollars in the fund and has been in it for fifteen years." He paused and raised one eyebrow. "And Mr. James P. Lewis, the manager of the fund, is a business genius!" he declared. I stared back without blinking.

It was far from an idyllic Orange County Saturday afternoon. I glanced out the window of Starbucks at the smoky skies, black from the ash of fires blazing across Southern California. I quickly checked my watch: 1:00 p.m. I had to leave no later than 2:30 if I wanted to be back to the church in San Diego in time to preach the 5:15 p.m. service. The dual life of pastor and fraud investigator may seem ill matched—and it's certainly no easy task attempting to tend a flock of parishioners while warning a nation of un-witting investors.

I flipped through the pages of the prospectus and listened with one ear to Kirshner while nodding periodically. My mind raced through several scenarios until my eyes rested on graphs and charts comparing growth rates, which averaged 38.8% annual returns. I hit a mental speed bump.

So the guy is a good money manager, I thought. *These type of consistent high returns may be unlikely but not impossible.* I knew that fraud is never found on the back-end, the "returns" offered to the investor. Fraud is found in the front-end, by how the person offering the high returns claims to be earning them.

Accountants and other professionals call this "sources and uses of cash." I call it the "if-then" test. *If* this mutual fund claims to be earning 38.8% annual returns for twenty years, *then* what can I find to independently prove that profitability? This fund's longevity worked in its logistical favor. To survive for twenty years, it was highly unlikely there was anything wrong, or it would have already shown up.

"How many people are invested in the Financial Advisory Consultant Funds?" I inquired.

"About five thousand people across the country."

"And how much do you currently have invested in this fund?"

"Between me and my father we have about two hundred fifty thousand dollars."

"What kind of due diligence did you and your father perform before you invested the first two hundred fifty thousand dollars?" I posed. It was like putting a quarter in the jukebox and hitting play.

"We called ten people who had been in the Financial Advisory Consultant Fund five or more years to make sure they had received their 38.8% returns," he proudly exclaimed. Kirshner was sharp and extremely likeable. He was a manicured mortgage broker and not naïve to the world of finance. He and his father were looking to more than double their two-hundred-fifty-thousand-dollar investment in the fund. But before they did, they wanted me to check it out and make sure it was legit.

"This is our life savings, Barry. We really need to know and be sure before we bump up our investment," Kirshner said. We both paused for a moment of agreeable silence.

His comment reminded me of why I first became involved with the Fraud Discovery Institute. Twenty years earlier people invested in my company and lost their life savings because I was a crook. In a strange way I felt that I owed Kirshner, and others like him. However, I disliked being put in the position of the last fence between him and his father, and their life savings.

After all, if I gave the deal a green light and ended up being wrong, they lost all of their money and I would be worse than a criminal. My slogan for that is "One and Done." As a fraud expert you can be wrong *one* time. Your reputation is damaged, but you can recover. However, if you are Barry Minkow, current fraud investigator and former perpetrator, and you are wrong one time, people lose money because *you* missed something. Then it's over. Period. I was experiencing a new kind of pressure even though I would have shrugged it off decades ago.

"How much are you going to charge me?" Kirshner asked.

"Promise you won't tell anyone?" I responded.

Not quite sure where I was heading, Kirshner looked at me and decided to play along. "Okay, I promise," he said hesitantly.

"Nothing," I whispered as I rose and grabbed the paperwork relating to the fund, "but you can never tell anyone."

⁓

"Hi, Barb. Any calls?" I asked as I drove south on the 5 South. (In California highways are graced with titles like "The 5" versus "I-5" elsewhere in the country.)

"Just one. Where are you? You do realize that you are preaching tonight?" she asked. Saturday night service—my secretary has a keen grasp of the obvious.

"Yes, I do realize that. I'm driving as fast as I can. I'm in Orange County headed back to the church." I searched diligently for a pen in the front seat cluttered with the usual empty water bottles, open CD cases, and cassette tapes of my favorite pastors. "Okay, go ahead."

"Carol called and wanted to let you know that her cancer is in remission. She appreciated your visit last night. Why were you in Orange County?"

"I'm scouring other churches trying to find a job with a secretary who will appreciate me."

"Good luck," she said flatly. Barbara Brown and I had begun working together seven years before when Community Bible Church had about a hundred and thirty adults. Now with over one thousand regular attendees, the staff had grown significantly and so had our mutual fondness and respect. "Are you on another fraud case?" said Barb.

"Looks that way."

"Does this involve a lot of money?"

"Well, that depends on whether you believe eight hundred million dollars is a lot of money." There was silence on the other end.

"I think you need to be careful, Barry." Barb was like a second mother to me, and I could hear that matronly concern shift into high gear. "People kill for that kind of money."

"Come on, Barb. I survived seven and a half years in prison. I'll be just fine. Call Carol and tell her I'll stop by to see her some time next week. And I'll see you soon."

The rest of the drive home was uneventful except for the two thoughts I could not get out of my mind. First, I kept dwelling on Fred Kirshner's answer to the question about due diligence: *we called ten people who had been in the Financial Advisory Consultant Fund five or more years to make sure they had received their 38.8% returns.*

As a perpetrator of fraud, I remember always using "satisfied investors" as primary evidence of the investment's authenticity. Consider the alternative. If people were unsatisfied and not receiving "high returns," then they would complain to the authorities, the media, and just about anyone else who would listen. Perpetrators are keenly aware of that fact and uphold one fundamental duty: keep investors happy. We strive to attain advertisers, not adversaries. After all, if investors are happy, they do not grumble to law enforcement or other protest outlets. Even more importantly, these backers become key advocates for the investment. Satisfied investors are used to pacify other prospective investors, telling them how great the deal is, how timely the payments are, and so on.

Consequently, whenever I hear that the primary attraction to the investment is other current investors I get alarmed. *But this deal has been around for twenty years*, I said to myself. *No fraud could persist that long. And besides, eight hundred million dollars is a lot of money. Not to mention the five thousand people involved in the fund.*

The second item to contemplate was the obvious question that everyone thinks but is afraid to ask, the one inescapable question that every fraud perpetrator offering high returns to lure investors fears the most . . . *Why would anybody who earns 38.8% annually need investors?*

I glanced at my watch again, located the phone next to a mountainous stack of papers, and made the next logical call.

"Don, it's Barry."

"Let me guess. You need something by yesterday and you're on a new fraud case," he quipped. I could practically see him smiling on the other end of the line.

"Everybody's a comedian. Listen, I need you to do a workup for me."

"Okay, let me grab a pen—and talk slow because I'm driving."

"Hurry up. I have to go preach in a few minutes."

Don Ray is the greatest public records researcher in the western hemisphere. I learned this firsthand back in 1987 when I was indicted. Don worked as a news producer for the local CBS television affiliate that covered the ZZZZ Best fraud. To my continued regret, he always was able to uncover facts about the case that I didn't want disclosed. Nevertheless, I respected him for his praiseworthy skills at searching public records. When I was convicted and sentenced to prison, we kept in touch from time to time. Later, when I began doing proactive work at the Fraud Discovery Institute, we became closer. Any fraud investigator will tell you that it helps to have a public records expert as a close friend.

"All right," said Don, "go ahead."

"The guy's name is James P. Lewis, and the company is Financial Advisory Consultants located in Lake Forest, California. He claims to be a mutual fund manager and has been in business twenty years. He has about five thousand investors nationwide," I declared.

"Twenty years is a long time. You're not thinking this guy is a fraud, are you, Barry?" Don asked with disbelief. *Back to the length of time issue again,* I thought.

"I don't know what to think until I see the research," I said. "Let's check him for licenses, Series 7, Series 66: check with NASD and the California Department of Corporations. Let's also verify if he has any tax liens or lawsuits. Oh, and include corporate records. I want to know who the officers and directors of Financial Advisory Consultants are—"

"I know the drill. We *have* done this before," Don interjected, "and you need this by . . . ?"

"I need this by the time I finish preaching," I said.

"Good, that gives me at least twelve hours."

"Very funny. Just e-mail me a preliminary report in the morning."

"Another all-nighter for Barry Minkow," he said. "You know my wife is becoming jealous of us."

"Tell her I owe her dinner at the restaurant of her choice. Now go to work."

"Yeah, yeah, yeah. . . . I'll have it for you, Barry. Count on me."

"Thanks, Don." I already knew I could count on him.

I swiped my Bible and the sermon outline off my desk and darted into the sanctuary. As I sat in the back and watched people filter in, I realized that the people I saw were uninterested in Barry Minkow, the fraud investigator. They were coming to church to hear about God, not Barry. Fraud was the furthest topic from their minds. This meant my preliminary concerns about Financial Advisory Consultants had to be set aside in favor of a sermon from the Gospel of Mark on the crippled man being lowered through the roof and healed by Jesus. These lightning transitions from one profession to the other were becoming increasingly difficult.

I hurried home that night after church and studied the materials from Financial Advisory Consultants. Kirshner had turned over the standard prospectus that was given to potential investors and about two years of one-page monthly newsletters. Lewis provided updates on the fund's activity in each faithfully distributed newsletter to all current investors.

The Growth Fund averaged returns of 38.8% annually while the Income Fund averaged 18% annually. Admittedly, I was no expert in the mutual fund business and therefore was unable to render an opinion as to whether these high returns were unusual. However, I did know how poorly *my* mutual funds had performed the last few years—nowhere near those kinds of returns. In fact I had lost money! I made a mental note to contact an expert in the mutual fund industry who could tell me if such returns are consistent or even possible with the mutual fund industry.

Something else leapt out at me from the newsletters. Lewis claimed that the Financial Advisory Consultants' mutual funds cumulatively invested in three primary areas: buying and reselling businesses (corporate takeovers, leverage buy outs, etc.), insurance premium financing, and equipment leasing. These three fields of business were the front end of the high returns he was earning for investors.

But his newsletters never mentioned a proper noun, perhaps an insignificant detail to the average investor. With ambiguous language like, "In May of 2002 we bought a large laundry company and sold it for a 2.9% profit for the month," the name of the laundry company was never provided, making it impossible to confirm the transaction. That struck me as odd, so I scanned the other newsletters. In every case there was never a proper noun included!

Other months of the newsletter revealed much of the same: "We purchased a manufacturing company and resold it for a 3.9% monthly profit and have three other deals in escrow." Although I could not yet be sure, this ambiguity was particularly disconcerting because it was something I used at ZZZZ Best to fool investors. For example, we claimed to be doing fifty million dollars in carpet restoration jobs on buildings that had been damaged by fire, smoke, or water. But when the auditors or investors wanted addresses for these job sites, we could never provide them because these jobs did not exist! I always made up a standard lie that went something like this: "We cannot allow unauthorized people on the job site at anytime because of liability issues. Therefore no addresses of the job sites can be given." It was a wall that we erected between good due diligence and our fraud. And it worked . . . for a while. I eventually got busted. But this guy—he'd been going strong for decades.

Maybe the accountants for the fund have this information, I thought.

⌇

Sunday morning at the church went smoothly. Preaching three services got my mind off of Financial Advisory Consultants temporarily. But as soon as I got home I knew what I had to do: make calls—lots of them. I had to contact current investors in the Financial Advisory Consultant Fund to get answers to questions that only they could provide. Investor calls were always long and tedious but yielded the most information. Although I didn't feel like talking after preaching three sermons, I needed specifics. I had the name of only one other group of investors that the client, Fred Kirshner, knew from Oregon. He was a retired pastor named Dale Japp, who along with his father and brother Jeff supposedly had millions invested in the fund. My job would be to get Japp not only to tell me all about the Financial Advisory

Consultant Fund, but also to provide me with names of other people he knew who were in the fund.

"Mr. Japp? This is Pastor Barry Minkow with Community Bible Church in San Diego. I am calling about the Financial Advisory Consultant Fund." I drew a long breath and waited for a response.

Technically I was not lying. I am the senior pastor of Community Bible Church in San Diego, California. And I used my real name and even disclosed my past criminal behavior. However, I had learned that when performing due diligence calls about investment opportunities, Pastor Barry Minkow is a lot less intimidating than Barry Minkow, co-founder of the Fraud Discovery Institute. Okay, so on my best days I'm a little sketchy.

"Yes, Pastor Barry, how can I help you?"

"Mr. Japp, I have a friend who is considering investing in the Financial Advisory Consultants income and growth funds and your name was given as a reference for the fund. Are you a satisfied investor?"

"Oh yes, Pastor! I am very satisfied. Our family has been investing in the fund for almost two decades. Never had a problem, and whenever we needed a withdrawal, our money was sent to us immediately."

"That's great, Mr. Japp. Do you have any financial statements on the company that have been prepared by a CPA?" I continued.

"No, we get a monthly newsletter and a statement showing our principle investment along with the returns we made for that month. This is a private fund, Pastor Barry. Mr. Lewis does not need audited financial statements like Fidelity or Janus."

"Right, right, Mr. Japp." Now wasn't the time to correct him. "I guess you have a point there. Hey, am I correct in assuming that you have been averaging 38.8% in the growth fund annually?"

"Yes, I have, and so have my father and brother."

"How does Mr. Lewis generate these large returns?" I asked, trying to suppress any shred of suspicion in my voice.

"He buys and resells businesses at a profit and then keeps a small ownership interest in those businesses for the fund. He also does large equipment leasing for medical doctors and insurance premium financing. That's how he is able to generate such large returns," he said, as if he had repeated the same scenario to others who have inquired; his statement sounded well rehearsed.

"Yeah, that's what the offering materials and newsletters seem to indicate. Are you aware of any of the companies he has bought and sold or any of the companies he has provided equipment leasing for?" I asked.

"No, I'm not, Pastor Barry. I leave the everyday business of the fund's operations to Mr. Lewis."

I didn't want to believe it! Every red flag for fraud was prevalent in this deal and I had just begun making calls. Before ending the call, Japp gave me three more investors' names and their phone numbers.

Three hours later, I had talked to a total of eleven investors in the Financial Advisory Consultants growth and income funds. Most of these investors had high six- and seven-figure investments with Lewis for many years and had brought all of their family members and friends into the fund. Additionally, the people I talked to shared a common desire to increase their principle investments, just like Fred Kirshner and his father. None of them had ever seen an audited financial statement nor were they able to identify any names of the companies Lewis allegedly bought and sold. The gravity of the situation began to weigh heavily on me. *Why did I agree to look into this?*

I stared out the window of my home office while nervously rubbing my fingers through my hair. Rereading the newsletters and offering materials one more time, I made mental notes of the red flags for fraud that I had already confirmed:

- no independent proof of profitability: names of companies bought and sold, or leasing clients, or insurance premium finance clients;

- control by a singular person: James P. Lewis;

- no audited financial statements or internal controls in the company;

- unusual high rates of return in a low interest rate environment;

- all new investors relied upon the word of current investors to make the decision to enter the fund.

The fund was growing daily. I had no choice but to move quickly.

A ringing phone interrupted my fingers clacking on the keyboard.

"Hello?"

"Barry?"

"Don? Is that you?" I asked.

"Yeah, I had to call you. The guy is a ghost. He *doesn't exist.*"

"What do you mean he doesn't exist?" The high-pitched tone of my voice indicated my trepidation.

"He doesn't exist. No lenders license, no broker/dealer license, no registration with NASD, and Financial Advisory Consultants isn't even a corporation. James P. Lewis filed a DBA back in 1985." He paused. We both knew what that meant. The man controlling an eight-hundred-million-dollar mutual fund for twenty years with five thousand investors across the country was not even incorporated.

⁓

I exhausted the rest of the evening mulling over the implications. If this fund were an elaborate Ponzi scheme, then how could it break the rules and survive for so long? How could intelligent doctors, lawyers, businessmen and women, and other professionals not notice the seemingly obvious intentional omissions of any proper nouns in the newsletters? Were they simply blinded by the high returns?

The clock was clearly ticking because new investor money poured into the Financial Advisory Consultant Fund on a daily basis. That much I knew. Then I thought about law enforcement. This was clearly a case for the Securities and Exchange Commission, and, because Lewis was located in Orange County, that meant the Los Angeles office of the SEC on Wilshire Boulevard. I half cringed at that realization. That was the same SEC office that prosecuted me sixteen years earlier.

On Monday morning I went to my office at the church, dug out a space on the desk, and began working. A tornado could do a better job organizing the place than I do. As I left the house, I warned my wife, Lisa, that it would be a long day. As usual, she was supportive. However, she was concerned because of the dollar amount that was at stake. I reassured her that most white-collar criminals are nonviolent.

"The operative word there is *most*, Barry, and that's what bothers me," she said softly, lines of worry creasing her delicate forehead. I didn't ignore her concern, but I had to press on.

There were four facts I needed to be sure of before I contacted the SEC. First, I called an old friend from prison who had been busted for a large insurance premium finance scam that brought down two banks. He told me to meet him in a bar in Los Angeles.

Pastors don't normally conduct business in bars, I told him.

"That's where I conduct business these days," he said. "You want information from me, that's where you'll need to come."

The bar was in downtown Los Angeles. The first thing I noticed when I walked inside was how dark it was. Candles glowed on the secondhand tables, despite the fact that it was only two in the afternoon. It might as well have been midnight as far as any patron was concerned. I blinked my eyes repeatedly.

How will I find Harry in this place?

A booming voice from the other side of the joint erased that concern. "Well, well, well, if it isn't the Preacher Boy!" said my friend in his thick Southern accent. I thought about crawling under one of the dark tables as he continued, "Fellas, this is Barry Minkow, the one-time Wall Street wiz kid turned pastor. You may have read about him on the front page of the *Wall Street Journal.*"

Harry was actually Harold "Smooth" Lang. He was about 6'3" tall and slightly overweight, with newly peppered light brown hair. His clothes were mostly wrinkled and his shirt untucked. It was clear that Harry was relaxed in the bar and certainly had the home court advantage on me. In the past people had made the mistake of underestimating Harry, which is how he liked it. Despite his general disheveled appearance, he was one of the smartest men I had met in prison. We stayed in touch mostly because his mother always wanted me to drag him to church. I had little success, but because of the love and respect I showed his mom, I knew he would see me and provide the information I needed.

Harry was convicted in the late '80s for orchestrating one of the largest insurance premium finance scams and bank fraud cases in American business history. He gave back most of the money, served five years in a medium security prison, and now was living on the balance of the money he didn't return.

"How's your mom?" I asked as I clambered onto a high stool next to him at the bar.

"She's doing great. At church everyday just like you, Preacher Boy," he said as he motioned for the bartender to come over. "What'll you have?" he asked, with one eyebrow raised.

"Diet Coke," I said.

"And bring me another beer," Harry insisted. I surveyed the bar. Lots of people were there at the bar and tables. Two televisions, one showing a repeat of a college football game, were anchored to the opposite walls. I was happy to notice that people had finally stopped staring at me after Harry's boisterous introduction.

"Harry, listen. I need some information on the insurance premium finance business," I stated. He nodded curtly as if to tell me to continue. "Well, this guy claims to be earning between 18% and 38% annually in that business. And I thought that since you wrote the book on that industry you would be able to tell me if those kind of returns are possible," I said.

He hoisted the newly arrived beer, took a swig, and wiped his mouth with the side of his hand.

"Maybe five years ago those returns were possible, but not today. Remember, Barry, the return is always dictated by what the consumer is willing to pay. And with interest rates low, the average consumer could place the premium on their credit card for less than that," he pointed out. He explained that people who buy insurance and do not want to pay the full premium for the year in advance would rather make monthly payments and use insurance premium financing to satisfy the annual premium for their house, car, or business insurance.

Harry continued, "So let's say your business insurance cost five thousand dollars annually and the insurance premium finance company offered to finance that premium over twelve monthly payments for 18% to 38% annually—and don't forget that is only what he is paying investors; he must be charging much more than that to the customer to earn a profit—then why not put the premium on your credit card which is averaging about 13% in this kind of environment? It just doesn't add up."

It was amazing. Someone who did not know Harry would never guess that such knowledge would come from a man who spent most of his waking hours seemingly half drunk!

"One more thing, Preacher Boy. Anyone who is in the insurance premium finance business in California must comply with the Department of Financial Institutions Industrial Loan Law." He paused to make sure I was listening. I was scribbling notes on the napkin that had been served with my diet Coke. I couldn't write fast enough. "They call them 'PFCs,' Barry, and they are highly regulated," he stated with authority. "My guess is your friend is not licensed."

"Thanks, Harry," I said as I got up from the bar. "Now how can I return the favor?" I asked. He stood up and placed his hand (thankfully not the one he used to wipe his mouth) on my left shoulder. He eyes locked with mine as he looked down at me.

"Pray for me, Preacher Boy."

Within five minutes of meeting with Harry, I punched in the number to the California Department of Financial Institutions where I confirmed that neither Lewis nor Financial Advisory Consultants had been licensed with that department. *Bingo!* Harry was right.

❧

Next, I needed to check the public records for the leasing side of Lewis' business. I had done enough leasing deals back in the ZZZZ Best days (albeit most of them fraudulent) to know that if Lewis was a lien holder on medical equipment or any other equipment for that matter, it would have to show up in a public UCC-1 filing. I drove back to the church and checked the public records. Neither Lewis nor Financial Advisory Consultants were Secured Party lien holders on any equipment.

Then, I needed to see if Lewis, his company, or the investment opportunity he was offering was registered or "blue skied" in the states where he was doing business. Laws were made to protect the public from just anyone asking to exchange your hard-earned money for the promise of lofty returns. In fact, and much to my shame, I was one of the reasons why such laws were created. Neither Lewis nor his company were registered in any of the states he was selling his offering—a clear violation.

The final step was to find out if the returns Lewis claimed were possible. I called Dustin Woodard, editor of the mutual fund category at About.com. Explaining the rate of return Lewis had earned over a twenty-year period, I asked him if it was unusual or out of the ordinary. I faxed him the prospectus for Financial Advisory Consultants and explained my concerns.

"Give me a few hours and I'll e-mail you a response," he said.

Within an hour I received the unfavorable written reply: "Any investment claiming 38% to 40% returns over a seventeen-year period must be fraudulent." It was time to contact the SEC.

∾

I sat placidly in my car and stared at the building. I didn't want to go in—it was *the* primary address of bad memories. My phone jingled insistently. It was Barb.

"Are we having a staff meeting today? Everyone is standing around waiting for you," she said huffily.

"Can't Pastor Jim do it?" I inquired with slight irritation. It's not that I felt it was unimportant, but at that very moment I was almost hyperventilating.

"Where are you this time?" she asked.

"I'm in Los Angeles in the parking lot of the SEC getting ready to go meet with a high-level enforcement lawyer on what I believe is the largest and longest running Ponzi scheme in American business history."

"What are you doing in the parking lot? Afraid to go in?"

"Yeah, a little. These people don't like me, and they certainly don't trust me," I said. "And I've got to lay out this case for them and turn over this evidence."

"No, they don't like the 'old Barry' from sixteen years ago. I think they'll like the new Barry."

"Do you like the new Barry?"

"Sometimes . . . when he communicates with me," she said with a hint of sarcasm but sincere warmth. (Did I forget to mention I am not terribly good at communicating?)

"Sorry about that. No staff meeting today. I've got to be the fraud guy.

Now if you'll excuse me, I think I've summoned enough courage to face the giant," I said, more for my benefit than hers.

"Go get 'em. And don't forget you have a wedding rehearsal tomorrow." Here I was trying to muster up enough courage to report a multimillion-dollar fraud while juggling my pastoral calendar! *Funny*, I thought, *both marriage and fraud can affect people for a lifetime.* I made one final check of my Financial Advisory Consultants file and made my way to the building.

᠆

"Mr. Tercero, nice to meet you. I'm . . ."

"I know who you are, Mr. Minkow. Come this way."

Following Tercero, I smiled at the receptionist who had not taken her disapproving eyes off of me from the moment I entered. Like I was going to steal one of the outdated *Newsweek* magazines that cluttered the waiting room table.

"You know, I cannot always see you on such short notice, Mr. Minkow," said Tercero pointedly. We entered a small, bare conference room and took seats in well-worn chairs on opposite sides of a rundown table. He promptly closed the door. The dull and stained white walls badly needed repainting. Tercero was all business, so I wasted no time and got right to the point.

I pulled out copies of the Financial Advisory Consultants offering memorandum, two years of their investor newsletters, Fred Kirshner's monthly statements, and a list of the eleven people I spoke with who confirmed the fund's size, scope, and duration.

"All this is very nice, Mr. Minkow, but do you have any investor complaints?"

"You and I both know that you don't need a complaining investor to shut down an unregistered security by an unlicensed broker dealer. We also both know that in a good Ponzi scheme there will never be a complaint from an investor—that's how we keep them going." Our eyes locked and I continued. "No, Mr. Tercero, there will not be a complaining investor in this case until you 'cease and desist' Mr. Lewis and prevent him from raising any further funds. Then you'll have your complaints. About five thousand of them if I am correct." I had his full attention. "I realize that I am not the most credible source, and that's why I brought you all the materials so you can confirm my findings."

He thumbed through the materials but made no facial expression. Either he was apathetic because of an understandable lack of trust or he had a great poker face. Thankfully, it was the latter. I spent the next thirty minutes walking him through each of the documents and explaining what I had learned. It did not take him long to connect the dots.

"How did you find out the names and phone numbers of all these current investors?" he asked.

I ignored the question. The FBI and SEC have their way of getting answers. And we ex-cons have ours. "I'm going to make a surprise visit to Mr. Lewis tomorrow morning at his Orange County offices," I interjected.

"Why?"

"Because before I issue a report alleging that this is a massive fraud, I want to see the offices and look into the eyes of Mr. Lewis. When you have spent seven and a half years in prison looking at guilty people, you get kind of a knack for reading people's expressions. Are you going to want my final report, Mr. Tercero?" He shifted the papers one more time and then tidied them into a neat pile.

"You're not going to meet Mr. Lewis and represent to him that you have been deputized by the SEC, are you?" he asked half jokingly.

⁓

It was 6:50 a.m. on Wednesday morning when I hung up the phone with Lisa and parked behind the Financial Advisory Consultants' offices on El Torro Road. I left at 5:00 a.m. to make sure I got there before 7:00. It was mandatory that I arrive prior to his secretarial staff. Fred Kirshner told me that they kept James P. Lewis well protected. I also remembered how early I got into the office when I was perpetrating my fraud. With the volume of lies necessary to keep a fraud of this size going, I knew Lewis needed an early start. Ten minutes later he proved me right.

After he pulled up in a luxury vehicle, I waited five minutes and then followed him into the office. It was a modest 1,500-square-foot floor plan with two visible offices and a reception area. Five people max could work in this area, and running a multimillion-dollar conglomerate (which is what Financial Advisory Consultants purported to be) consisting of divisions that included buying and reselling businesses, equipment leasing, and insurance premium financing was impossible with only five people. It struck me how other investors had visited these offices, known Lewis had no other locations, and still believed that he could run a billion dollar fund with three separate divisions from a miniscule office with five people on staff.

While standing in the unimpressive reception area, I remember one distinct train of thought before I met Lewis. Our church has a 1.5 million dollar annual budget with twelve full-time employees, and *this* guy is going to run million dollar deals and earn 38.8% returns almost single handedly from this place? Ha! I heard him conclude what must have been a phone conversation since there was no one else in the office.

"Mr. Lewis?" I called. Within minutes he came out to the front to greet me. He was rushed and did not have much time to talk but did allow me a few minutes to sit with him in his private office. Private offices for fraud perpetrators are not simply areas to house a desk and chair; they are war rooms. We take on the world from our supposed power seat: investors, bankers, skeptics, and auditors. It is where we create fraudulent documents and plan how to stay one step ahead of our enemies. I had a similar type of office at ZZZZ Best. My mind raced back to the many calls, meetings, and schemes I had planned from my war room.

I directed my attention to Lewis and knew beyond any doubt that he had plenty to hide. His heavy, shifty eyes held the kind of expression that no one else but another criminal would recognize, one that only comes from trying to stay one step ahead of everybody else.

I explained to him that I believed someone had plagiarized his offering materials for the fund. Indeed someone had previously plagiarized his offering materials, so I was able to hand him a set of the actual materials used. Although irrelevant to the case, it did buy me a few minutes with Lewis. I didn't want to start by telling him I was there to investigate him! I handed him a business card that disclosed my affiliation with the Fraud Discovery Institute and told him who I was. He remembered the ZZZZ Best case, and we talked a few minutes about my experiences.

He quickly reminded me of his next meeting, and I took that as my cue to exit. I reached out my hand to grasp his, and as I said my goodbyes I realized that I was looking in a mirror. Sixteen years earlier I was James P. Lewis—albeit on a significantly smaller scale. I truly felt sorry for him. Like me, he probably did not start out to defraud five thousand people out of eight hundred million dollars. Perhaps he had the best of intentions, but then one small compromise led to another and before he knew it, he was living a massive lie. I had seen it many times over the years. I had lived it.

I wanted to grab him by the shoulders, shake him hard, and say, "Don't you realize what you are doing? Don't you realize the number of lives you are ruining?" But even if I did, he would not have listened for the same reason I would not have listened had someone warned me. Lies, fraud, and deceit are never an end in themselves but rather a means to an end. They are manufactured because we have justified them through a series of convoluted rationalizations. I left that morning with an empty pit in my stomach.

Within six weeks of my visit to Lewis and the issue of my twenty-five-page report, the following story broke on the Associated Press news wire.

STATE, FEDS INVESTIGATING SOCAL INVESTMENT FIRM
By Don Thompson, Associated Press
December 11, 2003

SACRAMENTO—Financial Advisory Consultants, an Orange County-based investment firm, claims to have generated extraordinary profits for its clients over 20 years, but records indicate it has not registered with state and federal agencies that regulate financial advisers and investment funds.

The company's annual reports to clients give no details on the companies it says it has bought and sold, nor the investments it says produced an average annual rate of return of 38.8 percent from its growth fund and 18.9 percent from its income fund since 1983.

Its clients, some of whom have invested hundreds of thousands of dollars of their retirement savings with the company, said they are pleased with the consistently above-market returns reported by the firm in good times and bad.

But state and federal regulators have begun probing what at least one whistle-blowing client fears may be returns too good to be true. Regulators are examining documents provided by Barry Minkow, a convicted felon turned anti-fraud investigator for San Diego-based Fraud Discovery Institute.

When contacted for comment, company receptionists said that only President James Lewis could answer questions. He did not respond to numerous messages left with his office or on his cell phone, though his staff said he had received them.

He also had received but did not respond to letters sent by certified mail and overnight mail, although the certified mail receipt indicated it was received by the company, and his staff said he had picked them up. The Associated Press' offer to talk with a company attorney or other representatives drew no response.

In its literature, the company says it performs a variety of functions that state and federal regulators and financial experts say require government registration. Regulators in California, Oregon, Washington and at the federal Securities and Exchange Commission said they have no incorporation, licensing or registration for Financial Advisory Consultants or Lewis.

"We're trying to figure out who they are," said SEC spokeswoman Pauline Calande.

North American Securities Administrators Association spokesman Bob Webster said a lack of registration is a warning sign to investors, as is the lack of detail in the firm's reports to its clients.

"In investment, disclosure is king," Webster added. "An investor has a right to know what they're investing in."

Dustin Woodard, mutual funds editor at About.com, said the extraordinary returns, the lack of details and the word-of-mouth marketing make the company "very fishy."

"Certainly no mutual fund has had such a phenomenal track record," said Woodard, who is "highly doubtful that any hedge fund or investor pool could produce such results."

Large portions of Lewis' reports to investors were virtually identical to those used by another Southern California firm, Sunburst Financial

Systems of Palm Desert. Sunburst also borrowed from reports by a third company—MX Factors of Riverside—that state regulators have barred from accepting new investments.

While certain hedge funds and firms that deal with wealthy, "sophisticated" investors are exempt from some licensing requirements, Financial Advisory Consultants' investors present a different profile. They said they learned of the firm by word of mouth—often from friends, family or members of their church—and are satisfied despite a complete lack of detail on the investments made on their behalf.

Some, however, reported difficulties in getting access to their money.

Robert Liss of Aurora, Colo., said he tried to withdraw money from his account in September but was told he couldn't because the federal government had put a homeland security freeze on $8.4 million from investors in Syria and Iran.

Neither the U.S. Department of Homeland Security nor the U.S. Treasury could find any record of such an asset freeze.

Some of the other registered companies with which the 57-year-old Lewis is affiliated have run into problems with business associates and the government, records show.

Lewis is listed as a registered agent for Sun West International LLC, which was sued by Harrah's Entertainment Inc. of Las Vegas in 2001 after it stopped flying Harrah's guests to its casinos from around the nation. Harrah's sued to recover $377,000 in prepayments and $622,000 it spent on guests stranded when the company stopped flying, according to reports at the time.

A Sun West employee confirmed Lewis is the same person who runs Financial Advisory Consultants. U.S. and Canadian aviation authorities could find no registrations or aircraft ownership records for Sun West.

California Department of Insurance records show a James Paul Lewis at the same address as Financial Advisory Consultants had his insurance license revoked in 1989, while he was affiliated with Pi Omega Delta Insurance Services.

Financial Advisory Consultants, according to Lewis' 2001 report to investors, closed 26 projects in its growth fund and had a 40 percent profit, mostly by buying and reselling financially healthy companies in "ownership distress"—when partnerships or marriages break up, or an owner dies and the spouse doesn't want to run the business.

The income fund returned 18.9 percent in 2001 by financing insurance premiums and equipment leasing programs and providing corporate loans, Lewis reported.

Though the firm's reports provide no details on what companies were bought or sold, or its investments or loans, some clients interviewed by The Associated Press said they aren't bothered.

"They've gone out and made these investments, and we're the recipients, I guess," said John Streib of Bremerton, Wash. He said his investments have earned more than 30 percent a year for more than five years.

Minkow's client, who would not let his name be used, said he has invested about $150,000 and other members of his family about $500,000 with the firm over about five years. He said he has been able to withdraw substantial sums, but with a two-month delay after he asked for his money—as outlined in a company document that warns "the right of redemption is at the sole discretion of the Funds Manager, James P. Lewis Jr."

When asked to investigate the firm and Lewis, Minkow said he grew suspicious when he could find no records on Lewis or the company.

"He's nowhere to be found—he's a ghost," Minkow said.

Minkow this fall drew attention to two other Southern California companies, MX Factors and Sunburst Financial Systems, both of which promised investors high returns but were not registered to sell securities with the state. His client who raised concerns about Financial Advisory Consultants also was an investor in MX Factors, which the state Department of Corporations ordered to stop accepting investments.

Then, on Christmas Day, the next incriminating story hit the AP wire:

INVESTORS FEAR THEY'LL LOSE MILLIONS IN ALLEGED PONZI SCAM
By Don Thompson, Associated Press
December 25, 2003

SACRAMENTO—More than 5,200 clients across America trusted James Paul Lewis Jr. with their life savings, pouring hundreds of millions of dollars into his Southern California investment funds on the word of a few friends.

Many heard about Financial Advisory Consultants through fellow churchgoers, although professional athletes and at least one movie actor are said to be investors.

As their own retirement accounts sagged with the stock market, they marveled at Lewis' reports of consistently returning upward of 40 percent from one fund and 20 percent from another, year in and year out for two decades.

They scrambled to give him money, any caution or doubts pushed aside as they saw their fellow investors periodically withdraw as much as $250,000.

Their financial future came crashing down this week, when a federal judge froze the company's assets and the FBI carted away documents and computers from Lewis' three-room Orange County office suite.

No charges have been filed, but the FBI alleges Lewis was operating a "Ponzi scheme," in which early investors are paid with money from later investors. The federal Securities and Exchange Commission says the "fraudulent scheme" involved $813 million from more than 5,200 investors.

"It's a house of cards," said Barry Minkow, himself once imprisoned for seven years for defrauding investors through his ZZZZ Best carpet cleaning company. "It will go down as the longest-running Ponzi scheme in history, and the mutual fund that didn't exist."

Minkow, who now works as an anti-fraud investigator for San Diego-based Fraud Discovery Institute, provided state and federal regulators with documents questioning Lewis' legitimacy, also prompting an investigation and story by The Associated Press earlier this month.

When it was all over, the paper profits owed by Lewis to investors was $813 million, although the actual cash he received from investors was approximately $400 million. Lewis was eventually charged with fourteen counts of fraud by a federal grand jury.

At this point I think it is important to note that I have not always been on this side of the law . . .

RISE AND FALL

2 | WIZ KID

Growing up in Reseda, California, and attending Grover Cleveland High School, it did not take me long to learn an unstated rule: if you wanted a date with a beautiful girl (especially a cheerleader), you needed to have one of three things going for you.

First, you had to have looks. Well, Brad Pitt I am not. So that left options two and three. Option two was to be the star football player or to excel in some kind of respectable sport. For me, that did not occur until I went to prison . . . but I digress. That only left money. My only shot was money. If you did not have looks and were not a great athlete, there was still the possibility of landing a date with a cheerleader if you had money, especially if you had a nice car to go with it.

During my junior year in high school, I owned a 1972 Buick that was known as "The Bomb." I realize that language has changed since I was in high school, and that today, the word *bomb* can actually refer to something good, but in 1983 that term denoted anything but. My Buick was called "The Bomb" because it looked like one had hit it. An ugly gray primer covered the side panels; carpet cleaning equipment hung out the window of the back seat. High school girls are image conscious and do not want to be caught dead in a car that has to be started with a screwdriver.

Like most folks, I really wanted to be accepted in high school. But at lunchtime, while the in-crowd would gather to talk about the issues of the day, average guys like me were really not welcomed. That section of the cafeteria was reserved for the successful: drop-dead gorgeous cheerleaders, star athletes, kids whose parents had money or new cars, and so on. I didn't fall into any of these categories. And for me, the fear of going through high school unnoticed was far greater than the fear of not graduating.

I concluded that the best way for me to become included in the upper echelon of Grover Cleveland High School was to start a business and earn enough money to buy a nice, new, flashy car. Then I would finally land a date with a beautiful girl. Naturally, I already had one particular blond in mind. Her name was Lisa Petrow, and she was the dream of every eleventh grader—especially me.

Since carpet cleaning was the only business I knew, and since it was a relatively easy entry business (no tests to pass or licenses to secure), I concluded that this was my best opportunity. So, in October of 1982 with the help of Jerry Williams, a local loan shark from the gym where I worked out, ZZZZ Best Carpet and Furniture Cleaning Company was birthed out of my parents' garage. Jerry lent me sixteen hundred dollars and charged me two hundred per week—interest only. I used the money to purchase my own carpet cleaning equipment and business cards. I never intended to take this company public on Wall Street before I was legally allowed to drink. Like a lot of love-struck teenagers, I merely wanted to attract a girl, and if the cost of doing that was to own a carpet cleaning company and pay some loan shark two hundred dollars per week, then I was more than willing to comply.

And then it happened. For some odd reason, Diners Club sent me a credit card. That's right, at sixteen years old I had a credit card, and no one else my age could make that claim! Apparently anyone who filed a "DBA" and opened a business automatically qualified and was sent a credit card by Diners Club. Since then, credit card issuing policies have changed—maybe because of me.

Word spread quickly around Cleveland High School. Barry Minkow had a Diners Club card and loved to invite lots of people to nice restaurants and pay the bill. And that's when everything in my life changed. People, even the coveted in-crowd, began to include me in their group. I was invited to post-football game parties that were only reserved for the popular kids. I learned that people loved, included, and respected me while I was buying. So I bought all the time.

On almost every Friday and Saturday night, before the big evening began, I could be found with twenty-five of my closest friends at a nice restaurant signing a credit card receipt for everyone's dinner. It did not matter that my new business had cash flow problems. It did not matter that it was not a good business decision to incur all kinds of high interest credit card debt. It did not matter that the kinds of people that now accepted me loved my newly found purchase power and not me as a person. The results were worth it.

I had just learned a valuable truth about people: *money imputed respect*. Achievement in the business world makes up for a lack of looks or athletic talent. When I was buying, I was included. When I was buying, the respect and acceptance that I desperately desired came. I quickly determined that the one thing that must remain constant in my life was that I had to *keep buying* at all costs. Money became a narcotic that repressed my ability to reason clearly. "Right" was defined early on in my business career as forward-motion, and "wrong" was anything that got in my way of achieving.

Realizing that the carpet cleaning business was the vehicle by which I would gain acceptance and respect, I began to focus on making the company both successful, and more importantly, visible. Every time I went into a customer's home and cleaned their carpets, I would always be asked the same question: "How old are you?" And when I said I was sixteen, they almost always responded in the same way: "You're sixteen years old and have your own business? My son is stuck on drugs and doesn't even do his chores and here you are a businessman. What a great story!" I kept those responses in the back of my mind and decided to capitalize on them. I reasoned that the best way to get more attention and recognition was to tell the world about my story. And the best way to tell the world about my story was through the media. So one day I called the local network news affiliate in Los Angeles. I disguised my voice to sound older, and told a segment producer that I had just had my carpets cleaned by the sixteen-year-old owner of ZZZZ Best Carpet and Furniture Cleaning Company, and was pleasantly surprised by the fact that a high-school junior was running his own business.

"Why do we always hear tales about teenage drug abuse and high school dropouts but never success stories like this?" I questioned him. "What could be a better model for other young people than a guy who has defied the odds and started his own company?"

The producer was soon convinced that the story was newsworthy. I gave him the company phone number so he could set up an interview with this inspiring young entrepreneur. Luckily for me they didn't have Caller ID back in the eighties. I stayed planted in my shabby desk chair and waited impatiently for the call. In less than five minutes, the phone rang. "I'm trying to reach a Mr. Barry Minkow," said an inquisitive, deep voice.

A few days later a crew arrived to film the segment. My family's garage housed our humble headquarters. The story aired that evening, and the response was extraordinary. It wasn't just my family and friends who responded with enthusiasm. Radio stations, *Los Angeles Daily News*, and even my school newspaper called, wanting interviews. Prospective customers called, demanding that Barry Minkow personally clean their carpets.

At school, I became the new sensation. And this time it was not just because of the Diners Club card. I was the only student at Cleveland High publicly recognized as a businessman. Finding myself at last the possessor of a "cool" label, I became determined never to revert back to being labeled a nerd. The spotlight was mine now, and I was hooked on the attention. But my party did not last.

The bank where I had first opened the ZZZZ Best checking account called me and said that because I was only sixteen years old, California law prohibited me from signing on a legal, binding contract. And a checking account constituted a "legal binding contract." So they informed me that they were immediately closing my accounts and returning the checks I had written. There I was, a business, a company, with no bank and bounced checks to cover.

However, instead of quitting, I quickly concluded that successful businessmen who wanted to continue receiving public attention must be resourceful. As I mentally surveyed my limited options, I remembered Joe's Quickie Mart, which was located a few blocks from the garage office. I drove over to the store and walked into the back room where I knew I would find Joe, the owner.

"Barry! How are you, my friend?" he greeted me. Joe was a family friend who put long hours at the store and had single-handedly built it from nothing to a successful business. Many times, as a youngster, I had helped him stock the shelves. The pay was always the same—one six pack of Hostess mini donuts (chocolate, of course) and a can of cola. Even if there was no work when I showed up, he would create some easy task to justify giving me the free food. Joe was a good man.

"I'm okay, Joe, but I have a small problem." We shook hands, and he guided me to the cage where the soda pop was stored. We pulled up two crates and sat down.

"How's the carpet cleaning business coming?" he asked. I paused before answering and took note of the many boxes of inventory. I had seen this stuff a thousand times, but now that I was in business, it had taken on a different meaning. They were no longer just boxes, but dollars and cents. Joe was making big bucks, and I wished I were in his shoes.

"To be honest with you, I'm having trouble keeping a checking account open," I confessed. "It seems that until I am eighteen years old, I'm not allowed to sign any legally binding contracts. So I can't write checks or deposit my customers' checks." I paused and lowered my voice. "Basically, Joe, I'm out of business." He paused and thought for a moment.

"I'll tell you what I'll do for you. Just bring me your customer checks, and I'll cash them for you. If you need to pay a bill or something, I'll give you a money order made out to whomever you want. This way you can keep control of your business." The idea sounded too good to be true. I squinted at him.

"How much will you charge me for each check?"

"The normal fee for the check-cashing business is 5% of the face amount of the check. But for you, I'll lower it to 3%. Does that sound fair?"

"It sure does!" I exclaimed, and wondered how I could repay such a favor. "Can I do anything for you in return?"

"Well, my carpets at the house are pretty dirty. Do you think you can take care of them for me?"

"Say no more! I'll personally go out and clean them for you. How about Saturday morning?"

"That would be great."

I rose and shook Joe's hand, feeling a weight roll off my chest, and left the store with a whole new outlook on life. *Who needs those stupid banks anyway?*

I drove home as fast as I could and pulled into the driveway. Mom and her best friend Vera Hojecki were my two telephone solicitors. They would call perspective customers and ask them if they needed their carpets cleaned. Between the two of them they averaged ten sales a day—enough to keep two carpet cleaning crews working all day.

I marched into my temporary office and asked my usual question, "How many leads did you guys get?"

Both of them smiled, a signal that generally meant business was good. And considering that I was paying each of them $225 a week, I expected production.

"Any calls?" I asked.

"Just Jerry," Vera said. "He was a little upset because the two-hundred dollar check you gave him bounced." For the record, passing a rubber check to a loan shark's check is not one of your better moves.

"Don't worry, I'll call him back. And there won't be any more bounced checks around here. I just made a deal with Joe at the store to get money orders in exchange for customer checks. No longer am I dependent on these bankers."

"That's great, Barry," Mom replied, hoping that what I said was true. The calls from all the angry people with bounced checks were getting to her.

I got comfortable in my chair before I picked up the phone to call Jerry. "Jerry, this is Barry. Look, I'm sorry that check bounced, but I've got some good—"

"I don't want to hear it, Barry," he cut me off angrily. "My bank won't take any more of your checks." He was furious. "Every week you come up with some excuse about why you can't pay me, and I always let you off the hook. But now you owe me eight hundred dollars, and I need the money! I'm running a business, too, and I can't afford to let you slip through the cracks every week."

There was no way I could get anywhere with this angry man over the phone. My brief experience in business had taught me the benefits of persuading with eye-to-eye contact. "Are you going to be at home for a while?" I asked.

"Yeah, I'll be here for another hour or so."

"I'll be there in twenty minutes." I hung up and raced to my car. *Another fire to put out,* I thought. "I'll be back in an hour!" I yelled to my mother. "Take my messages."

I was certainly getting a crash course in crisis management. I needed to make some kind of arrangement with Jerry, because if I gave him eight hundred dollars all at once, I wouldn't be able to meet payroll. Besides, he shouldn't have charged interest for my first two weeks in business, because I had spent most of that time organizing, not earning income.

Within fifteen minutes I was pulling into Jerry's driveway. As I knocked on his door, I wondered how much money he was actually making in the plumbing supply business. He always carried around a lot of cash neatly folded in his pocket, and everyone, including me, seemed to owe him money. I wished I were in such a position.

"Come on in, Barry," Jerry called from his usual spot on the end of a large sofa. He was writing checks from his business checking account. "What's the excuse this time?" he asked.

"The bank closed my account again. They found out I was only sixteen years old."

"Why did they let you open the account in the first place?" he snapped.

"I don't know. I guess they didn't suspect anyone under eighteen years of age would need a business account. And based on what I've been through these past several weeks, I can see why." I was relieved when he smiled—almost laughed. "But don't worry, Jerry. I've made a deal with a check-cashing place near my house. They're going to cash all my customer checks for a 3% fee and give me money orders in return. And you know that a money order can't bounce."

"That's great. But what about the eight hundred you owe me? I've got to give a guy a big loan, and it's going to make me short."

I wonder how much weekly interest he *has to pay?* I thought. I was certain that my presentation about the money orders would buy me some time with him. But now he was in need, and there could be no more delays.

Regardless, I gave it one more try. "If you could give me a few weeks, I can catch up. Mom and Vera have set up some big jobs that I'll be doing personally, so I can keep all the proceeds. Meanwhile, I've got payroll in three days and an overdue phone bill." A glance at Jerry told me he wasn't buying it.

"Why is it that I'm always last on your priority list, Barry?" he complained. "Without me, you wouldn't even have a company!"

Jerry wasn't the kind of guy I wanted to rile. Even though I was on steroids at the time and fairly strong, he was much bigger and a lot more intimidating.

"I know, Jerry, and I'm not trying to jerk you around, but it's just that I'm hurting right now. I can't walk into a bank like a normal businessman and get a loan when cash is short. I don't have that option. In fact, I can't even open a checking account!"

He listened attentively—a good sign. Then he said, "I'll tell you what I'll do. Come back tomorrow with five hundred dollars in cash or money orders. I'll let the other three hundred ride until after the first of the year. But that's the best I can do for you." He looked at me, awaiting a response.

Although I couldn't afford the five hundred, it was the best deal I was going to get. "That's fine, Jerry. I'll see you tomorrow about two o'clock. If I'm a little late, don't worry. I get out of school at one, and from there I'll need to go to the convenience store."

"No problem. I'll see you at two, or close to it."

I got up, shook his hand in defeat, and left the house. On the way home, I thought about how I was going to juggle my funds in order to meet my many obligations. If I gave Jerry five hundred, that would leave me with only six hundred to cover payroll and the phone bill. But those expenses totaled close to a thousand dollars. I was in trouble. Where would I come up with the other four hundred dollars?

The good news was that this was Tuesday, and I had until Friday—payday—to figure it all out. Maybe I could generate enough business on Wednesday and Thursday to cover the four hundred. But because I was in school, Mike and his partner had to do all the cleaning. Since I paid them 50% of whatever they brought in, this took a big bite out of my profits. *When will I start making money?* I wondered.

When I arrived at the garage-office I asked my mom and Vera if there were any calls.

"Just one. The supply store called and said the check that you swore wouldn't bounce, did. They want one hundred fifteen dollars in cash no later than Friday."

I moaned. "Great! I'm falling in love with today." I plopped into my chair and rubbed my tired eyes. "Don't worry, Mom, I'll straighten out this mess." It was difficult to keep up company morale when every two hours, someone was yelling about a bounced check. But that was a price I had to pay if I wanted the fame and glory that came with running my own business at the age of sixteen.

I gathered the checks from the past two days, and after making a few phone calls, dashed out of the garage and headed to my new "bank." At the convenience store I would get money to pay Jerry and the carpet supplies store.

The buzzer sounded its usual warning as I went through the door. As a youngster, I had passed through this door maybe a thousand times. I remembered back to those summer days when my sister Sheri and I walked barefoot to Joe's convenience store, bought some candy and soda pop, and played hide-and-seek for the rest of the day. Back then I wasn't worried about things like payroll, supplies, or Jerry Williams. Maybe ZZZZ Best was forcing me to grow up *too* quickly.

Joe's voice woke me from my daydream. "Come on over here, Barry. Let's see how much you got for me."

"A little over six hundred," I replied, waving the checks.

Joe opened a drawer and took out a small box containing several blank money orders. He also pulled out a small machine with a handle attached to it. Adjusting the numbers on the machine, Joe inserted the money orders one after another, pulling the handle for each. And then to my surprise, he simply initialed the bottom of each money order, pulled off his copy, and handed me the blank original.

"Don't you have to fill these out?" I asked.

"No, I only imprint and initial the money order. You fill in the 'pay to the order of' section on the top." He pointed to it, and I filled it in.

Then I endorsed the back of my customers' checks, gave them to Joe, and was ready to go.

"Can you wait here a minute, Barry? I need to get my logbook in the back so I can record this transaction."

"Go ahead, pal. I've got a minute."

He walked to the back of the store—out of sight—while I leaned against the counter next to the cash register, wondering again how I was going to cover this Friday's payroll. I looked down at my three money orders and then, out of the corner of my eye, I noticed the small box of blank money orders. There within easy reach lay the solution to all my problems. If I took just two of them and quickly stamped in two hundred dollars on each, I would be home free.

I surveyed the store. It was empty. Outside, the busy sidewalk gave way to a street filled with traffic. Rationalizations and justifications flooded my thinking: *I have people depending on me for payroll. It's not like I'll steal the money and go buy drugs. I'd be stealing for a good cause. Besides, no one is giving me a chance. It's not my fault that the banks keep closing my accounts, causing me to pay service charges on each returned check. I'll figure out some way to pay Joe back. He'll understand. Even if I get caught, I won't get in trouble because I'm just a kid trying to run a business.*

I looked at the money orders again, then at the imprinting machine. Joe was still gone. I thought about the embarrassment of failure. The last thing I wanted was to go out of business and have everybody think I was a flop—again! One final look. No customers, no Joe.

I grabbed two blank money orders from the bottom of the box. By the time Joe noticed, I'd have paid him back. I pulled the machine around, set it for two hundred dollars, inserted the money order, and nervously pulled down the handle. It barely made any noise. Before I put the second money order in, I looked around again. I pulled the handle. What seemed like an eternity really only took minutes.

Quickly I slid the money orders into my pocket, put the machine back neatly with the handle facing away from me, and made sure the box of money orders was in its original place. I had committed my first real crime!

"Sorry I took so long, Barry. It seems my wife took the logbook home with her." Joe walked to his position in front of the cash register. "But that's okay. Need anything else?"

"No, Joe," I said, hoping I didn't look or sound suspicious. "I'll probably be back tomorrow if that's okay?"

"That'll be great," he said as I turned toward the door. "Oh, Barry . . . don't forget Saturday morning—the carpet cleaning at my house?"

A cold chill crawled down my spine. This was my friend. He had helped me when nobody else would, and I had just stolen four hundred dollars from him. Now I was going to his house to clean his carpets! Stealing from Joe was a mistake, but it had to be done, right? I had no other option.

"I'll be there at nine o'clock, my friend." Saying that killed me.

இ

I would later learn from my years in prison that I was not the only one in custody who could pinpoint a "money order" moment. A point in time when what I call *the anatomy of failure* took place: contemplation plus rationalization equaled consent. When we committed our first crime.

In fact, of the 2.3 million people that bust the seams of our federal and state prisons across the country, all of us have one thing in common—none of us planned on being there! But after meeting hundreds of men during my seven years and four months in custody, I learned that we each had a story where we could pinpoint that first crime when consequences did not immediately follow actions (no lightning bolt came out of heaven after I stole the money orders), and thus the behavior was subtly reinforced.

And so when the next financial crisis occurs we are classically conditioned to revert back to what worked before—fraud and theft. And this continues until the stakes become too high and finally reach the point where our actions can no longer be concealed. That is when we learn the flaw in our thinking.

But then it's too late.

இ

Instant notoriety temporarily overshadowed the feelings of guilt I experienced from stealing money orders from a friend. I may have stolen but no one knew, and, after all, I would pay Joe back and no one would be hurt.

My income increased steadily but not significantly as the months passed. It did not take me long to discover that operating a business without a checking account was difficult at best. Another test of my total commitment to ZZZZ Best's success came when I was searching for a bank. I decided to disclose my age in the hopes that a banker might identify with the human-interest side of the ZZZZ Best story and he or she would ignore the minimum-age law to give me a shot. It was during this search that I met Doug Fitzgerald at Town Bank in a nearby suburb.

Doug was highly experienced and had a keen intellect. I convinced Doug to open a business checking account for me if I promised to discuss ZZZZ Best progress with him at least three times weekly. I think he was pleased to become a mentor to an up-and-coming entrepreneur. I was happy to let him feel like he was helping a kid, but I knew better. I used my age to manipulate situations when the odds were not in my favor. In addition to Town Bank, Jerry Williams also used his influence at Second Savings, and I opened a checking account there as well.

To handle the extra business and stay ahead of mounting expenses, I hired additional telephone solicitors to work in the evenings and a second carpet cleaning crew. But Jerry's two hundred dollar weekly payment, continuing payrolls, and other expenses caught up with me, and I faced yet another financial crisis.

To make matters worse, Joe called, having traced his missing money orders to me. My biggest problem next to rationalization became denial. *If I can just hang on until school gets out, I'll be able to fix all these problems*, I thought. Since I could do most of the jobs myself, my profit margin would double and I'd climb out of debt—if I could survive until June. Thus began the rationalization which finally buried me. *If I could survive until . . . fill in the blank . . .* was my consistent mantra.

After Joe's call, I sat at my garage desk and developed a plan of action. I checked the balance in my checkbooks from Town Bank and Second Savings and realized that I was almost twelve hundred dollars short. Just then I came across a slip of paper from Town Bank that showed my current account balance. It was higher than what the checkbook revealed—presumably because some of the checks I had written had not yet cleared. I picked up my Second Savings checkbook and wondered how long it would take for a check deposited at Town Bank to make it back to Second Savings. *At least a couple of days,* I thought, *and definitely long enough for me to meet the payroll.* Within minutes I was on my way to Town Bank.

"Why are you depositing a check from one ZZZZ Best account to another?" an officer at Town Bank asked.

"Just transferring some funds," I said confidently. "Anything wrong with that?"

"No, Barry, not at all. I just wanted to make sure there was no check kiting going on . . . it's my job." She initialed her approval on the deposit slip. So what I was doing actually had a name, *check kiting*.

That weekend I worried about how long it would take for that check to hit Second Savings. If it bounced and Jerry found out, I'd be in big trouble. Not only would I have Joe after me, but Jerry and Doug Fitzgerald as well. I had to cover that check!

I am truly ashamed to admit what I did in order to cover the check. At the time I thought it was much easier to ask for forgiveness than permission. In racking my brain for a way to make money, I remembered my grandmother's jewelry.

When I weighed the option of taking a few items she may not miss with saving my company from ruin, Grandma lost. I didn't mean to hurt her, but I was going to hurt a lot more people, like my employees, if I didn't take some valuable pieces. If you've ever pawned anything, you know that you literally receive pennies on the dollar for what you sell. I hate to say that I considered the pawnbrokers to be thieves in light of what I was doing. I covered the check and survived another crisis.

As ZZZZ Best continued to grow, so did my confidence. Confidence blossomed to cockiness, and my parents found my behavior difficult to control. I was an eleventh grader who was earning wages for himself and his family. I was a force to be reckoned with.

When school let out for the summer, I was able to devote one hundred percent of my time to ZZZZ Best. During the day I cleaned carpets, and at night I ran the phone room. I slowly caught up with Jerry and made the payrolls. My grandmother did notice that some of her jewelry was missing. Unfortunately, everyone remembered I was the last one in her house before it was missing, and I was pinned with accusations. I fell back on my usual excuses and denials.

I decided to move the company from my parents' garage to the two-story Reseda Business Center on Darby Avenue, not far from my house.

The center was leasing industrial office space at very low rates. For three hundred dollars a month, I rented two upstairs offices in a building that housed automotive shops, cabinetmakers, and ironworkers. The biggest expense of the move was the phones. Pacific Bell wanted a thousand dollar deposit to install six telephone lines. As usual, I was not prepared for the reality of running a business and had to borrow more money from Jerry! Nonetheless, the thrill of housing ZZZZ Best in a real office setting far outweighed the price of Jerry's money. Much later I would learn that my pride would cost me far more than the interest ever did.

I hired additional solicitors and cleaners, hoping they would help cover the new expenses. This sudden expansion, along with the move, boosted company morale to an all-time high. I began to hold weekly mandatory employee meetings. To increase professionalism, I ruled that all cleaners and solicitors, including my mother, refer to me as "Mr. Minkow." I figured that since I had to endure so much as the owner of the company, I was entitled to some respect.

Throughout the summer of 1983, my relationship with Doug Fitzgerald deepened. He advised me to take out business insurance, provide employee incentives, and hire an accountant. I trusted Doug, but not enough to tell him about the check kiting, Grandma's jewelry, and the money order incident. After seeing an abundance of checks written to Jerry Williams, Doug inquired as to my relationship with him. I told him that Jerry had lent me some money but was not a partner in the company. He sensed that I wasn't telling the whole story about Jerry, but he never pressed the issue.

﹏

Doug was onto something I would later use to catch fraud. Even though I was trying to hide my debt to Jerry Williams, consistent payments to one person over a period of time revealed a financial relationship that I did not want to disclose. In like manner, companies who perpetrate fraud usually resort to hiding debt to create a more favorable balance sheet. Doug's inquiry into Williams taught me that repetitive payments to a particular person over a period of time was a vehicle employed to hide debt and the true financial condition of a company.

∽

To get the company into a positive cash flow situation, I reverted to my old check-kiting scheme. But after I let a few checks bounce, the banks were on to me. A furious Doug Fitzgerald called me into his office, presented the evidence of my crime, and asked me to explain myself.

I denied any wrongdoing and blamed the events on the rapid growth of the company. "I'm only seventeen, Doug! I can't keep control of everything." This excuse usually worked with everyone, except Doug!

He got out of his chair and moved to the end of the desk. Staring me in the eye, he gave me the following warning: "I like you, Barry, and I have a lot of respect for what you've accomplished. But if you're going to make it big in the business world, you're going to need integrity. That means you've got to be honest with your banker. I'm going to let you make payments on the overdraft that you have incurred as a result of the check kiting. But if you do anything like this again, I'll have to close the account." He stared into my eyes with quiet intensity. "You got it, Kid?"

"Yes sir, Doug," I said, putting on my most sincere and slightly peevish face. I apologized and assured him it wouldn't happen again. If only I had meant what I said, my life would have turned out much differently.

∽

I returned to Cleveland High School for my senior year as an object of great respect with teachers and students alike. Before then, only the star athletes received recognition, but the success of ZZZZ Best had changed that. I had attained my goal of being known and accepted by others and enjoyed basking in the glory of favorable attention.

The media continued to hail me as the seventeen-year-old boy genius. Most times I was completely willing to believe what they wrote, ignoring the truth of the depth of my deception. Banks and other financial institutions actually called me and solicited my business now.

The demands of running the company and going to school finally took their toll on my workout program. But because my ego wouldn't allow my body to deteriorate, I increased my steroid intake. At the time, the effects of steroid abuse were not widely published, and if I heard anything negative, I promptly ignored it.

On the business side, it was the same old, same old. The additional employees and the overhead of a real office once again depleted my available cash. I struggled to meet the weekly expenses and missed three or four "Jerry" payments. I was as bad off financially as when I started my business a year earlier. My inability to retain capital seemed to be the problem. There had to be a better way than scrambling from week to week—and I was determined to find it.

Doug Fitzgerald was happy that I had paid down the overdraft at Town Bank. Back in his good graces, I asked him to approve a business loan for ZZZZ Best. After all, I had been in business for over a year, employed almost twenty people, and had proved that the company could generate consistent income.

But when Doug explained that to qualify for a loan I needed assets, profit-and-loss statements, balance sheets, and the like prepared by an accountant, I was at a loss. Not only did I not have that stuff—I didn't even know what a profit-and-loss statement was! What I didn't know was killing my company.

I left the bank in a huff, swearing that I would find a banker out there who had heard my story and would make ZZZZ Best a loan without all those financial statements. But Doug was right. I spent most of my Christmas break traipsing from bank to bank and did not find one that would bend the rules. Most demanded a three-year track record before one could even be considered for a loan. Despite all the no's, I refused to get discouraged: if they wanted to block my legitimate avenues for raising money, I could always turn to some illegitimate avenues.

I determined that no matter what the cost, I needed to open another ZZZZ Best location to generate more income to help pay the expenses. My goal was to get one location running so well that it would pay the bills for both offices, leaving the income from the other office as pure profit. The cost of another office, I figured, would be ten thousand dollars.

The next scheme for raising funds hatched quickly. This time I defrauded an insurance company. I had insured my carpet cleaning equipment for almost twenty thousand, much more than the actual value. The insurance company had not done their due diligence to find out if the figure was inflated, and no one ever came to actually see what I had. The agent had told me that if the equipment were ever stolen, the company would cut me a check for any amount up to that figure.

The Reseda Business Center had no security to speak of, and many people had access to the upstairs office space. One afternoon, I waited until my last employee left and then I snuck back into the office and staged a burglary. I pulled out a few drawers, threw away old upholstery cleaner, relocated some carpet-repair tools, and went home for the evening, leaving my office people to discover the break-in the next morning.

I instructed my mother to call the police and have them make a report. That way I could quickly substantiate my insurance claim and get the money faster. Within days, an adjuster from my insurance company handed me a draft for the entire amount of my claim, twelve thousand dollars. I have to admit the whole episode was really easy—too easy. As I drove to Town Bank to deposit the draft, I thought about how I could explain this large influx of cash to Doug Fitzgerald.

I couldn't tell him I had been burgled of twelve thousand dollars' worth of equipment, because he had been to the office and knew I didn't have nearly that much stuff. I needed to come up with something else. I remembered that Doug knew that ZZZZ Best had occasionally worked some small, emergency water-damage claims for Trust Insurance. He knew that Gary Todd, a friend from the gym, was an adjuster for Trust, and that he had called on ZZZZ Best more than once to clean carpet damaged by water or fire. The payments were always made by draft.

I walked into the bank and told Doug that Gary had recommended ZZZZ Best to a friend who was an adjuster for another insurance carrier, that we had been called upon by this new client to perform restoration services on a large building, and that the draft was simply the money we had rightfully earned for services rendered. He believed me. He even gave me immediate credit on the draft, which enabled me to purchase supplies for ZZZZ Best's second location. I had successfully pulled off another crime, and each time it seemed a little easier to rationalize. I convinced myself of what I later learned other convicted white-collar criminals had—specifically that committing fraud as a *means* to a legitimate end and not as an end in itself was okay. As long as the use-of-proceeds for the theft or lies or stolen money orders was for the greater good, then dishonesty was justified. And little did I know then that the excuse that I had invented for Doug Fitzgerald would end up being the real fuel for the ZZZZ Best fraud.

⌐

I located the second office in Thousand Oaks. If running one office was difficult while going to school, trying to run two was nearly impossible. Instead of struggling to pay twenty people a week, I now had fifty to pay. Plus, I spent many hours traveling back and forth from Thousand Oaks. But with the expansion came increases in power and control. Being the boss of almost fifty employees kept me in constant demand, which helped me feel needed and wanted. My emotional health depended on how well the company was performing.

Unfortunately, the Thousand Oaks office ran into immediate problems because of management. The carpet cleaning industry was notoriously "easy entry," which meant it attracted its fair share of drug addicts and alcoholics, not to mention white-collar crooks like me! Consequently, to save the office, I moved my best telephone solicitor, my mom, to the office, who straightened out the problems, but not before my cash was again depleted.

On the ego front, the news was good. The competition had finally begun to take notice of ZZZZ Best. Larger companies, which had for years dominated the industry in the Los Angeles area, were now getting a run for their money by a seventeen-year-old kid! Our telephone soliciting and prominent yellow pages ads brought us a substantial volume of business. But, because of my lack of financial experience, we were unable to reap the benefit of these large gross sales.

As my eighteenth birthday approached in March of 1984, my parents were concerned about my college plans. Before I started ZZZZ Best, it had always been my desire to continue my education. But after tasting the fulfillment and fame of the business world, I changed my mind. After all, I was already well ahead of people who had graduated from college. I had a leg up on the rest of life since I had started so early.

As I turned eighteen, my family, friends, the business community, and the media heralded me as one of the top ten entrepreneurs of the 1980s. I had done a great job of concealing how I had achieved my success; no one knew who I really was. As for me, all I knew was that I was afraid of growing older and losing the "boy genius" designation. Once I was over eighteen, the novelty of "young guy makes it big" would wear off. The fear of losing that public attention kept me up at night. I began to understand how all those child stars felt as they aged and their shows got cancelled. But I refused to go out like that. I concluded that the only way to overcome the obstacle of age was to keep increasing the amount of stores, income, and number of employees.

The pressure I heaped on myself dramatically changed my philosophy about doing business. I put unrealistic demands on myself and evolved into an intolerant, impatient perfectionist who was never satisfied. Even on weekends I couldn't rest. If by accident I slept in one day, I'd have to explain to my family and friends how hard I had worked all week to justify some much-needed rest. I wasn't satisfied unless people viewed me as the hardest and most dedicated worker they'd ever seen.

With only ninety days of high school left, I tried to "tread water" financially until I could dedicate my full attention to the company. Although spring is usually the best time of year for the carpet cleaning industry, production in both offices was down. And because I was totally dependent on the day-to-day sales to pay the bills, I was in trouble. The cash demands of a company with fifty employees grew so great that I waited until after 6:00 p.m. on Fridays to pass out payroll checks, knowing that with the banks closed, they couldn't be cashed. This really upset the employees, many of whom saw through this tactic and threatened to quit.

One week several of my carpet cleaners tried to cash their checks early Monday morning while I was at school. With no money in the account, Town Bank turned them away. Just weeks from being able to devote my full attention to the company, I was in danger of losing it. But I'd been in similar predicaments before and knew what I had to do.

To resolve this latest crisis, I exercised my newly acquired legal rights (I was finally eighteen) by opening checking accounts at five different banks! I then took a few of the temporary checks from my new accounts and deposited over seven thousand dollars into my Town Bank account. Having gained the confidence of Doug Fitzgerald and others at the bank, I got immediate credit on the checks. This helped me to cover the payroll and avoid a massive walkout. But to avoid detection, I had to cover the temporary checks.

To do this, I staged a break-in at the Thousand Oaks office. This time, however, the adjuster for my new insurance carrier—the other company had canceled my policy after the first claim—said it would take a week before the draft would be ready. After I promised to pay him a thousand dollars interest plus the principal within a week, Jerry Williams lent me more money. I had pulled off another check-kiting scheme. I received the draft for almost seventeen thousand dollars six days later—just in time to cover the next payroll.

Rumors spread within the company that I had staged the Thousand Oaks break-in. Many felt two burglaries in six months were not probable, or at least were highly suspicious. I met this problem head-on by requiring all employees to attend a company meeting. I spoke boldly and blamed the break-ins on "jealous competition." I had a world full of people at my disposal where I could lay blame.

As my senior year came to a close, I was satisfied that I had accomplished every goal I had set for myself. Like most high schools, Cleveland had contests for "Most Popular," "Most Likely To Succeed," and many others. I was one of the few students who won two awards: "Most Likely To Succeed" and "Class Clown." In my eyes, the acknowledgement proved that ZZZZ Best had met my deepest need—acceptance! I didn't stop to see the irony in the two normally opposing awards. Class clown is usually reserved for goof-offs or people least likely considered to accomplish anything. For me it was fitting; it was my antics that kept me in business!

On the way home from a graduation party, I put my arm around my tired girlfriend and thought about what I had missed during high school. ZZZZ Best had prevented me from attending many football games, parties, and social gatherings. But that had been my choice. In fact, if I hadn't started ZZZZ Best, I probably would not have been invited anyway. I had willingly given up high school fun for big-time finance.

My date fell asleep, and as I sped down the quiet freeway that warm summer night, I knew my formal educational career had ended. I resolved to make an impact on the business world that no one would ever forget. I would meet that goal with great aplomb.

3 | UNLEASHED

I soon realized that people had taken advantage of my high school distractions. Some of my carpet cleaners were arriving at their scheduled appointments, suggesting that the customers call the company and cancel the job, and then cleaning the carpets for much less money, which they pocketed. I had lost a significant amount of business and fired one of the men involved. Out of school for only a few weeks, I was already seeing the benefits of hands-on management.

Next I promoted Mike McGee to be my right-hand man. A dedicated, hard worker who gave ZZZZ Best one hundred percent every day, Mike had been with me since the garage days and had earned my total trust. He looked up to me, and because I feared losing his respect, I didn't disclose my past or present crimes. Together we attempted to straighten out the company's many problems.

As the money from the Thousand Oaks burglary dwindled away, I considered new means of raising funds. I was tired of waiting until the last minute and then panicking to cover payroll. I wanted to stay ahead of the financial game. Two things helped me do this. First, I put a "Money Wanted" ad in the *Los Angeles Times*, hoping to find a willing investor. Second, I met a man named Paul Weaver.

Paul owned a construction company. Like Jerry Williams, he was very wealthy and often invested in other businesses. Though he was much older than I, we got along well and he had become interested in ZZZZ

Best. He was impressed by the fact that I ran my own business at such a young age.

One summer day in 1984, after Paul and I had finished working out at the health club, he came to visit my Reseda branch. After a quick tour of the facility (by then I had leased additional office space), we retired to my office.

"So, how much would it cost me to get in on the action, Barry?"

His question caught me off guard. I wasn't used to people asking to give me money.

"I don't know, Paul. What would you feel comfortable with?"

"Listen, Kid," he said sternly, "I'm a businessman. When I see a deal I like, I go for it." He took a deep breath. "I like what you've got going here and I want in. You tell me how much you want."

The good news was that he wasn't looking for a partnership or a percentage of the company. I would retain full control over ZZZZ Best, regardless. The bad news was that his money was going to be expensive. But I was used to that and hadn't quite figured out how I kept ending up in that situation.

"Well, I'm considering opening another office in Anaheim. But it's going to be pretty expensive. Can you afford twenty-five thousand?"

He didn't even blink. "Tomorrow I want you to go to my bank and pick up a twenty-five-thousand-dollar cashier's check." He got up from the chair and walked toward the door. "Every Monday, I'll expect you to give me twelve hundred in cash—seven hundred to reduce the principal and five hundred interest. Can you afford those payments?"

I smiled. That was much more money than Jerry had ever lent me. Should I have asked for more? "You bet I can. Anaheim is the perfect place for a new location. I'll 'clean up' over there."

"Write down my beeper number. If you ever need me for any reason, just call and I'll get back to you."

I wrote down his number, went over to shake his hand, and he strode off.

With all the internal problems and financial difficulties, I didn't think opening more locations was possible or wise. But because I needed to give Paul a legitimate reason for his loan, I was forced to expand before the company was ready. As I sat in my office, I thought about how angry Jerry would be if he knew about my new relationship with Paul. For that reason, I told

Jerry nothing about him. Unbeknownst to me at the time, I had learned another key ingredient to fraud perpetration—hiding debt.

༄

A few days later, Rick Price, an investor in the Los Angeles area, responded to my ad in the *L.A. Times*. To stay ahead of any future cash flow crunch, I agreed to meet with him.

After touring our offices, Price asked me some technical questions about the company's gross sales, net profit per store, and related financial conditions. Basically, he wanted financial statements. Unlike Paul and Jerry, who were street smart and knew how to hustle, Price was a professional who had made millions over the years.

To impress him (and to get some of his money), I needed someone who could prepare financial statements for ZZZZ Best. Through an acquaintance I found a public accountant who asked to see all my company records. Unfortunately, my records were in such poor shape he found it impossible to track my past business activity. But if I didn't have a profit-and-loss statement that confirmed the company's earnings, Price wouldn't lend me any money.

So I convinced the accountant, for a large fee, to prepare bogus financial statements and tax returns confirming large profits that didn't exist. Although Rick Price preferred CPA-prepared statements, he accepted the statements prepared by my public accountant and agreed to loan me thirty thousand dollars. Interestingly, his payment schedule was identical to Paul's: a weekly amount of about twelve hundred, with seven hundred to pay down the principal and the balance as interest, cleverly disguised as an "advisor's fee." Price also had me sign an agreement—something Paul and Jerry had never done—that forced me to pledge my company as collateral.

I was amazed how a man of Price's caliber would set up a loan requiring such high interest. But if he chose to be blinded by greed, I had no problem taking advantage of him. Or was he taking advantage of me?

My relationship with Doug Fitzgerald and Town Bank continued to improve. Doug allowed me to open a merchant account that enabled ZZZZ Best to accept MasterCard and Visa, making sales easier. He even eased up on monitoring my account, which allowed me to slip the large deposits from Paul Weaver and Rick Price in without incident. With this unprecedented cash surplus, I decided to start playing the part of the "big-time business-man." Until mid-1984, I had spent most of the ZZZZ Best proceeds on company expansion and paying people off. I still lived at home and drove an older car. I needed tangible personal assets to prove that ZZZZ Best was really making it.

So I went to Granada Nissan and purchased a brand-new, twenty-thousand-dollar 300ZX. To build my credit, I bought the car on credit, putting only six thousand down. Because 1984 was the first year for the 300ZX, many people stared as I drove down the highway. The car became my elo-quent rebuttal to skeptics who doubted that ZZZZ Best was earning big bucks. Then I purchased a brand-new, two-bedroom condominium in Canoga Park, one with a pool right outside my window. Although I couldn't move in until March of 1985, I was satisfied, since I had something signifi-cant to show for two years as a businessman.

The new car improved my social life considerably. Girls who had never given me a second glance were now anxious to go out with an entrepreneur in his flashy sports car. Magazines, newspapers, and local television shows also boosted my image with more tales of the "Amazing Barry Minkow Story."

❧

Mike had tried to tell me that opening the Anaheim office would be a mis-take; we didn't have the management depth to handle another location. But because I wanted it (the part he knew) and needed it as an excuse for raising additional funds (the part he did not know), he was determined to make it work. I relocated several key people from the two existing offices, hoping they could run Anaheim profitably. As a result, not only did the Anaheim office lose money, the other locations suffered from the loss of key people. Now I was stuck with three unprofitable stores and large, weekly loan payments.

To make things worse, one of my employees went to work for another carpet cleaning company and spread the word that I was losing big money and was in danger of going under. The rumor made the rounds of the com-petition and got back to all the ZZZZ Best offices.

As I fought to keep up company morale, a manager from one of my biggest competitors thought it would be fun to steal some of my employees right out from under my nose. I showed up at the Reseda office just as he was assuring two of my men that I was going out of business. Rather than make a scene, I asked him to step into my office. Once the door was closed, I asked where he got off coming to my office trying to steal my people.

We argued loudly before I asked him to leave. He warned that ZZZZ Best wouldn't be in business forever, and I brushed off his comment with the threat that no one would get in my way.

But in the back of my mind I knew his rumors had validity. My onetime cash surplus had dwindled to fewer than ten thousand dollars—far short of what I needed to pay the weekly bills. Once again I faced a financial crisis that could crush me—unless I thought of another way to raise capital.

I rushed to my car to make my daily deposit at the bank, but because of my unexpected visitor, I hadn't made it there in time. Not good for those who play the float in order to survive. Pausing at a stoplight, I looked over the two stacks of deposit slips—one for customers who paid by check and the other for customers who paid by credit card—and realized that the credit card slips were written in by hand, not imprinted. With so many crews in the field, it would have been impossible to give each an imprinter. As long as the customer signed the credit card slip, the bank agreed to accept the deposit.

If I used the names and numbers of my legitimate credit card customers to make up additional slips in large amounts and forged their signatures, I could raise immediate cash. Of course, the customers would dispute the charges, but that would take months. In the meantime, I'd have free use of their money. By the time I pulled back into the company parking lot, I had it all planned: the following morning I would start creating bogus credit card slips.

♒

Jerry had asked to meet with me privately a week earlier, but because I was otherwise occupied writing phony credit card receipts, I had been able to put him off until now.

"I'm not an idiot, Barry," he groused. "I see this Rick Price guy and Paul coming around the office. I know you're probably getting money from them . . . and I don't care." He waited for me to look up from my telephone messages. "I only care about me! You'd have nothing if I hadn't helped you get started."

"I know that, and I appreciate what you've done for me. You're my friend for life," I said, and returned to my work.

"Good, I'm glad you feel that way, because I want you to do something for me." I stopped everything and listened. "I see your new car and I want the same thing."

So, this was Jerry's price for my freedom. It was futile to argue with him. He was still a little stronger, a little meaner, and a whole lot more experienced than I. If I complied with the monthly car payments, I would be free to borrow and deal with whomever I wanted, without looking over my shoulder to see if he was watching. To me, that was worth two cars.

Jerry had loaned me money off and on in ZZZZ Best's early history. We'd never kept an accurate accounting, what with the heavy interest payments, so it wasn't clear what the principal balance was at any given time. We just mutually assumed I had a limitless obligation to him for making ZZZZ Best possible.

"No problem," I said calmly. I reached across the desk and shook his hand. "Let me know who to send the car payments to."

That's one lesson I learned the hard way. I needed to keep accurate records for the heavy loans. But the rest of my records, well, they could be slightly less accurate. Our company name at the top of the page was still ZZZZ Best, but that was all that was correct!

Jerry was satisfied with the car. He had gotten exactly what he wanted. As for me, I concluded that some battles weren't worth fighting as long as it didn't cost me the company. I knew there would come a time when I would be released from the clutches of Jerry Williams, and I looked forward to that day.

With my cash demands temporarily eased by the credit card fraud, Mike and I determined to spend more time shoring up the Thousand Oaks and Anaheim offices. From November 1984 to February 1985, I drove to Anaheim at least twice weekly. I enjoyed spending time in my car, away from the pressures of ZZZZ Best.

By February 1985, Mike and I had jacked up the company's productivity. Whether the locations actually made money was impossible to tell because of the heavy loans and expenses they were forced to absorb. Nevertheless, gross sales were substantially higher—an important point for those of us who lived week to week.

When I went to Town Bank to paint Doug Fitzgerald a brighter picture than usual, I learned that the bank had fallen on hard times and been forced by the FDIC to close its doors. Doug was moving to another bank, Third Union, and I immediately moved the company accounts along with him. Despite Doug's efforts, it took almost three weeks before I could open another merchant account and deposit more credit card slips. The delay nearly buried me. Once opened, I made up for lost time by running almost one thousand dollars' worth of phony drafts through the account daily. It wasn't long before they were on to me.

A disturbed and disappointed Doug Fitzgerald summoned me to his office one spring morning. He told me the bank had discovered that I had processed close to fifty thousand dollars' worth of bogus credit card charges. To protect themselves, they had frozen the ZZZZ Best accounts and bounced all my checks. Doug was powerless to help.

Faced with the possibility of losing everything, I asked Paul for a $30,000 loan. Based on my consistent payments on the first loan, he willingly gave me the money. Then I borrowed $12,500 from Jerry, promising to have it back to him in two months, with interest of course. Finally, I went to Rick Price. For months he and I had talked about a $45,000 loan and, because I was in trouble, I took his money as well. Within a two-week period, I raised over $80,000, which was enough to cover the bad checks and get a fresh start at a new bank, National Federal Savings and Loan. Doug agreed to give me a good recommendation if I promised (in writing) to pay back the credit card vouchers as they came in. I even put $10,000 in Third Union Bank as a gesture of good faith.

Even though Doug briefly interrogated me on the credit card incident—I blamed the fraud on "unscrupulous subcontractors"—it seemed the banks were more interested in recovering their losses than in prosecuting any wrongdoing. There were no legal repercussions. This made a lasting impression on me. As long as I paid the money back and nobody got hurt, I could do whatever I wanted.

⌒

To celebrate my nineteenth birthday, *Entrepreneur* magazine profiled me as the "Entrepreneur of the Month" for March of 1985. The publicity couldn't have come at a more opportune time. The credit card fraud had tainted my credibility with some in the financial community and with ZZZZ Best telephone personnel who took customers' complaints about overcharges. I used the entrepreneur "title" to corroborate the authenticity of ZZZZ Best, made sure all the employees read the article, and even sent a copy to Warner Center Bank, hoping to earn their trust. The media clearly imputed credibility, or in my case reestablished the credibility I had temporarily lost.

Also in March, I moved into the Canoga Park condominium, having furnished it for less than ten thousand dollars. Leaving home was tough, but it was time for Barry Minkow the businessman to take advantage of his success. I brought over Mom, Vera, and Mike, the three employees who had been with me since the garage days. They strolled through the condo and made the appropriate ooh's and ah's as they entered each area. They each possessed the one quality that I demanded above all else: one hundred percent devotion and loyalty to me, at all times.

The excitement generated by the *Entrepreneur* magazine award, coupled with the purchase of the condo, helped ease the pain of turning nineteen. Though I was getting older, my accomplishments (as far as anyone knew) were keeping pace with my age. I was still newsworthy.

My March celebration soon came to a sobering halt. The credit card drafts bombarded me in April, wiping out my ten-thousand-dollar cushion and causing Doug to call me daily. Fearing prosecution if I didn't pay, I delivered funds to Third Union Bank twice weekly. I also had to come up with the weekly loan payments to Paul, Jerry, and Rick Price. Company payrolls and expenses reached an all-time high. And large yellow pages ads, purchased in several phone books back when I thought the credit card fraud would last forever, were now coming due to the tune of almost five thousand dollars per month!

My larger problem was that of limited options. With my three investors "maxed out," I had no way to replenish my cash position. The three offices could not support all the expenses. Plus, I had promised to open a San Diego office soon. Several of my key cleaners and solicitors had their hearts set on relocating to ZZZZ Best's newest branch. If I didn't follow through, I would have a serious morale problem on my hands.

By the end of April, I was back to kiting checks, buying time until I could come up with a temporary cure for my financial ills. I fell behind in payments to Rick Price and was surprised when he cut me no slack and tried to foreclose against the company, assuming that repossessing my equipment would shut me down.

When the marshals handed me a subpoena to appear in court, I immediately went to a lawyer for advice. After reading the agreements, he told me that if the judge ruled against me, ZZZZ Best would be out of business. But for some reason, I wasn't scared. I had been through similar situations and had always come out on top. I was confident that once again I would figure out some way to solve the problem.

I went to court, and my defense was the truth—namely, that Price was charging me an illegal rate of interest on the loan. The judge believed me. In fact, he called Price a usurer, stating that he had no experience in the carpet cleaning industry and was therefore undeserving of his "advisory fees." He literally accused Price of disguising his "consulting" fees as a vehicle for an illegal, high interest rate loan. I had dodged another bullet. The ruling forced Rick Price to accept monthly payments on a significantly reduced principal balance.

⟋

Even with this victory, as May came to a close, I was in deep financial trouble. My checks began to bounce, and it looked as if my luck had run out. As I was sitting in my office, trying desperately to figure out some way to hold things together, the phone rang. The call changed the course of my life more dramatically.

4 | FRESH CASH

"Hi, Ralph, how are you?" I asked as I tried to focus on his call. "I'm good, Barry. How's business?"

"Good . . . good," I lied through gritted teeth. "How can I help you?"

"I've got a very special carpet repair job for you. It's in a townhouse development. The guy has a busted seam and needs a cleaning."

"No problem, Ralph. I'll have a crew over there tomorrow."

"Okay. But I need you to do the job personally. The customer is refusing to close escrow unless it's done right." There was a short silence before his voice dropped to a whisper. "He's supposed to be a mob-type guy, Barry. His name is Ron Knox. He's very wealthy and very dangerous."

Although I hadn't heard of Ron Knox, I'd heard the mob often lent money to small businesses. Ralph had my interest. "When do you want this job done?"

"Today if possible. Are you busy right now?"

"Yeah, but I can swing by there—"

"Listen, Barry," he interrupted, "I want you to be careful with this guy. He's got a reputation."

I shrugged off his concern. "Don't worry, Ralph. I'll be fine." I jotted down the address, picked up the keys to one of the trucks, and was on my way. I had seen movies and television shows that portrayed gangsters as loan sharks who "bust up people who don't pay." But I was desperate the day I pulled into Ron Knox's driveway, and I was willing to do business with anyone, even if it meant pledging my life as collateral.

～

"So, you're the wiz kid I keep reading about." Ron Knox was about fifty years old and impeccably dressed. From his seat at the dining room table, he was watching me glue together a seam in his hallway carpet. "I saved that February article in the *Herald-Examiner* that profiled your company. The press really seems to like you."

I smiled and kept working. "It's good for business, Mr. Knox. I never turn them down."

"Neither did I when I ran my own company," he boasted.

"Really?" I looked up from my work, pretending an interest in his past business dealings.

"Yeah. I started a company out of my house. After years of hard work, we went public and the stock was worth millions."

I didn't know much about stock and public companies, but I didn't want to let Ron know that. "What happened?" I asked curiously.

Ron got up out of his chair, walked to the kitchen counter, and picked up several articles. He brought them to where I was working and dropped them at my side.

"The government took everything from me because they said I didn't follow the rules. Once they put a jacket like that on you, it's only a matter of time before you fail." I glanced at the articles. Ron Knox and his company had been front-page news at one time. "But originally I started out like you did. In fact, we've got more in common than you think."

I removed the steaming iron, set it on its stand, and walked over to the dining room table. This was the opportunity I'd been waiting for. "I just bet we do," I said with a toothy grin. "Did you have trouble raising money and getting bank loans?"

Ron Knox moved and answered questions slowly and thoughtfully. He was in no hurry and kept things under control. "Sure I did. But I had some close associates who lent me money when I needed it. How about you?"

I took a deep breath and forced myself to look distraught.

"I'm not that lucky, Mr. Knox. I've got three stores, almost one hundred employees, and could grow even bigger if I had the capital. But for some reason, no one wants to lend a nineteen-year-old businessman any money."

Ron listened attentively. "How much money will you need to expand?"

I thought back to my first meeting with Paul, when I had given him a low figure in answer to the same question. I wouldn't make that mistake again. "About one hundred thousand dollars?"

"It costs that much to open a few rug cleaning stores?" Ron asked a bit skeptically. He probably wanted to hear a specific use for the money.

Knowing I couldn't lie about the cost of opening a carpet cleaning location, I remembered the time I had deposited a large insurance draft into my Town Bank account and told Doug it was for work done on a restoration job.

"No, it doesn't," I replied honestly. "But the company performs restoration services on buildings damaged by fire and water. And the bigger the job, the more money I need to buy materials and supplies to complete it."

"How many of these jobs do you have going right now?"

"Three," I lied. "One in Torrance, one in South Pasadena, and the other in San Diego. That's where my next office is going—if I can raise the money."

Ron pushed a few newspapers around on the table and picked up a pad and pen. After jotting a few notes to himself, he opened his briefcase and pulled out the February 1985 *Herald-Examiner* article.

"So you're the big Barry Minkow." His laughter eased the tension. "I'll tell you what I'll do for you, Kid." He scribbled an address on his notepad and handed it to me. "Later on today, I want you to stop by my office. Bring me your financial statements and some proof of these insurance restoration jobs, and I'll raise you all the money you'll ever need."

With great difficulty I restrained my enthusiasm. It had taken less than thirty minutes for Ron Knox to solve a problem that had hampered me for two and a half years. "I'm just about done here, so if you'll give me until four o'clock, I think I can get you everything you asked for."

He nodded with satisfaction. "Four o'clock it is. I'll look forward to it." On the way back from Ron's townhouse, I thought about the items he had requested. The financial statements were no problem; my accountant had prepared those for the Rick Price deal. But how would I prove I had thousands of dollars in restoration business? And what would happen to me if Ron Knox lent me the money and found out I was lying about the jobs?

Unfortunately, I had no other choice. I suppressed the "MOB BUSTS UP JEWISH BOY" headlines that passed through my mind and focused on what I needed to do to keep the company running. As long as Ron got his money back, nothing would ever happen to me. I hoped.

ꙅ

"This is Gary Todd."

"Hi, Gary, it's Barry. How's it going?"

"Good, partner. How's business?" he asked.

"Great! Is Partner Insurance keeping you busy?"

Gary had left Trust Insurance for Partner, mostly because of me. In 1983 I had abused our friendship by falsifying two Trust drafts. Gary hadn't been fired, but his superiors had questioned why he had entrusted claims to a seventeen-year-old kid. He resigned and was later hired by Partner Insurance.

"Yeah, I'm busy. But it keeps me out of trouble. What's on your mind?"

"Do you feel like making twenty-five hundred dollars for doing nothing?"

"Depends on what kind of nothing."

"Well, Gary, I'm going to level with you. I've got a guy who will lend me all the money I'll ever want—if I can confirm to him that I'm doing large restoration jobs. What I need are a few letterheads from Partner's and for you to confirm three or four jobs. To play it safe, I'll put your direct number on the letter so that when people call, they'll only reach you." I gave Gary a chance to think about what I had said before I continued. "If it wasn't a life-or-death situation, I wouldn't ask you this, Gary. But I'm hurting real bad, and I've got a hundred employees depending on me." The I'm-stealing-for-the-greater-good rationale had subtly become my constant chorus.

"All right," he said in a soft tone. "Come by and pick up the letterhead."

Amy, my secretary, trusted me. If I told her to type out contract verifications on Partner letterhead, she assumed it was for a legitimate purpose. Amy was an organizer, a hard worker, and someone who cared for me as if I were her own son.

With my financial statements, three phony restoration work orders totaling almost two hundred fifty thousand dollars, and the verification letter supposedly signed by Gary Todd in hand, I made my way to Ron's large, elegant office building. Before I went in, I contemplated whether or not I should go through with the plan. Would Ron Knox really harm me if he found out about my con? Was ZZZZ Best worth risking my well-being? I answered these questions with a turn of the doorknob.

An attractive secretary greeted me. "Yes, Mr. Minkow, Ron and Dean are expecting you. Just go right in," she said, pointing to the door opposite her.

"Well, I see you made it on time," said Ron when I stepped into the room. "Barry Minkow, I'd like you to meet Dean DeWitt."

We shook hands, and I sat next to Ron, while DeWitt seated himself at the desk.

"Did you bring the documents?" Ron asked.

"Sure did." I handed him the folder, and he began to examine its contents.

"So how long has ZZZZ Best been in business?" Dean asked.

"I started the company at age sixteen, in October of 1982. That's when the DBA was officially recorded. A few months ago my attorney advised me to form a private corporation, and I did."

"Are you the sole owner of the corporation's stock?" Ron interjected.

"I am."

"Why don't you just go to a bank and get a loan for your business?" Dean asked.

Already I didn't like this guy because he wasn't buying into the Minkow song and dance right away. But if I was going to save ZZZZ Best, I needed to answer his questions. "Banks and I have never gotten along," I admitted. "When I opened the company, several of them closed my accounts because I was underage. When I turned eighteen and tried to get a loan, they explained that I needed a three-year track record plus hard assets to pledge as security."

Ron passed some of the documents to Dean, and they read in silence.

Eventually Dean looked up. "If we call this Gary Todd guy at Partner, will he verify these contracts?"

"Yes, he will." My heartbeat thumped almost audibly.

Ron motioned to Dean, who left the room with his letter from Partner, then turned to me. "How much will you make on these contracts?"

I had to think of a figure. "About eighty thousand dollars in profit when all is said and done." Lying had become second nature to me.

Ron nodded and looked back at the financial statements. "Assuming everything checks out, I'll raise the money for these projects from a few friends of mine, and we can split the profit on the jobs. Does that sound fair?"

"Sure does," I replied brightly. In reality, I was desperate; I had bad checks to cover. "The problem is, I have to purchase some materials immediately or I could lose one of these contracts. How long will this whole process take?"

Ron smiled. "I just met you, Kid. Slow down—I'll take care of everything."

Just then Dean DeWitt came back. "It checks out," he told Ron. I breathed easier. Gary had come through again.

"We need to fix these financial statements," Ron said.

"No problem," Dean answered. "I'll get Carl Stowe on it right away."

"Good. And then we'll take him to some banks and see if we can't arrange a line of credit," Ron said.

I was concerned. Bank loans take a long time, and that was one thing I didn't have. "I appreciate the effort, but I don't think any bank will lend me money. And I've got jobs to complete now!"

The two men looked at each other and smiled.

"Never let it be said that I stopped progress," Ron replied. "Come by my house tomorrow and pick up ten thousand dollars. That should get you started. Then I'll meet you here late next week and have one of my associates give you another twenty-five. That will buy us enough time to arrange a bank loan, or if that doesn't work, to raise some money from Lee Herring."

"Who?"

"He's a close friend," Ron said. "I'm supposed to be broke, so I've got to finance my business ventures through friends. But you don't need to worry about that. Just get these jobs done and run that company. I'll take care of the rest."

After a few questions, I got up to leave. But then I remembered the agreements Rick Price had asked me to sign before giving me any money. "Will you want me to sign any loan documents, Mr. Knox?"

"For now, that won't be necessary, Kid. Just pay me back and everything will go smoothly. . . . I trust you, Barry. And I'm helping you because you remind me of myself when I started out."

∽

I covered most of the bad checks with the ten thousand dollars. While I was waiting for the twenty-five thousand, Ron Knox visited the office. I introduced him as a friend doing business with the company.

Mike and Amy came to me immediately after he left. Ron worried them; they had heard he was reported to have crime connections. I downplayed our relationship, assuring them that I was in complete control of ZZZZ Best. Yet, deep down I knew that was no longer true.

Dealing with Ron Knox inspired me to work out more regularly. Although I'd never decreased my steroid use, the stress of running ZZZZ Best had forced me to miss many workouts. Ron scared me, and that got me into the gym. He drove a large, black Cadillac, the kind driven by the bad guys on television. He called me often and had his finger on the pulse of my daily activities. I wasn't naïve enough to believe that muscles would stop bullets, but a consistent workout program did give me more confidence in dealing with the new realities of my business life.

Late Friday afternoon I walked into Ron's office building. Traffic on the highway was heavy as people rushed home to begin the weekend. No one seemed to notice or care that I was about to sell my soul to the devil.

The secretary was answering phones as I entered the office. She motioned for me to go right in. I found Ron Knox by himself. "Hi, Kid! How's business?"

I felt like telling him the truth: if I didn't get the twenty-five thousand, all one hundred of the payroll checks I'd just issued would bounce. But I hoped I sounded believable when I said, "Business is good. We're anxious to get those restoration projects started."

"I want you to take a look at these." Ron handed me financial statements and tax returns for ZZZZ Best for 1983 and 1984.

The documents were much more detailed than my accountant's had been—professionally prepared, with footnotes. They also showed higher earnings and an inflated balance sheet. I was proud to be president of the company represented by these statements.

"What do you think?" Ron asked.

"They look great. No bank will turn me down for a loan now. Who did these?"

He paused before answering. "Carl Stowe. He owns some retail shops and has an accounting business on the side."

Just then the intercom buzzed. It was the receptionist. "Donald is here to see you, Ron."

"Send him in."

The second I saw Donald Snyder, I stopped perusing my new financial statements. He had slick dark hair pulled back into a short ponytail, and he scowled as he filled the doorframe. He was carrying a paper sack.

"Donald Snyder, meet Barry Minkow," Ron introduced us. I rose from my chair and went over to shake his hand.

"I read about you in the papers," Donald said brusquely.

I smiled nervously and nodded. Donald was an intimidating man.

"Does the Kid know the rules?"

"Since it's your money, I thought I'd leave that to you," Ron said, smiling.

Donald tossed me the brown bag. "You pay every Tuesday. I don't care how long you keep the money as long as you pay every week. You got that, pal?"

I got it. The same deal as with Paul and Jerry, only Donald came on ten times stronger. "No problem. I can handle that. Should I give the money to Ron every week?"

Donald looked at Ron. Ron nodded.

"Yeah, just give it to him," Donald agreed.

I couldn't resist the temptation to peek into the sack.

"It's all there, Kid. You don't have to count it. Twenty-five thousand dollars. Listen, Ron, I've got to go downtown, so unless there's anything else, I'll call you later."

"That'll be fine, Donald. I'll be home most of the night."

Before he left, Donald wanted to tell me one more thing. "Look, Kid, I don't know you. The only reason you're getting this money is because of Ron. But if you miss payments or try to beat me for the money, you'll have problems—big problems."

He didn't need to threaten me, but it worked anyway. I was scared. "You won't have any problems with me, Mr. Snyder," I replied.

He stared at me for a second with an enigmatic smile, lightly patted me on the cheek—just like in the movies—and was gone.

"Before you leave," Ron began, "I want you to sign these tax returns so we can submit them to a few banks." I promptly obeyed. If I could say at the end of any given day that the only illegal thing I had done was sign a few fake tax returns, I was doing well.

My newest pal also informed me that he had rented office space in the Reseda Business Center, right down the hall from the ZZZZ Best main office. I knew what he was really doing was tightening the reins and groaned internally at his announcement. Having Ron Knox and his "associates" hanging around my main office was at the top of a worse-case-scenario list. People would think the mob had taken over my business. Still, I was in too deep to say no; I needed the bank loans he was arranging.

As I turned to walk away, I realized that I didn't know what my weekly payment was on Donald's loan. "By the way, Ron, how much do I give you every week for this money?"

"Five points a week, Kid—that's the going rate."

"How much is that in dollars and cents?"

"Twelve hundred and fifty dollars a week—interest only," he said sternly. I should have known.

⸎

"Barry Minkow, I'd like you to meet Lee Herring and Julie Kennedy," said Ron Knox as I entered Lee's home. Ron had set up the meeting in hopes of raising one hundred thousand dollars from Lee and a few of his friends.

"Did you bring the documentation with you?" he asked. Ron wanted Lee and Julie to see the phony financial statements, the letter from Gary confirming the three restoration jobs, and the work orders substantiating their dollar amounts. I handed him the neatly assembled file folder.

Lee was a nice man who, according to Ron, loved pursuing this type of financial adventure. Julie was extremely attractive and a good listener. She had just been through some rough times and was looking to improve her cash situation. Both were said to be wealthy and anxious to invest. In fact, Ron had made it clear that if I could impress Lee, I could raise endless amounts of money because of his many contacts.

Ron did most of the talking; I simply sat back and answered questions. The investors were told that ZZZZ Best needed approximately one hundred thousand dollars to complete the three projects. The offer was simple: the two could each invest up to $100,000 and in return would receive 2% a week (in cash) as interest on their money, until the principal balance was paid off.

"How can you afford to pay us that much on our money, Barry?" Lee asked.

"The profit margin on these jobs averages 30% to 35%. If we're doing $250,000 worth of restoration work, the company will net over $80,000 for three months' work. So, the cost of the money is absorbed in the large profits." I was getting good at this. I knew all the right words and could even look people right in the eye and lie to them. By the time I left Lee's house, I knew the loan was a done deal.

～

The meeting with Lee and Julie also taught me an invaluable lesson about fraud perpetration and, much later, fraud detection.

When raising money, con artists have to create a use-of-proceeds for the funds with a believable story to explain how they can achieve higher than normal returns (in my case 2% per month). My lie was that these returns were possible because of the margins available in the restoration business. I was banking on the fact that neither Lee, Julie, nor even Ron had enough knowledge about the restoration industry to say, "Hey, I'm a former carpet cleaner and there is no way restoration work has average gross profit margins of 30% to 40%." My fraud presupposed that people's inexperience in the carpet cleaning industry would prohibit them from independently proving my high-profitability claims. And, in almost every fraud case I later investigated,

I always began by looking at that proof-of-profitability question. If a deal was fraudulent, the profits would be as well.

༈

Lee, Julie, and one other person made up the first investment group. The large influx of cash allowed me to pay Paul off completely, catch Jerry up, pay the company's outstanding debts, and open my fourth office in San Diego. Mike and I had learned the secret to opening a successful office: we introduced our company with a large direct mailing to thousands of homes and followed up with telephone soliciting. This helped us generate large amounts of business and start off profitably.

The opening of the San Diego office also helped me create a diversion. Because the restoration jobs were phony, ZZZZ Best could not stand up to the strict scrutiny that would certainly come as the company grew. However, if I had four offices all over California and a hundred and thirty employees, I could divert attention from the phony restoration business to the area of the company that was legitimate: the carpet cleaning. As a result of implementing this technique of diversion, I later redefined the term *fraud* as "the skin of the truth, stuffed with a lie."

At ZZZZ Best the "skin of the truth" was the carpet cleaning stores which really existed. The "stuffed with a lie" were the restoration jobs that did not exist. In uncovering fraud, knowing this diversion technique helped me to break many cases because every fraud has a skin of truth which exists solely to conceal the lie. The only way to catch a financial crime in progress is to differentiate between the two.

Despite the success in San Diego and a cash position that allowed me to stop kiting checks, we still had major problems. By early August, rumors had spread throughout the industry that ZZZZ Best was a "crime-owned" company. When I wasn't in the office, Ron Knox would come in and order Mike and Amy around, even telling them that he owned the company. Lee was unhappy; Ron made it hard for him to speak with me unless he was present. My nightmare of losing control was becoming a reality.

Donald Snyder called me from a pay phone on a Tuesday in late August. "Where's Ron?" he demanded.

"I don't know, Donald. But I've got your money. Do you want me to bring it to you?"

There was a long silence before he spoke again. "Yeah, Kid, where do you want to meet?"

"Well, it's almost lunchtime. Why don't we meet at Louie's? I'll meet you there in twenty minutes—I'm buying," I added. Though I feared Donald, I couldn't see the harm in trying to get on his good side.

When I arrived, he was sitting at a table in a dark corner, away from the crowd. Donald wasn't much for socializing.

"Been waiting long?"

"No, just got here. What's good here anyway?" he asked, studying the menu.

I glanced around and pushed a sealed envelope across the table. "It's all there, Donald, twelve hundred and fifty dollars." He looked at me as if I had said something wrong. Hoping to correct myself, I blurted out, "Uh, I usually get the barbecued ribs."

The expression on his face had changed. "How much did you say is in here?"

"Twelve fifty—that's what I've been paying Ron every week." He bowed his head and shook it slowly. "Was I supposed to pay more?"

"No, Kid. I was only charging you a thousand a week. Ron marked it up on you and didn't bother telling me. That's going to cost him."

"Listen, Donald, I don't want any trouble. If he finds out I told you, he'll come after me."

"No, he won't; I'll make sure of it. Now just what is your arrangement with Ron?"

Because he seemed genuinely concerned, I told him everything—except that the restoration jobs were phony. He heard me out and instructed me to say nothing to Ron.

"It's one thing to try and beat a guy like you," Donald grumbled. "But to use my money to make a score behind my back without telling me—that's a different story. He'll pay, Kid, you can bet on that."

"Is he going to give me trouble?" I asked, concerned. Donald was out of patience.

"Look, Barry, I told you I'll handle everything. Just pay me every Tuesday and take care of Lee by yourself. I'll do the rest. You got that?" He pointed across the table at my chest.

"I got it, Donald. I got it."

༄

True to his word, Donald settled matters with Ron—there was no sign of him. The Reseda employees were once again happy and content. Especially Amy and Mike. Although he didn't know why the sudden change had occurred, Lee enjoyed communicating with me directly. The rumors of my involvement with criminals behind the scenes faded as company morale returned to normal.

With Ron no longer watching my every move, I decided to buy another car. A friend was selling a barely used red Ferrari 308 for fifty-five thousand dollars. I put forty thousand down, took possession of the car, and paid off the remaining fifteen on time. The first day I drove it, I knew it was the car of my dreams. People everywhere stared as I sped down the street, radio blasting.

While I was showing off my new Ferrari around the San Fernando Valley, I wasn't worried about Ron Knox or Donald Snyder. I was so used to controlling what was in front of me that I wasn't watching my back.

Big mistake.

5 | RON RETURNS

I've got to see you right away!" exclaimed a panicked Donald Snyder one Tuesday morning. "We've got problems." Donald ordered me to meet him in the parking lot of a library. He was waiting by his car when I pulled my Ferrari into the busy lot

"What's the problem?" I asked nervously as I slammed the door shut.

"It's about Ron."

"What about him?"

Usually Donald was calm and in control, but this time he was noticeably distraught. Something big was brewing. "Look, Kid, I can't see you anymore."

"What do you mean you can't see me anymore? I've been making my payments on time, haven't I?"

"That has nothing to do with it. This guy Knox has some very good friends back East. He went to them about what happened between him and me over the money and they told us—me—to back off."

There was no love lost between Donald and me, but dealing with him was much easier than dealing with Ron. For one thing, Donald didn't think he owned my company. "Does that mean he's going to be hanging around me again?"

"I don't know what he's going to do. I talked to him this morning, and he told me to have you meet him at Derrick's Diner in about an hour."

"What if I don't want him around anymore? What if I told these guys out East that I like you better? Don't I have any say in the matter?" I demanded angrily.

"You'll do as you're told!" he yelled. "And you won't cause any problems. You got that, Kid?" He was staring at me intently. I had said too much.

"Yeah, I understand," I replied dejectedly and watched as Donald walked to his car, got in, and sped away.

⸺

"Just coffee," I said to the waitress. I glanced at my watch—I was early. I tried to sort out in my mind just what Donald meant by "Ron's friends back East." Up until that morning, I had had no idea that people elsewhere in the country knew about or had any interest in ZZZZ Best.

I stared out the window at the car wash across the street and wished I were one of the minimum-wage workers busily wiping down the cars. True, they weren't driving Ferraris, but they didn't have a Ron Knox in their lives, either, or his friends from out of town.

"I see you're on time," Ron said as he approached the table. I had been so preoccupied with the activities at the car wash that I hadn't seen him walk up. He slid into the booth and leveled his gaze at me. "Well, Barry, I hope you've learned your lesson." He smiled and made sure I was looking at him before he added pointedly, "No one gets away from Ron Knox."

"I've been paying everybody on time," I said, trying to change the subject. "Lee's people are happy, and the jobs are going smoothly."

"How's the Ferrari driving?" he asked sarcastically. I wondered how he knew.

"Good," I said. "One of the few benefits from the restoration profits."

"Well then, you won't mind me asking for my profits from these jobs, will you?"

"No. When they're finished and we get paid, you'll get your forty thousand."

"Unfortunately, I can't wait that long. I have some associates who produce movies. They need money now to finish a project."

I knew I could get as much as I needed from Paul. I had good credit with him, so if Ron pressed me, I could come up with the money. But I wanted to stretch it out as long as I could.

"What kind of movie can be produced for forty thousand dollars?" I asked, stalling for time.

He sipped from his glass of ice water before answering. "A porno movie. We shoot them on video and then duplicate them. It's big business, Kid, and I've got to have the forty thousand now!"

"All right, but I'll need two days to get an advance from Gary."

"I don't care how you get it. Just bring the money to my house in two days. I also want to pay off Donald and get rid of him. But that can wait until you finish the jobs."

"Anything else?"

"Yeah, one more thing. Have the Feds come to see you yet?"

"The Feds? Who are they?"

"The FBI. They'll probably visit you and ask a bunch of questions about me and my involvement with ZZZZ Best. I suggest you tell them that we have a legitimate arrangement. And whatever you do, say nothing about the financial statements or Donald's loan, understand?"

"I understand, Ron. They'll get nothing out of me," I promised.

"Good, Kid." He smiled. "I knew you'd do what's best for you."

༄

Paul was more than happy to lend me as much as I wanted. He had grown accustomed to getting the weekly interest payments from me for over a year. I borrowed one hundred thousand dollars and paid off Ron and Donald. The rest I put in reserve, knowing the weekly interest payments to Lee and Paul would soon catch up with me. Even with his money, Ron had made it clear that I was still obligated to include him in all future restoration contracts. *There's just no getting rid of this guy*, I thought as I sat in my office.

The phone buzzed. It was Amy. "Barry, there's a Charles Hunter here to see you. Should I send him in?"

"You bet, Amy. Send him right in!" I said excitedly. Charlie Hunter had been a friend of mine for years, and right then I needed a friend.

I greeted him at the door. "Come on in, Charlie. What a surprise." He smiled and gave me a hug. "Can I get you some coffee?"

"No, Barry, I really don't have time. I just stopped by to talk to you for a few minutes."

"Sure, Buddy. What's on your mind?"

Charlie slid his chair up to the desk and asked in a soft tone, "Are you in some kind of trouble, Barry?"

"Trouble? What do you mean?"

"You know I'm your friend. You can level with me. The word on the street is that you're involved with Ron Knox. Is that true?"

There was no reason for me to lie to Charlie. "Yeah, I'm involved with him," I answered reluctantly.

"Are you into him for some big money?"

"Not him personally, but I owe one hundred thousand dollars to a few people he introduced me to. Why do you ask?" Charlie glanced at the closed door. "The guy's no good, Barry. He's a user. The only thing he wants from you is control of your company. And he'll stop at nothing until he gets it." Dumbfounded, I stared at Charlie.

"You'll never get rid of the guy. He'll milk you dry until there's nothing left."

"Great!" I stood and walked around the desk. "Is that what you came by to tell me? That I'm doomed?"

"No. I came to offer you some help."

"What kind of help?" The pressure was getting to me. I paced the office, rubbing my hands through my hair and fighting back tears. "According to you and everybody else, I should just kill myself before this maniac ruins me."

"Will you listen to me, Barry? I never told you this before, but I have a few friends who might be able to help you get rid of Knox. If you're interested, I want you to come by my house this Saturday and meet them."

"What good is that going to do? This Knox guy's got powerful friends back East who have an invisible shield around me," I moaned.

"If I didn't know for a fact that my people could deliver you from Knox and his friends, I wouldn't be here."

Charlie was serious. And I was desperate. "What time Saturday?"

"How about noon? Is that good for you?"

"Yeah," I said, turning to my seeming deliverer. "And thanks for saving my skin."

෴

As I pulled into Charlie Hunter's neighborhood early that Saturday morning, I was looking for more than just relief from Ron Knox. I was also looking for the freedom to run ZZZZ Best the way I wanted. If Charlie's friend could provide that, I was a buyer.

After introductions and small talk, I took a chair at a table with Stanley Robbins, Robert Fuller, and Charlie. Stanley (he preferred "Stan"), a forty-ish chain-smoker with a shock of brick-red hair, was quick-witted, funny, and according to Charlie, extremely well connected to important families back East. He owned several houses across the country, a condominium in Southern California, and was always looking for a good deal.

Robert Fuller was introduced to me as a "stock market wiz." Supposedly the Securities and Exchange Commission had been forced to change some of its procedures because of his past efforts. Fuller was about sixty-five years old, heavyset, with a strong personality bordering on intimidating.

Stan was clearly in charge, though. When he talked, Charlie and Robert listened. He asked me simple questions about Knox: how we had met, how much Donald had lent me, who his contacts were, and what my current financial obligations to him were. I liked Stan. He seemed genuinely interested in helping me and expressed no desire to take over.

"If you don't tell me the whole truth, I can't help you, Kid," Stan concluded.

I gave him my version of the whole truth—which, of course, excluded the phony restoration contracts.

Robert was more interested in the daily operations of ZZZZ Best: each location's monthly income, the number of employees I had, and my expansion plans.

After nearly two hours, the three men had a thorough understanding of my relationship with Ron Knox and how ZZZZ Best operated.

"You should be proud of yourself, Barry. You've built yourself a heck of a company," Stan said as he puffed on his cigarette. "And I'd like to help you out . . . but only if you want me to."

Everybody looked at me, awaiting a response. "I'd like you to help me, Stan. But how? Knox has me boxed in."

Stan paused. "You let me worry about that. If you want my help, I'm going to need your cooperation. You must do exactly what I say."

I was willing, but I needed to know more. "What would that entail?"

"First, you must cut off all communications with Knox. Don't accept his calls, and, whatever you do, don't call him." I tried not to smile too big.

"But what if he comes by the office? How do I ignore him then?"

"I'm going to need to bring one of my guys out from back East to hang out with you for about six months. He'll move in with you and follow you around wherever you go. That way if Knox tries anything, my guy will be there to . . . take care of business."

"Who is this guy?"

Stan glanced at Robert. "His name is Phil Cox. He's one of the toughest people I know. He'll be perfect for this job."

"Kind of like a bodyguard?"

"Yeah . . . you could say that . . . a bodyguard."

I liked the idea. Only important people had bodyguards. "How will I pay him?"

"Just put him on your payroll for eight hundred dollars a week. I'll take care of the rest. But it's important that he come out right away. If you want Knox to leave you alone, I need to get busy."

"Sounds fine to me, Stan."

"Good. Now, I'm not pushing you or anything, but I have a dear friend who has a financing company. I'm sure he can raise you all the money you need for these restoration projects—for a lot less than Knox's people are charging. You interested?"

This was too good to be true. Not only was I going to be delivered from Ron Knox, I was also being offered an unlimited amount of funds. "I'm very interested in that kind of deal," I said. "In fact, I'd be willing to split the profits with you on all the jobs you're able to arrange financing on."

"If that's what you want. But, remember, I didn't force you to make that deal." Charlie and Robert smiled at Stan's comment.

"I know," I replied. "I offered, and I've got no regrets for doing so. Raising money has always been my biggest problem."

"Stan, can I add something?" Robert interjected. Seeing Stan's nod of approval, he turned to me. "Have you ever thought about taking your company public? I mean, if raising money has been a problem for ZZZZ Best, going public makes good business sense."

I thought back to when Knox had mentioned going public back in the original meeting at his townhouse, but I still didn't know what it meant. And the last thing I wanted was to appear naïve. "How long would it take for me to go public, and how much money could I make?"

Silence again. My three new partners exchanged looks, struggling to communicate to each other with their eyes.

"I could probably get it done for you in about ninety days—around February," Robert replied. "As for the money you'll make, it really depends on how the deal is structured."

"You'll also have to hire a lawyer and an accountant to do the paperwork—but once that's done, you'll put ZZZZ Best in the big leagues," Stan added.

"That's right," Charlie said. "You'll be known all over the United States by those who purchase your stock."

"And since you're the sole owner of the company, you'll retain control because you'll be the majority stockholder," Robert said, emphasizing the point.

Whatever else going public meant, to me it meant fame, big money, and total control—everything I had ever wanted.

⌣

My personal life was also a lie. I had a steady girlfriend who was practically living with me. Her name was Donna. She was kind and considerate and really loved me. I, on the other hand, was a cheating con man—but kept it well hidden from Donna.

"I love it, Barry!" Donna squealed as we toured the five-thousand-square-foot house in the new Westchester County Estates. "Can we please buy it?" Although we were not married, I owed Donna for her loyalty and wanted to share my dream home with her.

The broker had dropped the keys by my office. The two-story mansion boasted a huge living room, family room, dining room, two fireplaces, a large kitchen, and even quarters for a live-in maid. After reviewing Carl Stowe's financial statements, the broker had assured me that if I put down $250,000, I could easily qualify for a loan to purchase the property. Although they were asking almost $800,000, I knew I could get it for $750,000.

Raising the down payment would be simple. I would use the money I received from Charlie and Stan to pay off Lee and Paul. Then I'd reborrow from them much more than that, using my flawless track record to support my request. Once I'd acquired the house and taken ZZZZ Best public, I would finally prove to everyone that I was a big success.

This method of paying investors back and then reborrowing larger amounts is another commonly-used technique of financial fraud perpetrators. I had never read about it in a book or seen it on television; like other fraud techniques, I learned it through experience. I would convince people to invest, pay them their returns on time, and then set them up for the next big deal—in my case, the next big restoration job. I always had a use-of-proceeds for their funds and constantly appealed to my track record of payment as a reason for them to reinvest.

❧

When Phil Cox arrived on the scene, he looked the part of the typical hood. He wore dark sunglasses constantly in an attempt to hide a face that had been damaged on numerous occasions. He was not a large man but carried himself with confidence. He dressed neatly, and I was told he carried a gun. Phil had earned a reputation as a legitimate tough guy through years of loyal service to people like Stan Robbins. We got along well, and I actually think he liked me. Most importantly, once the word got out on the street that he was living with me, Ron Knox stayed far away. To me, that was worth the eight hundred a week.

After several meetings with Stan, Charlie, and Robert, it was agreed that I would hire a securities lawyer known personally to Robert Fuller, and Roger Voss, a CPA from the Midwest, to assist me in going public.

They had worked together on previous deals and even though my company was two thousand miles away, they seemed eager to take on the new business.

We also made what came to be known as the big "stock score." ZZZZ Best would merge with a dormant, public company—a shell company—out of Salt Lake City. I would actually buy them out on paper, thereby automatically becoming public. After secretly purchasing one million free-trading shares of that company's stock at five cents a share, right before the acquisition was announced I was to split the shares up evenly among Stan, Charlie, Robert, and me. Because my partners had several Wall Street connections who, according to them, would create a market for the stock, it wouldn't take long for the shares to increase in value dramatically.

We did this with financing arranged for me at a company on the East Coast owned by an associate of Stan's. To keep the restoration projects separate from the stock deal and ZZZZ Best, we formed a company called Security Insurance Services. We leased office space where Charlie, Robert, and Stan would operate the business. Things were moving fast, even for my usual breakneck pace, but I didn't care.

There was no turning back now.

⁓

"Two gentlemen are here to see you, Barry," Amy said over the intercom. Before I had time to ask who these men were, she continued, "They're with the FBI."

My heart sank, but I didn't hesitate. "Send them in."

The two men, dressed in suits and carrying briefcases, entered the office and sat down across from my desk.

After brief introductions, one of them said, "Mr. Minkow, we're here to talk to you about your relationship with Ron Knox. You do know him, don't you?"

Knox had warned me at Derrick's Diner that the FBI might visit, but I hadn't believed him. I was scared and caught off guard. "Yes, I know him," I answered calmly, trying not to raise suspicion.

"Well, Mr. Minkow, the word on the street is that he's shaking you down pretty good through some steep loans." They watched to see if I would react. I didn't, but I recalled that Charlie had heard the same rumor.

"Look, Mr. Minkow, you're not a target of our investigation. We know this Knox guy has infiltrated ZZZZ Best, and we want to help you get rid of him," one of them added.

Did these men know about Fuller, Robbins, and Hunter? I wondered.

If they didn't ask about them, I wasn't going to offer any information. I worded my response carefully, "Assuming that what you say is true, how could you guys help me?"

"We want you to testify in front of a federal grand jury about your business dealings with Ron Knox. If you cooperate, we can put this guy away for a long time."

So, they weren't aware of the phony restoration contracts or my new relationship with Stan and his friends. They were preoccupied with Ron Knox. That was fine with me.

After asking a few more questions and showing me several photos to see if I could identify various individuals, they left their cards and promised to keep in touch. I immediately called Charlie and Robert at the Security offices and told them about my surprise visitors. They were satisfied with the way I had handled the interview and gave me explicit instructions to let them know whenever the FBI contacted me again.

～

November and December of 1985 were busy months for ZZZZ Best.

We opened our fifth office in Santa Barbara, increasing the number of employees to almost two hundred. To keep pace with the growth, I hired additional office personnel, purchased several computers, and leased more space in the Reseda Business Center. I worked daily with the securities lawyer and Roger Voss, gathering the information they needed to complete the merger.

Gary Todd and I decided it was time to place some of the phony restoration contract paperwork under a different company. With so many "investors" having Partner letterhead with Gary's name on it, he feared getting caught. We opened a small, one-man office across town, had letterhead printed, and made it the official headquarters of Reliable Appraisal Company—an independent adjusting company owned and operated by Gary Todd.

Without the burden of chasing after funds, I was now able, for the first time in my business career, to focus the majority of my time on ZZZZ Best. I hired a public relations firm to get the biggest bang for my publicity buck. At nineteen, I was about to be the president of a public company. This was big news, and I wanted everyone to know about it.

The employees at the Reseda office quickly became accustomed to seeing Phil hanging around. He was quiet and stayed out of the way, which made my life much better than in the days when Knox had been in my life. And when I moved into my new seven-hundred-fifty-thousand-dollar home, Donna *and Phil* moved in with me.

"Sit down, Wonder Boy," Stan said as I approached the table at Alex's Restaurant, where he had asked me to meet him to discuss Ron Knox. As usual, Robert and Charlie were with him.

"Everything's set with the loan company," he reported. "Within ninety days, you'll have five hundred thousand dollars, and by May, you'll have a two-million-dollar credit line available."

"That's great, Stan!" I didn't try to hide my excitement.

"There's one catch. It's going to cost you a fifty-thousand dollar kicker on the five hundred thousand and two hundred fifty thousand on the two million. Can you handle that?"

"No problem, Stan. I'll give the money to Robert once the loan comes through, and we'll be set."

"Good. I've got to leave for New York next week, but I'll be back. You're in good hands, so don't worry about anything."

"Is everything set for January on the merger?" I asked.

"Yes, it is," Robert said. "But as soon as the deal closes, Roger Voss needs to come out and start working on a year-end audit. Are your earnings good?"

The correct answer to that question was, "Who knows?" With all the loans, kickbacks, and car payments, I had no way of knowing exactly how the offices were doing. I had to lie. "Yeah, every office is making a profit. Even Santa Barbara is doing well, and it just opened."

There was silence at the table as the three men thought about my remarks. "By the way, Kid, Knox is going to sue you," Stan said at last.

"What?"

"Apparently the guy is desperate for money. But don't worry. We've talked to our people back East, and they told us that if he sues, you're free to do whatever you have to in order to protect yourself."

"What does that mean exactly?"

"That means that we're going to get you a lawyer we can trust to defend you. If he thinks it's a good idea for you to testify against Knox, we'll let you—as long as you say the right things."

I had a lot to hide and wasn't too keen on going before a grand jury. But I didn't want them to know that. "However you want to handle it is fine with me. When will the suit be filed?"

"Any day now. But just forget about it. Give it to Robert, and he'll set up a meeting with the lawyer."

"Is it safe for me to travel from office to office, or will I have to be constantly looking over my shoulder for Knox?" I asked, trying to stifle the ripple of fear that tingled down my spine.

Stan smiled. "It's safe. Just make sure you take Phil wherever you go." He pointed toward the restaurant restrooms, where Phil was leaning against the wall, watching my every move.

⟋

"ZZZZ Best Taken Public by 19-Year-Old Founder." This headline blazed from the business section early in 1986. The news brought an onslaught of inquiries from across the country. My public relations firm had to work overtime to keep up with the requests.

Robert had proved himself to be an expert at generating interest in ZZZZ Best stock. Just weeks before the deal closed, he flew to New York and persuaded several brokerage firms to create a market for our stock, and the stock rose from five to fifty cents a share in two weeks! Since I was the majority stockholder, that made me worth millions—on paper. I had learned that some securities law prohibited me from selling any of the six million personal shares I had gained through the merger for two years. But I could sell the 250,000 shares of free-trading stock from our four-way split—as long as no one found out about it.

Becoming a public company dramatically increased morale at ZZZZ Best. We had accomplished something the competition could only dream of, a point I reinforced at weekly company meetings: "So, who would you rather work for: ZZZZ Best, a company that will one day be the General Motors of the carpet cleaning industry, or some loser local company that's going nowhere fast?"

As news spread of my goal to one day go nationwide, carpet cleaners from several companies tried to join the ZZZZ Best team. What a difference from a year earlier, when I worried about the competition stealing my people and how I was going to meet payroll!

6 FINANCIAL FRENZY

Perpetrating such a large fraud required all my time and plenty of planning. First, I had to constantly create more phony restoration contracts, complete with verification letters from Gary, to justify the loans I was receiving through Stan, Robert, and Charlie. Their money-raising efforts, though formidable, never seemed to go far enough. The interest payments depleted whatever cash surplus I had accumulated, causing another cash crunch. Also, Robert, Stan, and Charlie asked to be put on my payroll, which cost me thousands a month. Their deliverance from Ron Knox had come with a steep price tag.

To stay ahead of commitments, I embarked upon a multi-pronged, all-out borrowing spree. I reborrowed from Lee, Julie, and several of their friends, despite specific instructions not to from Stan and company. I approached banks, hoping that since ZZZZ Best was now a public company, I'd qualify for loans. And I did! Three different banks all lent me money, either personally or through ZZZZ Best.

With the assistance of Jerry Williams, I also figured out a way to defraud leasing companies. Here's how it played: between February and July of 1986, I asked several leasing companies to loan ZZZZ Best money to buy equipment. I told them that Jerry, who was an authorized distributor for Benson Equipment, was selling me specially-made units called Benson Super Cleaners for $forty-five hundred dollars each, available only through him. (There were no such machines.) To strengthen the ruse, Jerry agreed to buy back the nonexistent machines if I failed to pay. The leasing companies made out the checks to Benson Equipment. Jerry claimed a percentage, gave me the balance, and ZZZZ Best made the payments on the leases.

I used the proceeds from the bank loans and leases to open two additional ZZZZ Best locations, Lancaster in March and San Bernardino in April of 1986. Robert had told me that if I wanted the stock to go up, I had to "make things happen," like opening more locations even though the company wasn't in a strong enough position to support them. He was right. By my twentieth birthday, the stock had soared to almost three dollars a share.

This made aging easier for me. I had accomplished something in my twentieth year that, as far as I knew, no one else my age had accomplished in the history of American business. I couldn't legally buy a beer, but I headed a public company. That was newsworthy enough to keep me in the limelight for at least two more heavenly years.

But when it came time to make payments, my cash victories evaporated. I needed to raise money that I didn't have to pay back, and selling my undisclosed two hundred fifty thousand free-trading shares was my only option. Before I could do that, I needed approval from the top, and that meant a meeting with Stan.

෴

"We've got nearly three hundred employees, seven locations, and ten restoration projects going, Stan! That's why I need the money!" I exclaimed from the backseat of Robert's limousine, parked inconspicuously near a restaurant.

"I can probably get John Brady and somebody else to buy them," Robert said calmly. "That would keep the sale from putting too much pressure on the stock."

John was a stockbroker Robert knew. When Robert said to buy, John and other brokers asked, "How much?" Robert had considerable influence on Wall Street.

"I think the Kid's not telling us something," Stan stated pointedly to Robert and Charlie. "I think he's probably giving money to someone he hasn't told us about yet. Is that true, Kid?" he demanded. Stan never asked a question he didn't already know the answer to. There was a long silence.

Charlie had asked me for two hundred thousand dollars to buy some property. I advanced him the money against future profits from the restoration projects, swearing never to tell Stan or Robert about the loan. I tried to resist the temptation to make eye contact with Charlie, but failed. Stan was too street smart; he saw right through the deal and leveled his gaze at Charlie.

"Charlie, where'd you get the money to buy that land?" Stan asked loudly. He was visibly upset. There was another long pause. I had blown it. "Well, I'm waiting!"

"Look, Stan," I interjected, trying to change the subject, "I promise that everything will be okay as soon as I sell this stock. You, Robert, and Charlie can keep your shares. I'm only asking to sell mine."

"What's the status of the Knox lawsuit?" Stan asked Robert.

"I've got a lawyer for the Kid now. He understands the delicate nature of the situation. We're going to have Barry cooperate against this guy with the Feds," Robert replied.

Stan nodded, apparently satisfied with the answer, and then turned to me. "Have the Fibbies been to see you again, Barry?"

"Yeah, one of the men came by again, this time with somebody new. They said the same thing as before: 'We know Knox is extorting money from you and wants to continue to do so. Help us and you won't be sorry'—that kind of thing."

"Did you mention any of us?" he questioned.

"No!"

"Did they ask about us?"

"No. They're so focused on Knox that nothing else matters."

"Good." His attention shifted to Fuller. "Robert, sell the shares in blocks. I don't want any pressure on this stock, so take your time and do it right."

"No problem, Stan. I'll take care of it immediately," Robert responded.

"Anything else, Kid?" Stan asked.

"Not right now, but I'll keep you posted," I replied quickly, thankful the inquisition was over.

"All right, you can leave." As I climbed out of the car, Charlie was right behind me. "But you stay," Stan said to Charlie pointedly. "We've got something to discuss."

⌇

"It's time for you to make some big money, Gary," I said. "I want you to go full time with Reliable, and I'm willing to finance the expansion." I had no other option. It was only a matter of time before Gary Todd would get caught confirming nonexistent restoration jobs.

As he sat in my office that spring afternoon, I could tell that he was thinking about the fringe benefits of running his own company full time. "What's your timing on this transition?" he posed.

"I want you to do it now. I'll give you the money for everything you need."

"What would be my responsibilities?"

"Good question." I stood up and paced the well-worn office carpet. "It's really twofold. First, you'll verify all ZZZZ Best contracts. Second, I want you to try to legitimize these restoration projects by actually obtaining some real insurance business and assigning it to ZZZZ Best."

"I doubt I'll ever be able to substantiate millions of dollars' worth of jobs," he objected.

I raised my hand. "That's not what I'm after. I just want you to get us some real work and keep my investors satisfied. You got the idea?" I said pleasantly.

Gary silently considered the offer for a moment. "How many employees will you let me hire?"

"I don't care. Hire as many as you want. If they can bring in business, hire 'em! I'll cover the payrolls."

Gary was sold. "Cut me a check so I can get started, and I'll have a functioning office ready within a week."

⌇

"Carl Stowe, you are a hard man to track down," I said as the two of us chatted in my second-story office.

Carl was a tall, thin man of about forty-five, and extremely intense. We had been introduced through Ron Knox and had kept in touch ever since. Whenever I needed phony financial statements or tax returns, Carl delivered—for a price, of course. He also occasionally tried to raise money for ZZZZ Best, but was never successful. It may have been this lack of success that showed him just how phony ZZZZ Best really was. Though I never initially told him the whole truth about my relationship with Ron Knox and the restoration projects, he saw through everything. He'd also been preparing all the doctored financials. I liked Carl. He knew I was a fraud, but he still admired what I had accomplished at ZZZZ Best.

"I keep busy, Barry. I've got to make a living somehow," he jested in response to my statement. My decision to increase Carl's involvement in the company was based on his accounting expertise. I needed an audited financial statement for Roger Voss and didn't have the time or the ability to create the necessary paperwork. Carl was someone I could confide in and trust. No longer was it Barry Minkow versus Knox, Fuller, Robbins, Cox, Hunter, Lee, Paul, Jerry, the banks, and auditors. Now it was Barry and Carl.

"Carl, I have here a list from Roger Voss that details all the documents he must have to complete the audit. As you know, you need to create most of the stuff." I handed him the three-page letter and gave him time to review it. "Stan and Robert want this audit completed no later than August."

"Who are they, and how do they fit into ZZZZ Best?"

Although I trusted Carl, that information was on a need-to-know basis. Not wanting to raise suspicion, I downplayed the relationship. "They're just friends who helped take me public. There's absolutely nothing to worry about with them. They're pulling for us."

The crease in his forehead relaxed. "Good. Well, it's going to take me a few weeks to create all these bank statements and documents, but I can get it done. I also need to go meet with Roger a few times to explain things."

"That's fine with me. How soon can you get started?"

"Right away . . . but I've got one question. Let's say we pass the audit, then what?" He paused to choose his next words carefully. "I mean, where's the cure? You can't just keep borrowing from Peter to pay off Paul and expect to survive. One day it's going to catch up to you."

Carl was right, except for one thing. I pulled open the top drawer of my desk, took out my ZZZZ Best stock certificates, and handed them to him. "By January of 1988, these shares will become free-trading. My plan is to survive until then; sell a million shares at, say, ten dollars a share; and then pay everybody off once and for all. If I can keep things going until then, I'll be able to solve all my problems and make you a very wealthy man."

Carl was impressed. I did have an ultimate goal, and it included putting an end to ridiculous interest on loans and phony restoration contracts. "Well, if we need to survive for another eighteen months or so, I'd better get busy." He turned on his heel and exited the office.

Although I did not know it then, I had fallen for the supreme falsehood of fraud perpetration: fraud is a means to an end and never an end in itself. I told myself that lies to banks, investors, and auditors were not really wrong as long as I had a plan that would ultimately pay everyone back. As long as no one got hurt, there was no crime. Normally when financial fraud is exposed, a cure emerges out of the rubble. It's the "dream deal" that could have repaid everyone, the fraud perpetrator's equivalent of hitting the lottery. However, the likelihood of hitting the lottery is far greater than the odds of any fraud cure actually working.

I was also wrong about people not getting hurt.

∽

"Hello?" I slurred groggily into the phone. The clock on my nightstand said 2:30 a.m.

"Barry, is that you? It's Robert." He sounded panicked; judging by the time, it wasn't going to be good news.

"Yeah, what's up?"

"It's Charlie. They beat him up pretty good."

"Who did?"

"I can't tell you over the phone, but Stan called and wanted me to make sure that you don't talk to or meet with Charlie anymore. Do you understand?"

I hated Robert's condescending use of that phrase. "Yeah, I understand. Who did it?"

He didn't answer my question. "That's not your concern. Just run the company and do as we tell you."

⌇

June and July were busy months. Mike and I traveled frequently to all seven ZZZZ Best locations, trying to boost sales and build mature management. Business was good, considering we had expanded much too quickly. We wanted to expand again, into northern California, by no later than July. The more locations we opened, the easier it was for Robert to hype up the stock by likening ZZZZ Best to 7-11 convenience stores. The stock soon soared to over four dollars a share.

Carl Stowe was doing well with Roger Voss. Whenever Voss requested more information, Carl responded swiftly. The audit would be completed on time. Through the audit process I learned more about accounting than I ever wanted to. Real life was my university.

To verify the restoration projects, Carl used the Reliable Appraisal Company's letterhead provided by Gary Todd. Gary had established the insurance adjusting company and hired three adjusters and a secretary who was instructed how to handle all ZZZZ Best-related calls.

The cash demands and weekly expenses of a company with over three hundred and twenty-five employees pushed me toward two additional investors. One of them set up a one million dollar loan for ZZZZ Best at a bank in Los Angeles. An executive in the oil business who enjoyed investing in profitable ventures also signed on. I told them I needed the money to complete restoration projects, for which they would receive 50% of the contract profits. With their funds I opened our first northern California office and put a big dent in the two-million-dollar loan Stan had set up for me.

By the summer of 1986, Alan Hoffman, a man who was supposedly well connected, had replaced Charlie Hunter. According to Robert, Alan "had a lot of juice" and supervised a great deal of "family business" in California. Phil had known Alan for some time and trusted him with his life. I found him to be a nice, quiet man who never boasted of his influence and always treated me with respect.

The first thing Alan did was handle Ron Knox by showing Ron's friends

89

from back East canceled checks proving that I had paid Knox over five hundred thousand dollars. By mid-summer of 1986, Ron Knox was out of my life forever! This was a tremendous victory, but it didn't help my cash crunch.

About this time one of my associates told me he knew how to raise fifteen million dollars that I wouldn't have to pay back. An investment banking firm could do it through a public stock offering. He explained the difference between ZZZZ Best going public through a merger (as we had done in January of 1986) or by actually selling shares and receiving the proceeds. The idea appealed to me. Fifteen million dollars would pay off the two-million-dollar loan, Lee Herring, and Paul Weaver, and would cover all my other expenses. But the clincher for me was the prospect of a statewide tele-vision advertising campaign—including commercials in which I would star. I would happily feed my avaricious ego.

But first I had to get approval from my business partners. Without Stan Robbin's blessing, I couldn't do anything. Not wanting to discuss such matters over the phone, I drove out to Stan's condominium. Stan was holding court at the dining room table in his normal attire—underwear with no shirt or shoes, smoking cigar in hand. A large audience, mostly longtime friends visiting from the East, was in attendance, listening as he spun tales from his past.

I got the usual welcome as I entered the room, "Hey, Stan, the wiz kid's here." But I wasn't in the mood for laughs or stories. I needed Stan to approve the public offering and provide buying power for the stock through his East Coast connections. Unfortunately, he was so preoccupied with his friends that I was having trouble getting his ear.

I needed to shift his focus to me. I took off my shirt, shoes, and pants and sat down next to Stan in my underwear. Then I snatched up one of his cigars, lit it, and puffed away. There we were, two shirtless wheeler-dealers sitting around a table smoking cigars. The guys loved it, and the ploy worked. I had Stan's full attention.

I gave him an abridged version of the deal while he listened attentively. When I had finished, he looked me right in the eye and said, "You're crazy, Kid. But that's why I like you so much. And since this deal means so much to you, I'm going to let you do it." I gave him a big hug and the traditional kiss on the cheek and put my shirt, shoes, and pants back on.

Just before I got out the door, Stan hollered his final order, "Just don't let me down!" Stan's final warning echoed in my mind. In order to keep my word to Stan and to my employees, I'd have to pull off the biggest con of my life. This would be much harder than my other cons because Wall Street pros would investigate my claims about ZZZZ Best before I could raise any money.

But they were going to meet their match. By this time, the end of July 1986, I was a seasoned con man with years of experience in deception on my résumé. With the company on the line and my secret partners looking over my shoulder, I would do whatever it took to get the deal done.

7 FINANCIAL FIX

So, what's the balance in my business checking account?" I asked my secretary, en route to one of the biggest business meetings of my young life.

"You've got $152,800, and after we pay today's checks, you'll have $22,900!"

Must be all those payroll checks clearing at once, I thought.

"Okay," I said aloud, "and thank you very much for your help. By the way, did you get the candy I sent you?"

"Yes, Barry, I did. And thanks. I'm the talk of the bank!" she said proudly.

The woman deserved more than candy. She always alerted me ahead of time whenever my business checking account was overdrawn. In a critical position, she was able to give me immediate credit on large checks, which allowed me, on occasions (unbeknownst to her), to float funds through an elaborate check-kiting scheme.

"I'll be making another deposit tomorrow at about ten o'clock. You'll be there, won't you?"

"Of course."

"Look forward to seeing you then. Bye for now," I said in my sweetest voice. I hung up the car phone and slapped both hands against the steering wheel. There was only $22,900 left. The weekly cash demands were draining both me and my accounts. I needed the funds from the public offering to keep afloat until that wonderful day in January of 1988 when I could sell some of my stock and pay everyone off permanently.

Big meetings were no problem for me. By now I was a skilled con man who could lie to anyone, anywhere, at any time, under any conditions. This meeting was with a banker named Howard Kane. Bogus financial statements and other information about the company had impressed Kane. That was good. But something bothered me about meeting with him. Maybe it was because he had flown all the way from the East Coast just to see me. Or perhaps it was dawning on me that if I didn't convince him to raise the fifteen million dollars, ZZZZ Best would go under. I simply owed too many people too much money.

Leaving the freeway, I headed for our 12:30 p.m. lunch meeting. I had time for one last call.

"Hello," said a weary voice on the other end of the line.

"Well, Carl, this is it. This is the big cure!" I said. "If we pull this one off, I can stop kiting checks and quit worrying about having enough cash to meet our expenses."

"Just think, Barry, with fifteen million dollars, you won't need to depend on people like Lee Herring and Paul Weaver anymore. This can almost be a normal business!"

I laughed and got down to business. "Listen, we're going to have to make another deposit tomorrow, so get things ready."

"No problem," he replied. "Are you ready for the meeting? We've got a lot riding on it."

He didn't need to remind me. "I'll be fine, my friend," I said confidently. "You just make sure the checks don't bounce, and I'll handle the rest."

"I just didn't want you to get cold feet. After all, we're in the big leagues now—Wall Street. Get it?" he said enthusiastically.

"Yeah, I got it." I paused to think for a moment. He was right. This would be the biggest con of my life. "Don't forget, Carl, we're not raising this money to run to Europe and leave everybody stuck with the bills. We're going to meet payrolls, pay back investors, and develop a legitimate and profitable company. And if that happens, everybody's a winner and nobody gets hurt." I said this more to reassure myself than Carl.

"You don't have to convince me," he replied. "I'm with you all the way to make sure we survive until January of 1988. Once everybody gets paid and there are no victims, then there will have been no crime." The relief was evident in his tone.

"Right on, Carl!" My conscience was temporarily appeased.

"Hey, I just pulled up to the restaurant. Take it easy, man."

"Good luck!" he said in parting.

I tossed the valet my keys and walked purposefully to the entrance; sweat from the oppressive July sun threatened to drown me in my three-piece suit. I much preferred wearing a tank top and shorts, but for fifteen million dollars, I was willing to dress up. The maitre d' led me to a table on the outside patio. Kane was early.

After we had made our introductions and placed our orders, Howard Kane smiled and said, "So, why should I raise all this money for you, Mr. Minkow?"

"Because I'm building the nation's largest carpet and furniture cleaning and restoration company. And by raising ZZZZ Best the funds we need, you'll be on the ground floor of a guaranteed winner." Lies raced out of my mouth like an Olympic runner in full sprint.

"Is that so?" he replied, arching an eyebrow. "Tell me what you would do with an influx of fifteen million dollars."

I paused long enough for him not to suspect that I had a well-rehearsed answer. "Well, Mr. Kane, to begin with, I want to open ten new carpet cleaning stores. Each will cost approximately two hundred fifty thousand dollars to start but will be profitable within sixty days. We know this based on the eight offices that are already open and functioning. I also want to use about seven million to buy materials and supplies for our ongoing restoration business. If I can finance a hundred percent of these jobs, I'll no longer need partners and investors. This will increase my profitability tremendously, because I won't have to give up half my action." I gave him a moment and allowed him to absorb what I had said. "Additionally, the company will invest four million in a massive television advertising campaign that will dramatically increase our commercial and residential penetration in the marketplace. The balance of the funds will be used for working capital." As I spoke, I never took my eyes off his face. First rule of lying, don't break eye contact.

"Those are ambitious goals," he said as he sipped casually from his glass. "Do you have the management to back you up?"

"Yes, I do. My policy has always been to promote from within. Every one of our current managers started out as a carpet cleaner or a phone solicitor and worked his or her way up. My people know we are in the process of building a massive empire, and they want to grow with the company."

He nodded in approval, and I warmed to my subject. "My policy with personnel is simple, Mr. Kane. We're going places at ZZZZ Best, and our track record proves it. We continue to open new carpet cleaning locations every other month, and company morale is at an all-time high. People from other companies would give their right arm to be a part of our management team because they want to be with a winner," I said excitedly. He was listening attentively.

"Well, Mr. Minkow, it seems that you've done your homework. But going public isn't easy. I've got to hire lawyers who will investigate your company thoroughly. It will take about four months to put together a prospectus, and then you'll need to fly all over the country to present your company to the investment community. Are you ready for that kind of commitment?"

The word *investigate* always scared me. The last thing I needed was a pack of Wall Street lawyers I didn't know buzzing around my office and diligently examining my company for four months. But I had no choice, if I wanted to keep ZZZZ Best—and myself—alive.

Knowing that the best defense is a good offense, I boldly stated, "Of course I am. I wouldn't be here wasting your time if I weren't prepared to invest all my efforts into the deal. When do we get started?"

His smile told me that he was convinced. "I'll make a few calls when I get back East and have my lawyers contact you immediately. I'll also want you to fly out in a few weeks and meet some of the stockbrokers who will help sell the deal."

"Sounds great!" I responded. "Are we agreed on fifteen million?"

Kane did not hesitate. "I'm in agreement with that figure. Just do your part and get through the four months of constant meetings with lawyers, auditors, and investigators, and I'll worry about raising the funds."

"You've got a deal." I stuck out my hand to seal it.

"Deal." Kane shook my hand.

We raised our glasses and toasted the success of ZZZZ Best. The rest of the time was spent answering the usual inquiries about how I got started in the carpet cleaning industry at such a young age.

After lunch, I rushed straight back to my office. Carl Stowe was waiting for me.

"We've got it, buddy!" I announced jubilantly. "Fifteen million dollars!"

Carl pounded his fist on my desk in excitement. "Right on, man!" he shouted, then quickly sobered.

"But what do we need to do to get it?" Carl had enough experience in raising money to know that even the smallest of bank loans required huge amounts of paperwork.

"Relax, my friend," I said reassuringly. "All we need to do is satisfy these Wall Street big shots and we've got the money!"

The expression on Carl's face reflected serious doubt. "I don't know, Barry. If going public were easy, everybody would be doing it. These guys might not fall for the restoration con."

"Carl, listen to me!" I shot out of my chair and circled the desk. "I've been waiting for the one big deal that would solve all my financial problems since the days in the garage. And I'll be dammed if I'm going to let a bunch of Wall Street stuffed shirts stand in the way of my only opportunity to get all of these people off my back!"

He could see the determination in my eyes and allowed my words to sink in before asking, "How long will this whole going public process take?"

"From start to finish, four months. But that's four months of intense meetings, tons of paperwork, and a significant amount of traveling. For fifteen million dollars, I'm willing to put up with it." I leveled a searching look at him. "How about you?"

"You know where I stand, Barry—right next to you, all the way."

I filled Carl in on the rest of the details. By the time we had finished, we were ready to take on Wall Street.

≈

Howard Kane's first demand was that I obtain highly respected law and accounting firms. I followed his recommendations and hired a nationally recognized law firm and an internationally known accounting firm. David Lundy, the member of a high-powered East Coast law firm, was placed in charge of my deal. He was a likable, intelligent man who never forgot a detail. When conversing with him about the company, I had to watch my words carefully so I wouldn't contradict myself. I spent a great deal of time with David in the following months, perhaps too much, because I was beginning to like him as a friend and felt guilty for lying to him about ZZZZ Best.

Matt Paulson was in charge of the project for the accounting firm. Quiet and reserved, yet easy to talk to, Matt was very thorough and seemed always to be asking for one more document relating to the restoration projects.

While I courted Kane, Lundy, and Paulson, Carl Stowe created volumes of documents to substantiate our restoration business. He made up invoices from suppliers that didn't exist. He reconciled bank statements and tied them into ledgers so that the company appeared to be making big profits. By using blank checks from Reliable Appraisal Company, Carl even made it look like Gary Todd's company had paid ZZZZ Best millions of dollars.

Gary also did his part. When the Wall Street lawyers or the accounting people called Reliable, he provided good recommendations and verified ZZZZ Best's contracts. Meanwhile, carpet cleaning sales were up. Mike increased our residential business by successfully opening three new locations: two in northern California and the other in Monrovia. This pushed our figure of total employees to well over four hundred.

Mike was also the perfect man to put in front of the investment bankers, auditors, and lawyers because he did not know about the phony restoration business. As far as Mike was concerned, that was Carl's department. He ran the residential carpet cleaning stores and boasted about how great ZZZZ Best was because he believed it. In fraud perpetration the rule of thumb is to let as few people know about the fraud as possible, for obvious reasons. The more who know, the higher the likelihood of getting caught. By keeping my people blissfully ignorant, they could promote the company wholeheartedly because they were not hiding anything. That didn't stop me from feeling terrible about lying to Mike.

The rapid expansion, coupled with the pressure of going public, forced me to put in fifteen-hour days. My health suffered greatly as a result. I continued taking steroids, fighting a never-ending battle to retain my strength.

Robert, Stan, Alan, and Phil placed few demands on me during these busy months. The frequent meetings at Stan's condominium dropped off to once or twice a week. It was in their interest that I complete the public offering. After all, Stan and Robert still owned half a million shares of free-trading ZZZZ Best stock that I had purchased for them at five cents a share.

～

"I won't be home 'til about 4:00 a.m., Donna," I said into my cellular. "I'll be at the financial printer all night, putting the final touches on the public offering."

"Do you want me to wait up for you?" she asked kindly.

I laughed. "Of course not! Go on to sleep. By the time you wake up tomorrow morning, ZZZZ Best will be an official Wall Street success."

"How's your stomach feeling? Have you been throwing up blood today?"

"No. I'm all right," I lied. I leaned over to the rearview mirror of my BMW and studied my face. The streetlights exposed dark rings under my eyes. *Steroids are no substitute for sleep*, I said to myself. They were taking their toll on me physically, and Donna knew it.

"When this deal's done, can we spend more time together?" she asked hopefully. Donna enjoyed all the new cars and the house in Westchester County Estates, but she wasn't seeing much of me.

"Yes, Honey," I replied automatically. "But after the completion of this offering, I'll be forced to travel more."

"Can't I go with you?" she pressed.

I didn't want to make any promises to her I couldn't keep. Traveling was an opportunity to spend time with other women. It's what every business executive did, or so I thought. "We'll see, Honey . . . listen, I've got to go now. I'm almost at the printer's. I love you."

"I love you, too," she whispered.

The cool December air helped perk me up as I arrived at the printer at 10:00 p.m. I waved to Phil who was following closely in his own car, and watched him park half a block down the street. *If Matt Paulson and David Lundy knew I had a live-in bodyguard who had a questionable past, they would never do business with me*, I thought as I sauntered in the main entrance.

The place reminded me of a high-class hotel. The waiting room was beautifully furnished with velvet sofas and chairs. Original paintings hung on the walls, and the carpets didn't have a spot on them! When the staff realized I was the company president, they treated me like a king, escorting me down a long, well-lit corridor. Brass baseboards sparkled, reflecting the recessed ceiling lights. This was like no other printing company I had ever seen.

We finally arrived at a large conference room for this one last meeting with the lawyers and accountants. As usual, everyone was there ahead of me. A large table covered with documents dominated the room. David Lundy, Matt Paulson, and several other people from their firm were joined by other lawyers and investment company executives. Each had the task of proofreading the final prospectus before it went to print and making all the necessary revisions. I had never before seen anything like a financial printing operation. With their high-tech equipment, they had the capacity to produce thousands of full-color, glossy prospectuses and distribute them via air nationally in a matter of hours. This was definitely the big leagues. No one needed this kind of service unless he was raising major dollars and using them to print materials.

It took four hours to go through the prospectus. Even though it was late, I was too keyed-up to be tired. I imagined walking into the bank with millions of dollars. Instead of throwing me out for not being old enough, they'd be begging for my business! I wondered how it would feel not having to worry about meeting payroll each week. Then there were all those people I owed, many of whom thought they owned me. I couldn't wait to be delivered from their greedy clutches.

The only things that remained after the prospectus were the legal documents. As president and chairman of the board, my signature was required on nearly every one. David Lundy handed me a stack of papers to sign. As I sat there and scanned the documents, I recalled what one of the lawyers had told me about lying to the Securities and Exchange Commission: "You'll go to jail for a long time if you defraud the SEC." His words haunted me.

It's not too late, I reasoned silently. *I can stop the public offering now and minimize my potential punishment. Until this deal becomes effective and the stock is sold to the public, I'm not guilty of defrauding the SEC.*

It seemed like only days since my financial problems had been in the neighborhood of several hundred dollars instead of several million. Time had simply added more zeros to the tally. I again looked down at the papers and feigned inspecting them. Sweat beaded up on my forehead. I glanced at my watch; it was 3:20 a.m. Defrauding thousands of people through a public stock offering was incredibly different from stealing a few money orders or overcharging customer credit cards. How had things gotten so out of hand?

I had to have courage. This deal would supposedly make me the youngest person in U.S. business history to take a company public on Wall Street. I would raise fifteen million dollars. And I was only twenty years old! Besides, I had people depending on me. Employees and investors needed to be paid. Stan was counting on me. The ultimate goal was still the same: to keep ZZZZ Best running until January of 1988, when I would be home free!

I ran my fingers through my hair and rubbed my neck. The long day was catching up with me. I thought briefly about my high school friends who were now attending Cal State University, Northridge, living free from stressful decisions in frat houses. But I had chosen a different route. I wanted the fame. I wanted the glory. I wanted everyone to know who Barry Minkow was. I wanted magazines, newspapers, and television shows singing the praises of the "Boy Genius."

I straightened the stack of legal documents on the table and grabbed my pen. I began signing. Page after page, signature after signature. The more I thought about the money, power, and glory, the faster I signed. At 3:55 a.m., my hand raced across the last page, and I handed the stack to David Lundy.

"Here you go, sir, signed, sealed, and delivered," I said with a grin.

David looked at me intently. "You should be proud of your accomplishments," he said. "It's not every day that a guy who is not even allowed to drink legally takes a company public." He offered his hand, but I hugged him instead.

If he only knew, I thought. *If he only knew.*

8 BAD SERVE

The year 1987 started off great. The fifteen-million-dollar public offering had sold out in December of 1986. I had used the leverage from that to obtain additional bank loans, a total of ten million. ZZZZ Best's stock value was pushing nearly fifty million, making my share worth just shy of twenty-five million dollars.

On the advice of Howard Kane, I hired Thomas Meyer, a public relations man. Meyer was known for taking one small company's stock from two dollars to over two hundred dollars a share. Even Robert Fuller respected the way Meyer's firm was able to move stocks.

But I had trouble getting along with Meyer. He was just like me; he had to be in control. He criticized my staff and even hurled insults at me on occasion. Many times I felt like telling him off, but I resisted the temptation because he was making me a hero on Wall Street. In just four months (January through April 1987), Meyer singlehandedly took the stock from four dollars to over eighteen dollars a share, which put the company's stock value at just under three hundred million. My own stock was worth over one hundred million dollars!

As planned, I used some of the extra cash to do the television ad campaign. The three funny commercials instantly became hits, exposing how the competition often used "bait and switch" tactics on unsuspecting customers. I took great pleasure in starring in each of them, hoping to become so famous that I'd be noticed everywhere I went. It worked. By the end of

February, I couldn't go anywhere in California without being recognized. Somehow that made the lying, manipulating, and conning a little easier to take.

With the company growing in popularity, we opened nine new locations between mid-December 1986 and mid-May 1987: three in Arizona, two in Nevada, and four in northern California. We even began to manufacture our own private-label carpet cleaning chemicals. All this pushed our employee total to well over twelve hundred company wide.

But the biggest news of 1987 was the KeyServ deal. I learned in early February that Northern Foods, a British company, wanted to sell one of its American subsidiaries, KeyServ Inc. KeyServ was Sears Roebuck's nationwide authorized carpet cleaner. When customers called Sears for carpet cleaning, KeyServ did the work. Sears got between 10% and 15% of the sale, with KeyServ retaining the balance. KeyServ's annual revenues topped eighty million dollars.

I saw acquiring KeyServ as a way to instantly fulfill my dream of becoming the General Motors of the carpet cleaning industry.

There were just two problems: the twenty-five-million-dollar price tag, and the fact that with almost three thousand employees, KeyServ was three times the size of ZZZZ Best.

When I brought the deal to Thomas Meyer, he assured me that he could raise the money for the acquisition. "I'll get your foot in the door with the investment bankers, but you have to sell them on the deal," Meyer told me.

I studied KeyServ's financial statements and business strategies, looking for areas needing improvement. I also flew to New Town Square, Pennsylvania, and met with the company's top management. Once finished with that, I was ready to sell the investment people.

At my first meeting with the corporate finance people, I responded to every one of their concerns. If they had a question, I had a reasoned answer. Within hours they were satisfied enough to move forward. Truthfully, I think the proposed dramatic increase in stock price persuaded them more than I did. They were to receive a substantial portion of stock for funding the acquisition. Once again, unbeknownst to me at the time, I was utilizing what would later become a very popular tool in future Wall Street frauds: I was attempting to use my company stock (which was fraudulently inflated through bogus earnings and undisclosed debt) as currency to help purchase a legitimate company in hopes that my fraudulent earnings would somehow get lost among their legitimate ones.

Carl Stowe and I viewed the KeyServ deal as the final link in the chain that would lead us to January of 1988. Since the investment banking firm was offering to raise an estimated forty million, we would use twenty-five million to buy out KeyServ and the balance to hold us over until January.

We soon figured out that the fifteen million dollars from the public offering and the ten million in bank loans would still leave us short on cash. The "profits" being paid to investors for the nonexistent restoration deals were depleting ZZZZ Best's cash surplus at an alarming rate. As was the ad campaign. One of my advisors hauled reams of computer printouts to my office in early March to deliver the news. "Mr. Minkow, these commercials are killing us!" he said.

"What do you mean?"

"Well, between the production costs and the air time, we've spent almost two million dollars."

"So?"

"The problem is, we've only taken in twenty thousand in business."

"How do you know that?"

"Because we used a special 800 number in the spots. The sales off that number total only around twenty thousand dollars in business." He paused as I rubbed my cheek. "I think we should cancel all future television ads before we lose another two million."

He didn't understand. I didn't care about the cost-effectiveness of television advertising. I cared about every resident of California instantly recognizing my face.

"Don't cancel them," I said softly.

"What?" he asked in amazement.

"I said don't cancel them! It's called identity. We're going to keep running these commercials until ZZZZ Best becomes a household name."

My advisor was astonished. He gathered up his printouts and walked to the door. "Or until we go broke," he muttered as he left.

I chose not to respond.

～

"Come on, Barry, you're going to be late for your own birthday party!" Donna called up the stairs.

I was taking my time getting dressed and could hear the flood of people coming through the door to celebrate my twenty-first birthday. I made my way down through streamers and balloons and all the trappings of a gala affair. Donna had done an outstanding job preparing the house for my special day.

Though I hated turning twenty-one—I was now officially an adult and no longer legitimate heir to the titles "Boy Genius" or the "Whiz Kid of Wall Street"—I took comfort in my accomplishments: twelve hundred employees, the fourth hottest stock on Wall Street, the KeyServ deal, and connections with powerful criminals who worked hard at keeping me alive. Yes, I had made a difference.

I stopped by the front door and greeted a few arriving guests. The place was jam-packed with people. Inside, there was standing room only, and outside, a line of people waited to get in. The house looked more like a swank nightclub than a residence.

"Did you invite the whole world to this party?" I asked Donna.

"No, Barry. Just your close friends and those who would be offended if they weren't invited. Just relax and have fun," she said as she kissed me on the cheek.

"I think for next year's party we're going to need a bigger house," I replied.

I turned around and bumped into Vera, the second telephone solicitor I had hired way back in the garage days. "Look at this place, Barry," she said excitedly. "All these people love and care for you. Isn't it great that they're here for you?"

"Yeah," I replied softly.

She gave me a big hug and went on her way. But what she said stuck with me. *Did all these people really love me?*

I made my way to the living room and found several of my top managers laughing and talking. They paused in their conversation and greeted me warmly. I thought about what Vera had said and then asked myself what they were doing here. It's not because they love me, but because I sign their pay-checks! I faked a smile, shook a few hands, and strode into the family room, where Matt Paulson, David Lundy, and several of my financial advisors were chatting. They were only here because of the hundreds of thousands of dollars I've paid them in fees. My frustration increased.

I threaded my way through the crowd and into the backyard where several of my investors were admiring my swimming pool with its tiled Z on the bottom. I wish I had all the interest back that I've paid these people over the last two years. Do they like me for me, or for the "juice"?

As I made my way back inside, I noticed Phil Cox hanging on the perimeter, watching my every move. When my gaze met Phil's, I thought about Robert and Stan. Just two weeks earlier, they had sold their half million shares of ZZZZ Best stock at eight dollars a share. I wondered why. The stock was going up and the KeyServ deal would close shortly, which was sure to push the stock up even further. *Do they know something they aren't telling me*? I suppressed the thought and dove into the crowd.

Finally, I wandered into the kitchen, hoping to find at least one person who honestly loved Barry Minkow because he was Barry Minkow. One of my best friends from high school was there talking with Donna. I looked closely at both of them, hoping to see two reasons for stifling my paranoia. But then I remembered the one thousand shares of ZZZZ Best stock I had bought for my friend just the week before. As I focused on Donna, I saw the five-thousand-dollar diamond ring she wore on her finger. Had I bought her too? Maybe not intentionally, but . . . ?

A sick feeling settled heavily upon me. Weak-kneed, I climbed the stairs to the peace and quiet of my bedroom, where I threw myself across the bed and cried.

〜

The phone wakened me from my dream world. *It's a little early for a phone call*, I thought. I picked up the receiver.

"Barry, is that you?" asked the voice on the other end of the line.

"Yeah, it's me. Who's this?"

"It's Thomas Meyer. Have you read your morning paper yet?"

Meyer had a house in a posh L.A. suburb and often flew out from back East for extended periods. For him to call me at home this early it had to be serious.

"No, I haven't," I responded. "Should I?"

"There is a negative article about you in the front page of today's metro section."

"How bad is it, Thomas?"

"It's pretty bad, Barry. It talks about your past involvement with credit card fraud. Your stock is already down half a point. When are you going to be at the office?"

"I'm on my way."

"Good. I'll call you in half an hour. We're going to need to prepare some kind of press release to explain this thing away."

So much for an easy day. I rushed down the stairs and out to the porch where I stooped to grab the *L.A. Times*. My heart rate increased as I pulled out the business section. There it was. My picture in the top right-hand corner next to a bold-print headline: "BEHIND WHIZ KID LIES TRAIL OF FALSE CREDIT CARD BILLINGS." I almost collapsed but fear pressed me forward.

There was no time to stand there and read the article. I had to get to the office fast. I roared out of the driveway and got on the phone to John Brady, the stockbroker who had been introduced to me by Robert Fuller. He monitored ZZZZ Best's stock and alerted me to every significant change.

"John, it's Barry. Is everything all right?"

"I just tried to call you at the office. Have you read the article yet?" His voice betrayed him. He was extremely disturbed.

"I've got it right here in front of me. It's old news, John. Nothing to be concerned about," I said in a convincing tone.

"I hope you're right, Barry. The stock is down seven-eighths."

"Listen, John, we're going to be preparing a press release to respond to this article, so don't worry."

"But, Barry, I've already had two clients call with sell orders," he argued. "They read the article and called me immediately."

"Well, why didn't you stick up for me and assure them that nothing was wrong with the company?" I yelled into the receiver.

"Take it easy, pal. I didn't know what to say," he exclaimed in response to my attack.

"If any other stockholders call and want to sell, let them know you talked to me and I said everything was okay. Emphasize the fact that this credit card nonsense is three years old! Have you got that?"

"Yeah," he answered in defeat.

I sensed his grave disappointment. "Listen, I've never let you down since I've known you, and I'm not about to start now! I've told you this thing is nothing. I'll have it all worked out within a couple of days. In the meantime, do your best to prevent people from dumping the stock, okay?"

By the time our conversation ended, I was within five minutes of the office. Why did this thing have to break four days before I close the biggest deal of my life? I was panicking. I pulled into the parking lot and rushed to my office. It was only 7:15 a.m., and the phone was already ringing off the hook.

I snatched the receiver on the fourth ring. "This is Barry Minkow."

"Thomas Meyer, Barry. Listen, I'm going to set up a conference call with a few brokers from New York. They have some questions they want answered about the article. I think it's important for you to speak with them before this thing gets out of hand."

"I agree. What time do you want to do it?"

"Now!"

"All right. But I just got in, and there's no one here to answer the phones, so we might be interrupted," I explained.

"That's fine. I'll get us cross-connected. Just hold on."

As I waited, I read the article from start to finish. It was damaging because it alleged patterns of criminal behavior and denial. Thankfully it didn't mention the phony restoration business. As long as that isn't discovered, I can overcome all this other stuff, I decided.

"Barry, it's me. Are you ready?"

"Sure, Thomas. Put them on," I said with a sudden burst of assurance.

"Barry, this is Byron Buckley from Johnston & Lang. I've got a couple of associates on the line with me, and we just want to ask you a few questions.

Is that okay?" I had met Buckley a few months earlier. He ran the Los Angeles office of Johnston & Lang and had been very enthusiastic about ZZZZ Best stock.

"Go right ahead, gentlemen. Ask away."

"Has anyone from your investment banking firm called you yet to cancel the forty-million-dollar funding for the acquisition?" asked Buckley.

"No, sir. I haven't heard anything from our people, and I don't expect to. I would be very surprised if they reacted at all to this outdated news story."

"Well, are you going to prepare a press release of some kind to neutralize this article? There's a lot of selling pressure on the stock right now."

"Mr. Meyer and I were discussing that earlier," I answered. "We'll make a public statement that will explain the entire situation and put this whole credit card issue to rest."

"What actually happened, Barry?" asked Buckley. "I mean, how were all these customers overcharged?"

Telling Byron Buckley the truth was not an option. "I had some dishonest carpet cleaners who worked for the company a while back who overcharged customers to increase their commissions. When I found out about the scheme, I fired them and paid back all the victims. What more could I do?"

"I understand what you're saying and I believe you," said Buckley. "If I didn't, I wouldn't be talking to you now. But the public isn't aware yet of your side of the story, and we need to make them aware as soon as possible."

"I plan on doing that today, sir."

"Good. Meanwhile, let me know if you hear from your investors. The best thing you can do right now is close that financing deal. That would immediately silence the critics and stop the selling."

"That sounds great to me, Mr. Buckley," I replied. "I'll do whatever I can to get it done."

"Keep us posted and I'll call you later."

"How's the stock now?" I asked before he hung up.

"It's down one and a half," he answered. The conversation ended.

I sat back and massaged my temples, feeling the preliminary shooting pains of a migraine. There had to be a way for me to stop the freefall. For every point my stock dropped, I personally lost six million dollars in net worth.

The intercom buzzed. It was Amy—in early as usual. She was typically concerned. "Are you all right?"

"I've been better. You know about the article, I suppose?"

"Yeah, but don't worry, Barry, everything will be okay! I've got faith in you!" she said kindly. "Can I bring you some coffee?"

"Sure, and bring two aspirin with you. Also, because of this article, the phone's going to be ringing off the hook today, so just put the calls through as fast as you can. It's called damage control," I said.

"No problem. I'll be in there in a few minutes."

The phone buzzed again. *More good news*, I thought drearily. Disappointment has a very bitter taste.

"Sorry to bother you again," Amy said, "but Miles Harris from the investment banking firm is on the line. He says it's important. Do you want to talk to him?"

Only two weeks before, Harris had been publicly generous with praise at the convention that brought the KeyServ and ZZZZ Best management teams together. Now I feared even taking his call.

"Put him through, Amy," I said. Then, I addressed the caller with forced enthusiasm: "Hi, Miles. How are you?"

"Not good, Barry. I'm sure you're aware of this morning's *L.A. Times* article?"

"Of course I am, Miles. I told you this story might come out sooner or later. The contents don't surprise me in the least," I lied. I had disclosed the likelihood of some negative publicity, but I had played it very low-key. Naïvely, I suppose, I hadn't expected the story to be so bold and hard-hitting, nor to be given front-page metro status—with my photo, no less.

"Well, Barry, the story concerns me and a few of our top executives. Before we close the forty-million-dollar funding, we want to reinvestigate this entire credit card deal."

"But that stuff's three years old, Miles," I objected.

"Since it's our money, we'll be the judge of what's relevant to investigate," he snapped. "I want to fly in our investigators immediately. They'll spend the weekend with you and ask detailed questions about the contents of the article. If your answers can be independently verified, everything should be okay. If not, we'll back out of the deal immediately."

The article had put a lot of heat on Miles. He was supposed to know things like this and have answers prepared. But the news had caught him off guard. My downplaying approach to the incident had actually backfired on me. Now he was professionally embarrassed and determined to get to the bottom of this alleged credit card fraud.

"That's fine with me. I'll spend the three-day Memorial Day weekend answering questions. Whatever information they need, I'll provide," I promised. Amy slid the coffee in front of me. I took the aspirin and hoped that it would work quickly.

"Good," Miles replied. "I'll set everything up and have the investigators meet you at your office between eight and eight-thirty tomorrow morning."

"Are you guys going to say anything to the press?"

"We have nothing to say at this point. Right now we need to concentrate on completing the investigation."

There goes the relaxing weekend, I thought as we disconnected. This investigation worried me. Until this article, no one had been looking for fraud at ZZZZ Best. I was the wiz kid entrepreneur underdog who had overcome youth and built an empire. But now, the authenticity of the Barry Minkow story was in doubt. These investigators would come looking for impropriety, and that kind of scrutiny terrified me. I knew I should inform Byron Buckley about the call from Miles. But if I did, he might turn sour on ZZZZ Best. That phone call would have to wait. I glanced at my watch. I had already been through an entire day of aggravation, and it was not even 8:00.

"Barry," Amy's voice crackled over the intercom, "Channel 2 News is on the line. They want to know if they can come out and do an interview with you. What should I tell them?"

I mentally reviewed my options. *Maybe I can use this free airtime to defend my integrity*, I thought. For years I had used the media to convince the public that ZZZZ Best was legitimate. Now I needed to attack the critics head-on and systematically answer their questions. By creating a stage and putting on a performance (as I had done only weeks ago at the convention with the KeyServ and ZZZZ Best management), I could get out of this mess, too.

"Ask them if they can be here before two o'clock, Amy." Within minutes, she had confirmed a one-thirty interview time.

"That's great!" I responded. "If any other media people call, tell them I'll make a formal statement here in my office at that time."

"All right," said Amy. "Can I come and straighten your desk before they get here?"

I smiled. The desk was nearly invisible beneath mounds of paper—not a good impression for the evening news. Amy always thought of that sort of thing. "Sure," I replied. "Come in around twelve-thirty."

My attitude suddenly took a 180-degree turn. My television presence had never failed me in the past, and I felt confident that I could neutralize this story before it really blew up. I walked to the window and peeked through the blinds at my employees, answering phones and setting up carpet cleaning appointments. *These people work for me!* I thought proudly. *And there's no way I'm going to let them down!*

"Barry?" Amy said faintly. I darted over to pick up the receiver. "It's Stan. He says it's urgent."

9 INTO THE ABYSS

"Stan, how are you?" I said cheerfully. "Well, it's the wonder boy," he quipped. "How are you, Wiz?"

"I've had better days," I replied. "I'm sure you're aware of the problems I'm having with the media."

"As a matter of fact, I am. Do you think it would be possible to get fifteen minutes of your time today, Mr. Wonder Boy?" It was unusual for Stan to call me directly, normally Robert or Phil was the messenger, and more unusual that he wanted to see me on such short notice. I unhappily concluded that it must be serious.

"Of course I can spare fifteen minutes for you. What time do you want to see me?"

"How does now sound?" His voice had lost its brotherly tone.

"Now, Stan?" I was caught off guard. "Can I make it later on this afternoon? I don't mean to put you off, but I've got a lot going on with this article, and I need to be here for a few hours. How about four o'clock?" I asked tentatively. Stan did not like to be put off.

"If that's as soon as you can make it, I'll see you then."

"Great! I'll see you no later than four today. How are you feeling?"

The unwelcome sound of a dial tone was his response.

I stood and paced the office nervously. *Why is Stan so anxious to see me?* I wondered. The last thing I needed was a problem with him.

Just then Amy chimed in on the intercom, "It's the branch manager from Citizens Credit and—"

"Put him through," I interrupted. Citizens Credit was where I had my main business checking account. I owed the bank three million and planned to pay it back when the merger financing was completed.

"Hello, how are you this morning?" I asked cordially.

"I'm doing fine, Barry. But I think we have a small problem."

Problem was not a word I enjoyed hearing from my banker. "What might that be, sir?" I said respectfully.

"I'm going to have to call your loan, Barry. I hate to do that, but based on the information in today's paper, the bank is quite concerned about ZZZZ Best's credibility." My head spun. *One lousy article and the bank's going to jump ship on me*, I thought angrily. *What fair-weather friends they turned out to be.* "Sir, I think there's a big misunderstanding about this article. This whole credit card thing is old news and has nothing to do with our current operations," I protested.

"I'm sure that's true, Barry. And after the loan is paid back, we can go over it in more detail. But for now, the bank would feel more comfortable if the loan were paid in full. According to our agreement, the bank has the option to levy your checking account to pay the loan."

"You can't levy my checking account! All my company checks will bounce! I'll be out of business!" I yelled as I jumped out of my chair.

"Relax. I didn't say we've decided to do that today, Barry. I'm merely stating that we have that option. But I would like to see a significant reduction within five days, or I will levy the account to protect the bank's interest."

This was devastating news. I couldn't pay back Citizens Credit unless the investment money came through. And since the investment firm had just delayed the deal, I was in real trouble. But I couldn't let the bank know this.

"That's fair enough. Give me five days, and I'll make a major reduction in the loan." I paused to let the offer sink in. "By the way, tonight on Channel 2 News, you'll see my official reply to today's article. I would appreciate your watching the program."

"I'll do that, and I'll get some of my associates to do the same. Perhaps you can earn back some credibility with a strong explanation."

"You can bet I will," I countered. "And have a nice weekend."

I hung up the phone and called the only person who could help in this situation—Carl Stowe. I wasn't about to take on the world single-handedly any longer. "Carl, it's Barry. I need to see you right away."

"What's wrong, partner? Is everything all right?" Carl was a late riser and had not yet seen the article.

I filled him in on my day so far: the *Times* story, the plummeting stock, the investors, Citizens Credit.

"Was there anything in the article about the restoration business?" he asked.

"No, Carl, and that's what amazes me. They don't have a clue as to what's really going on, yet everyone's still jumping ship. But don't worry. I'm going on television in a few hours, and then I'll publicly put this thing to rest."

"I'm on my way. What's the stock trading at now?"

"The last I heard, it was down a point and a half."

"Don't worry, Barry. We'll handle this problem and close the investment deal. We've done it before when the chips were down, and we can do it again."

My phone was blinking, indicating another incoming call. "You're right, pal! See you in a few."

I quickly hung up and asked Amy who it was. I glanced at my watch. It was 10:00 a.m. This was turning out to be the longest day of my life.

"It's John Brady, Barry. He says it's important."

"Put him through." I wondered if I'd ever receive another call that wasn't important. "Yes, John, what's going on with the stock?"

"Everything bad," he said over the background clatter of a brokerage office on a trading day. "Unless you're on the short side. It's down two and three-quarters, and there's a ton of selling pressure. You have any idea who's doing all this selling?"

I tried to brighten John's mood by telling him how my upcoming press conference would take head-on the issue of the old credit card billing story. "That should slow the selling," I said. "You can count on me, John. I'll call you later."

As the conversation ended, I remembered the time John and I had gone to a ballgame together. We had a great time laughing and joking. John believed in ZZZZ Best and me. *What will happen to him if this all falls apart?* The whole thing had gotten totally out of hand.

The intercom, or rather, the harbinger of doom, buzzed again.

"Barry, Rhonda Ames from Union Bank is on the line," Amy said.

"I'm falling in love with today. Put her through." I owed Union Bank seven million. "Hi, Rhonda. How are you?" I asked when she came on the line.

"That's a question I should be asking you, Barry. Is everything all right over there?"

"Of course it is," I responded through gritted teeth. "Just a little bad press—nothing I can't handle. I'll be holding a press conference later to explain everything."

"I've noticed your stock is down quite a bit today. Have you heard from the investment banking people?"

"No, I haven't. They were prepared for this article because I disclosed the problem to them weeks ago." *Liar, liar.*

She changed the subject. "When are you going to be able to pay the loan back?"

The last thing I needed was another five-day mandatory pay-down. "I'd say within the next thirty to forty-five days, I should be able to clear the debt."

"Can't you do it any sooner?"

"Well, Rhonda, I have over twelve hundred employees to pay every week, not to mention my normal expenses. I planned on paying you back in late June when I'm in a better cash position."

"Yeah, but with this latest article, my boss is a little concerned. He wants the loan paid now, and by our loan agreement we have the right to demand that the note be paid at any time," she insisted.

I was getting a harsh lesson in finance. Whenever a bank got a little nervous, it had the right to call a loan. Somehow that rule didn't seem fair, but I was in no position to argue.

"I'll tell you what I can do, Rhonda. Why don't you fax me a personal guarantee letter for the loan, and I'll sign it and return it to you immediately. That way, you not only have ZZZZ Best's guarantee, but you also have my personal guarantee. And since I'm worth over one hundred million, that should increase your comfort level."

"I'm glad you suggested that, because that's one of the reasons I called. The bank definitely wants your personal guarantee on this loan. Also, I think you should be aware that we've frozen the funds in your business checking account."

"You did what?" I yelled. "Did you bounce my company checks?"

"No, but I'd suggest you not write any more checks against the account," she said.

I didn't push the issue. Only a seven-million-dollar cashier's check made out to Union Bank would change her mind. "If that's the way you want it, I'll stop writing checks on the account." It wasn't like I had a choice in the matter.

"Good. And I'll fax the personal guarantee form as soon as I hang up. I'll also tell my superiors that the loan will be paid in full within thirty days."

"No problem, Rhonda."

I slowly replaced the receiver and rested my head in my hands. With my cash at Union Bank tied up, I didn't have enough money to meet next week's payroll. Where in the world is Carl? I grabbed the phone.

"Amy! Where is Carl? He was supposed to be here an hour ago!" I snapped.

"He called and said he had to go to the bank and then see one of the investors. He forgot to tell you that when you called." She sensed my disappointment. "I would have told you sooner, but you've been on the phone."

"That's okay, Amy. By the way, Union Bank will be faxing a document for me to sign. Just bring it in when it arrives."

"I'll be looking for it," she said. "Want me to pick you up some lunch?"

"No, I'm not hungry, but thanks for offering."

I looked at my watch—11:17 a.m. In less than five hours' time, my world had crashed: the banks had called their loans, the investment firm had postponed the deal pending an investigation I was sure to fail, Stan wanted to see me, I was out of cash, and my stock was dropping by the minute.

Amy walked in with the fax. "That was quick," I commented. "These people must be worried." I signed the form. "Go ahead and fax it back to them and mail the hard copy to Rhonda Ames's attention."

"Yes, sir," she replied. "Barry, I know you're swamped, but there's a managers' meeting going on downstairs in the conference room. I really think you need to make an appearance to pick up the morale."

"Who's going to pick up mine?" But she was right. "All right, Amy, I'll be there in a minute."

I trudged out of the office, down the stairs, and into the conference room. Mike McGee was addressing the store managers in the mandatory, biweekly staff meeting. His tone was troubled, the atmosphere in the room subdued. I walked to the front, hoping to bring enthusiasm and encouragement to a dejected management team.

"Good afternoon, ladies and gentlemen," I greeted them cordially. "I realize that the article in today's *L.A. Times* has caused some concern. But I don't want you to allow it to affect the morale of this company. Mr. McGee has been with me for almost five years and can testify that we have continually overcome every obstacle that has been set in our path. This will be no different."

I walked back and forth, trying to generate some momentum. "People are jealous of winners and that's why they want to see us fail! But nothing's changed on our agenda. We're still going to become the biggest carpet and furniture cleaning company in the United States!"

I don't know if I was convincing them, but I sure wasn't convincing myself. My delivery lacked its usual confidence and buoyancy. Too many things were happening and my adrenaline couldn't keep up. I noticed Amy motioning to me from the back of the room. The press was early.

"Unfortunately, I have to cut this short, but I want all of you to continue as if this article never appeared. 'Business as usual' will be our motto." I strode off to an audience reaction singular in my career as a public speaker: dead silence.

In my absence, a dozen or so reporters, cameramen, and radio people had swarmed into my office. Lights were glaring, cameras were mounted, tape recorders were adjusted, notebooks were poised, and I was worried. If I couldn't convince my own sympathetic audience, how am I going to persuade a hostile one?

"We're ready, Mr. Minkow, if you are," a voice directed from the crowd.

I pulled my chair into the well of my desk, ran a comb through my hair, and straightened my back. The pressure was on and my fate was in my own hands—just as I wanted it to be. "I'm ready."

"Four, three, two, one. Mr. Minkow, can you comment on why your stock went down four points today?"

The question startled me. I didn't know the stock had dropped that much—I had personally taken a twenty-four-million-dollar hit. My knees went weak.

"I believe the drop in our stock can be attributed to an article in the *L.A. Times* that described a past problem we encountered with some dishonest carpet cleaners. They had overcharged some customers, and when I found out about it, they were subsequently fired. There really isn't much more to it," I said, trying to minimize the offense.

"Is it true that the Securities and Exchange Commission has ordered a formal investigation of ZZZZ Best?"

Again I was caught off guard. This was the first I'd heard of any SEC investigation. I hated being on the defensive. In past television interviews, I had been in charge and had dictated the pace. "I'm not aware of any such investigation."

Before I could expound further, another reporter waved a copy of our company prospectus in the air. "Mr. Minkow, in your prospectus it states that you completed a seven-million-dollar restoration project in Sacramento. But when I checked to see if ZZZZ Best had filed any permits for such construction, none were found. In fact, ZZZZ Best doesn't even possess a contractor's license. Can you explain this?"

The minute I heard the phrase "restoration project," I knew my days were numbered. They were on to me. How in the world did they connect my past credit card fraud with the restoration business? I groaned inwardly.

But I couldn't leave the question unanswered. "I'm going to have to refer that question to our legal staff. They are better equipped to answer that. I've got time for one more question," I said, trying to cut my losses, but I was really only fueling the fire.

"Is it true that your investors have backed out of the financing for the acquisition?" someone asked.

"That's false!" I snapped. "They have done no such thing. That's all for today."

I walked briskly out of the office and stopped at Amy's desk. "I'll be back in an hour," I told her. She knew intuitively that I was in big trouble.

I got in my car and sped to Stan's condominium. I glanced at my watch—it was only 1:15 p.m. Will this day never end? I should have been more concerned with how, not when.

As I drove, I attempted to systematize my many problems. I had overcome insurmountable odds before, but this challenge was clearly the most difficult. I took a deep breath and cranked the stereo, which had worked in the past. I was no quitter, but in my heart of hearts, I knew it was only a matter of time before my empire collapsed. My eyes started to water. The thought of failure scared me more than anything else. I longed to be shaken from this bad dream and told that everything was all right. Smiling people walked along the street; happy kids played in the yards. I wished I could trade places. I wanted to be anyone but me.

⸎

I parked behind Stan's condo and let myself in. "Stan!" I called loudly. "Are you there?" I was one of the privileged few who didn't have to knock.

"Come on in, Wonder Boy. I'm in the kitchen."

I walked in, gave him the ritual kiss on the cheek, and sat down. Here I am, barely twenty-one years old, kissing gangsters as if I've known them for years. How did I get myself into this mess?

Stan studied me. "You look terrible, Kid."

"You're one to talk," I said jokingly. Stan was wearing his standard uniform, underwear with no shirt, while puffing on a cigar. "I've had a hard day," I continued. "No, let me rephrase that. I've had the worst day of my life!"

Smoke rolled out of Stan's mouth as he smiled, staring at me the same way he'd looked at Charlie Hunter that day in the limousine. I was nervous.

"You can't be mad at me over this article, Stan," I protested. "I warned you about it the minute the reporter started calling and asking questions three weeks ago."

"What I have to talk to you about has nothing to do with the article," he replied. "I called you here to tell you a few things I didn't want to say over the phone." He put his cigar in the ashtray. "You're being investigated by the L.A. Police Department."

"I'm what?"

"I didn't stutter, Kid. ZZZZ Best, and you specifically, are the target of a major investigation," he said in a serious tone.

"What else can go wrong?" I replied in disbelief.

"I'm telling you so you can watch your back and be careful what you say over the phone . . . which leads me to my next point."

"More good news, I suppose?" I said sarcastically.

Stan got up, walked to the sink, and filled a glass with water. He drank it slowly before proceeding. "You've got a leak in your ranks, Kid."

"What's that supposed to mean?" I snapped.

"What that means," he said, "is that someone from within your ranks is spilling their guts about what's going on at ZZZZ Best." He walked back to the table and eased himself into a chair. "So far, this individual has told certain people that the Sacramento restoration job was a fraud."

"Who's the leak, Stan?" I demanded.

"We don't know yet, but when I find out, I'll tell you. I warned you time and again about those bozos who hang around you." Stan had never liked Carl Stowe because he knew Ron Knox had introduced us. He also didn't seem to care for others I associated with.

"What do you want me to do, Stan?" I asked softly.

"There's nothing you can do, Kid. Much of the damage has already been done. It's only a matter of time before they bury you. I'm giving you the freedom to do whatever you want to try to save the company." He picked up his cigar. "But, in my opinion, it's too late."

"Are you going to pull your people out of the stock?" I asked. I knew the answer.

"What do you think?"

"I think that I don't have a fighting chance." I wanted to leave, but I had one more question. "Is that why you sold out early, Stan?" My question sparked his interest. "Did you know then that it was only a matter of months before I fell?" I waited breathlessly for his reply, but he said nothing. "I've got to get back to the office." I got up, gave him a quick kiss on the cheek out of respect, and headed for the door.

Fighting back tears, I called Amy on my way back to the office to check on my phone messages. "Hi, Amy, it's Barry."

"I'm glad you called. The phone has been ringing off the hook. Everybody is yelling and demanding that you call them right away."

I passed a playground and saw little children playing baseball. I thought back to my Little League days and wished I could relive them. ZZZZ Best, the company that I had fought so hard to build, was crumbling. I pictured the failed interview with the press. They knew about the phony restoration business. I recalled Stan's words about the leak.

"Who called?" I struggled to ask.

"Rhonda Ames, Miles Harris, Citizens Credit, John Brady, Thomas Meyer, Byron Buckley, Robert Fuller . . ." The phone clattered to the floorboard.

I pulled over and cried, and then I thought about suicide.

10 | END OF THE ROAD

I rang Amy back to tell her I'd be there in fifteen minutes. My vision was blurred with tears, so I remained at the side of the highway.

The phone rang again. *Now who?* I thought.

"Barry, it's Sheri. How are you?" It was my sister.

"Well, honey, I'm struggling. How are you?" The traffic raced by. I looked out the window; no one seemed to care that my life was unraveling. Maybe Sheri would.

"I read the article in the paper and talked to Mom. She said the stock was down almost four and a half points! Are you okay?"

"I don't know, honey. I'm trying to hold things together, but everybody seems to want to jump ship."

"I won't, Barry! I love you, and I'm behind you all the way. You've made it through tough situations before, and you can do it again!" she said with startling conviction.

Her simple words of encouragement strengthened me. Maybe there was a way out. I had made it through difficult times before and had always come out on top. Maybe this temporary setback could be turned into another Barry Minkow "victory." I couldn't just give up. I had to try. There was too much at stake.

"Listen," she went on, "I'm going to Europe for two months with a friend. But I'll be pulling for you. Hang in there and don't let this thing get you down."

I sat up straighter and put my favorite cassette into the tape deck, "Eye of the Tiger," the theme song from *Rocky III*. But before I cranked up the volume, I had to say goodbye to my sister. "You'll never know how much this call means to me, Sheri. I'll love you forever, and I'll be thinking of you while you're away."

"I'll miss you, too. Now go get 'em!"

As I turned up the stereo, I looked in the mirror and wiped away the tears. The music shot bolts of energy through my veins as I headed for ZZZZ Best headquarters. "It ain't over 'til it's over!" I said to myself.

⌇

"Amy, hold my calls. I need to coach Mike about the investigators."

"Okay, Barry, but can I go home now? It's almost seven."

"Sure you can. And thanks for helping me through this nightmare of a day."

"Anything for you, Barry. Make sure you get something to eat. I'm worried about your health."

"Yes, Mother," I joked. She left.

"Okay, Mike, here's the deal. The investigators from Washington will be here tomorrow morning and they're staying all weekend, including Monday." He was listening attentively. Mike was scared. He wasn't used to high-pressure situations.

"They'll ask both of us questions about the credit card fraud, and our answers have got to be consistent," I said, pacing back and forth.

"But I don't know anything about the overcharges, Barry. What am I going to say?" he asked nervously.

"Well, I want you to tell them that we had a group of carpet cleaners we hired from another company who worked for us as subcontractors. Because they were paid on commission, they inflated some of their sales by increasing the dollar amounts on the credit card slips. When we found out about the overcharges, we fired the people involved and paid back all the customers." Mike was resting his head in his hands. "That's the story. I want to keep it simple."

"What if they ask for names?"

"Good question. Tell them the incident happened so long ago that you'll have to check the files. By then I'll have thought of something."

"So we're going to lie to these people, Barry?"

"Yeah, we're going to lie to them! This stupid credit card thing is almost three years old, and nobody lost any money because of it," I said sternly.

"But these guys are trained investigators. They'll catch us. I don't think it's a good idea."

I stomped over to his chair and leaned close to his face. "Listen to me, Mike, and listen good! When you came to me you had nothing! I'm the one who brought you two new cars and a new house. I'm the one who gave you a great job with this company! And if I say lie, you're gonna lie! Do you understand me?" I didn't often yell at Mike, but too much was riding on this investigation.

"Very good, Mr. Minkow," he murmured unenthusiastically. "I'll do exactly what you say."

"Good. I'll see you here tomorrow morning at eight o'clock."

೧

"It's the smartest thing you can do, Barry. It shows the investment community that you've got nothing to hide," Thomas Meyer said.

"What's the name of the firm you want for the independent investigation?" I asked as I yawned into my bedroom phone. It was now 9:30 p.m. on the fateful day. I didn't feel up to arguing about retaining a law firm to conduct an independent investigation of the allegations made against the company.

Thomas gave me the name of a prominent L.A. firm. "I'll arrange everything over the weekend, and they'll start work on Tuesday morning," he said.

"How am I supposed to deal with the investigators for the investment firm and these lawyers at the same time?" I asked.

"I'm not talking about a long, drawn-out process. Both of these investigations shouldn't take more than two to four weeks."

"But I've got a company to run, Mr. Meyer. I can't spend the next four weeks talking to a bunch of stuffed-shirts."

"If you want to save your company, you'd better find the time!" he answered.

"All right," I said reluctantly. "I'll get it done."

I gratefully climbed into bed and rethought the events of the day. Maybe I can skate through these investigations and close the KeyServ deal. But then I remembered Stan's words: "You've got a leak, Kid." Who was this leak, and how did he know that the Sacramento restoration job was a fraud? I had to find out more.

Then there were the banks. They were scared and wanted their money. I couldn't deposit any new funds into either Union Bank or Citizens Credit, because they'd use the money to offset my loans. But I had all kinds of expenses and the employee payrolls, which had to be paid with checks. I'd have to open a checking account at a new bank. And I'd have to come up with some money to put into that checking account, just to keep things going. Our funding had been postponed; I'd already reborrowed from Paul and Lee. Where could I get some big money fast?

Pat Chapman came to mind. As the successful owner of a manufacturing company, he admired my ambition and had offered to help me any way he could, even to loan money to the company. We had met several years earlier and had immediately hit it off. *He's good for at least a million*, I thought. I was sure he would help.

The second source I thought of was the investment firm in New York. The company had lent me five million against some of my restricted ZZZZ Best stock. Unfortunately, I could only use these funds to buy securities through a stock-trading account I had set up at the company. But I had a hunch that my account representative there might approve a one or two million cash advance against the account. Between Chapman and the New York investment firm, I could feasibly raise enough money to survive until the investigations were over.

I closed my eyes that night, determined not to give up without a fight.

⁓

"Mr. Minkow, we're going to want to interview you and Mr. McGee separately," announced the investigator from the investment firm.

I nodded. "That's fine with me, sir. You can meet with me first, and then with Mr. McGee. Is that okay with you?"

"Yes, but before we begin, I'll need all the documents relating to the credit card fraud, including the names and addresses of the men responsible for the crime."

I reached into a desk drawer, pulled out a thick file, and casually handed it to the investigator, trying not to look as if I were holding anything back. "This is all the information I have. The customer invoices and proof of their repayment are included," I told him.

"What about the names of those responsible?" he pressed.

"Well, sir, since it all happened almost three years ago, I'll have to dig that up for you. I don't have it offhand."

He looked at me intently and then briefly reviewed the contents of the folder. "Before I can complete my investigation, I'm going to need those names, but I suppose this is enough to get started."

After the interrogation, I spoke to Thomas Meyer. "It went well," I said. "They asked me questions on the credit card fraud for three hours, and I answered every one of them. I even gave them a tour of the facility and showed them the systems I've installed to prevent such a thing from happening again. Now they're talking to Mike."

"Good," he said. "I've talked to the law firm, and they're ready to begin. Two of their men will be at your office at nine o'clock Tuesday morning. Are you completing all your restoration work on time?"

"Yeah," I lied. "We're right on schedule. Why do you ask?"

"Because we're going to prepare a press release so the company can officially respond to all the allegations made in the article. I also want to include some positive information about the restoration business. It'll definitely help the stock."

"Sounds good to me, Mr. Meyer," I said excitedly. "Call me later."

I hung up and enjoyed a few moments of peace and quiet. With the stock market and banks closed, the office phone lines were silent. Then I set out to raise some money. I called my contact at the New York investment firm at a private number and talked him into a two million dollar bridge loan.

"Don't let me down, Barry," he warned. "I've got to have that money back in four weeks."

I assured him he'd have it, and called Pat Chapman and arranged to meet with him the following morning. Then the phone rang.

"Barry, is that you?" It was Gary Todd.

"Yeah, pal. How's it going?"

"Not good, Barry. I've got to see you right away." It wasn't like Gary to demand a meeting on such short notice.

"Is there a problem?"

"A big one. But I can't talk about it over the phone."

"All right. I'll meet you at Derrick's Diner in ten minutes."

Before I left, I looked down toward Mike's office and saw that he was still with the investigators. *Hope that's going well.*

As I navigated down Reseda Boulevard, I tried to think of what could possibly have gone wrong with Gary and Reliable Appraisal Company. Had the media called him? Was he having financial problems?

ॐ

Gary arrived five minutes after I did. He looked worried. "You look like you haven't slept for a week," I said. "What's wrong?"

"Thanks a lot!" he barked. "You don't look much better."

"So what's the big news, Gary? You're making me crazy trying to figure it out."

"Do you remember a man by the name of Paul Dennis?"

"Yeah, he was that guy who did some part-time work for you. What about him?"

"Well, it seems that he went to your accounting firm and told them that the Sacramento restoration job was a fraud."

"What!" I yelled. "How on earth does he know anything about our restoration business?"

"I don't know for sure. I think he overheard you and me talking on the phone and just put two and two together." I frowned and then slammed my fist on the table.

"Don't worry, man. I know it looks bad, but we can still make it," Gary said.

I resisted the temptation to yell at him for allowing Dennis to learn about the restoration business.

∽

So that's the big leak Stan warned me about, I thought on my way to see Pat Chapman early the next morning. I had tossed and turned most of the night, trying to figure out how to salvage the company's relationship with the high-powered accounting firm. If they were to resign based on what Dennis had told them, the press would jump all over the fact that our accounting firm had quit, and they'd force me to further substantiate the restoration business, which I couldn't do. Although I knew Meyer, Lundy, and others involved with ZZZZ Best would soon find out about the Dennis allegations, I decided not to tell them. *It's important that I look as surprised as they do when the news hits*, I thought as I pulled into Pat's driveway.

After a warm greeting and a brief tour of the house, we sat down in his dining room. "I hate to bother you on a holiday weekend, Pat, but it's really important," I began.

"No problem, Barry. Anything for you," Pat replied cheerfully.

"I appreciate that." I felt uncomfortable about asking him for so much money. Even though I'd raised millions of dollars over the past three years, this time it was different. Maybe it was because I was there in Pat's home. Or maybe it was because I liked him so much. Lying to potential investors had become second nature to me. But then I realized what was bothering me: in the past I'd always borrowed, knowing I could eventually pay the money back. This time I wasn't so sure. Deep down, I knew that if the investigations turned out badly, or if the accounting firm confirmed Dennis's story, I'd be through, and Pat would lose his money.

Nonetheless, I set those feelings aside and did what I did best—lie.

"Pat, I need to borrow at least a million dollars short-term, so I can complete a few of the restoration jobs. Two of the banks called their loans Friday, and that's put me in a real bind. I need your help, and I'm willing to give you my house as collateral."

"That's a lot of money, Barry. It's going to take me a week or so to raise that much. Can you wait that long?"

I nodded, relieved that he seemed so willing to help me with no questions asked. "Sure. If that's what it takes, I can manage 'til then."

"Good, then I'll get my lawyer on it right away. He'll want you to sign a few documents, but that shouldn't delay things. Is that okay with you?"

"It sure is, Pat. And I really appreciate your help." I ambled over to him and shook his hand.

"There are not too many people I'd lend that kind of money to on such short notice, but I trust you, Barry, and I'm happy to help."

I couldn't look him in the eye.

⁊

"What's the stock trading at now?" I asked John Brady on Tuesday morning.

"It's down almost a point, and there's a lot of selling pressure on it. It's about to go below ten dollars a share," he commented.

"Relax, John. We'll be making an announcement Thursday morning that'll help bring the stock back up," I said. "I'll call you later."

I arrived at the office at 7:00 and spent the morning on the phone. Stockholders from across the country were demanding explanations for the stock's drop. At 9:00, I was served with the first of many stockholder class-action lawsuits. David Lundy called to tell me the SEC had begun investigating ZZZZ Best. My twelve hundred employees desperately needed encouragement, but I was just too busy.

The investment firm investigators peppered me with questions about the credit card scam for most of the afternoon. Apparently Mike's story and mine didn't quite match. By 3:00, the accounting firm had made the Dennis allegations known to everyone, including David Lundy. And at the closing bell, ZZZZ Best stock had dropped below ten dollars a share. The pressure overwhelmed me, but I refused to give in. ZZZZ Best was my sole reason for living. If it died, I died.

For the next twenty-four hours, I helped prepare a press release that I hoped would stop the stock's fall. I swore to Matt Paulson at the accounting firm that I had never had any financial dealings with Dennis and that none of his allegations had any validity. He was skeptical. Too many things were happening, too many questions unanswered.

On Thursday, May 28, 1987, I rose up at 3:55 a.m. to get to the office by 4:30. I had to call the wire service at least an hour before the market opened back East. It was dark and quiet as I pulled into ZZZZ Best headquarters. When I went to unlock the door, I realized I had forgotten my keys, but I didn't have time to go back to the house. There I was, standing alone in the ZZZZ Best parking lot at 4:30 in the morning with no keys and my whole company crumbling around me.

"I should have gone to college!" I muttered as I smashed my elbow through a window.

In minutes I was on the phone, dictating a press release to the wire service. The press release implied that the investment banking firm's independent investigation had cleared the company of any wrongdoing. Though the stock had dipped below eight dollars a share, I was confident this announcement would turn the tide.

And when the market opened, the stock began to go up—slowly, but steadily. My confidence was suddenly restored. This seemed a sure sign of victory.

The L.A. law firm's investigators met with me again that morning. Instead of being intimidated, I answered their questions with confidence and enthusiasm. *They are not going to get rid of me without a fight!* I said to myself. When they left my office that morning to interview Carl Stowe and other ZZZZ Best employees, I was sure they believed me.

I spent the rest of the morning watching our stock creep back up to almost ten dollars a share, restoring the confidence of people like Byron Buckley and Lee Herring, at least temporarily.

I spent most of that weekend on the phone with Thomas Meyer. The investment firm had threatened to pull out of the KeyServ financing because our press release implied that their investigators had cleared us. Meyer had fought hard to hold the deal together.

On Sunday evening, Miles Harris called me at home.

"Barry, our lawyers have advised us to terminate our agreement with you for the forty million dollar financing," he said sternly. "You'll have to make a public announcement early tomorrow morning."

"So all that time I spent with the investigators was for nothing?" I protested. There was no arguing with him. I had to make the announcement and try to find another investment banker to do the financing.

On Monday, June 1, I was once again at the office by 4:30 a.m., keys in hand. I knew that sending this new release over the wire would hurt my stock, but I had no choice. If I failed to disclose that the investment firm had terminated our agreement, I would be in even deeper trouble with the SEC. The stock took a beating as the market opened and dropped below seven dollars. While I worked on holding the company together, Meyer worked on getting another investment banker, without success.

Nevertheless, I couldn't give up. I had over twelve hundred employees depending on me and hundreds of stockholders hoping that there was enough Barry Minkow "magic" left to pull ZZZZ Best through yet another crisis. The lawyers who were still investigating insisted on examining all the company's canceled checks for the past two years. When confronted with the checks I made out to Robert Fuller, Phil Cox, and Stanley Robbins, I explained that these men had worked on the restoration projects, but the investigators weren't convinced. They also came up with two pages of questions and contradictions on the restoration files for Carl Stowe to resolve.

Another hurdle I faced daily was the media. They smelled fraud, and just as a shark trails the scent of blood, they wouldn't stop digging until they had unearthed the truth. Some reporters even flew to Dallas, where I had recently claimed ZZZZ Best was doing $13.8 million in restoration work. There they contacted local newspapers, the city clerk's office, and even the Dallas Chamber of Commerce, trying to find a building that had recently suffered nearly fourteen million in damage. When they found no corroborative evidence, they reported it. Once again I could do nothing, because there was no Dallas restoration job.

The noose was tightening.

⁓

"Did you write these checks?" asked Matt Paulson, placing two canceled checks on my desk. Many months earlier, Gary had asked me to lend a friend of his some money. I had written a couple of checks to Gary's friend and had promptly forgotten about it. Now it was coming back to haunt me. Paul Dennis, the whistleblower, was that friend!

I stared directly at my signature on the checks and said, "I don't remember offhand, Matt. I'll have to check."

Less than seventy-two hours later, Paulson sent me a resignation letter. I had lost my accounting firm.

∽

During the next two weeks, the pressure mounted. Both Citizens Credit and Union Bank insistently demanded payment. News about the resignation of the accounting firm spread through the investment community and pushed the stock down even further. The investigating lawyers started to pose questions I couldn't answer. One concerned a letter sent by a "Mr. B. Cautious" to the accounting firm after they resigned. It contained a detailed explanation of the restoration fraud. How in the world could anyone know so much? If that wasn't bad enough, the money I had obtained from the New York investment firm and Pat Chapman was dwindling fast. But I was determined not to declare defeat.

On Saturday morning, June 27, I was looking forward to spending the day with the girls' softball team I had been coaching. That spring I had been approached by a parent of one of the girls and agreed to coach as a community service. The position had actually given me a much-needed break from my fast-paced life. This weekend we were playing a tournament in San Fernando that the team had qualified for by winning the league championship. I thought back to that championship game as I sped down the freeway. Less than two months earlier, it now seemed like years. So much had happened in such a short time.

The phone rang. It was one of my board members.

"Barry, can you stop by my office? Several of us are here—and the attorneys, too; we need to talk to you."

"But I'm on my way to a big softball tournament."

"It'll only take ten minutes. Can you please come over?"

"All right. I'll be right there."

They're not calling me for an emergency meeting on a Saturday to give me a raise, I reflected. I arrived within fifteen minutes and greeted two of the investigating attorneys and several board members.

"Barry, we're sorry to call you in on such short notice, but we have a serious problem," one of the board members said. "The investigators have informed us that unless they are given the addresses to all the restoration jobs, they will not be able to complete their investigation." All eyes focused on me.

This is it, I thought. *I'm through*. I could do a lot of things, but I couldn't provide addresses for jobs that didn't exist. I had done my best to hold things together, but as soon as they made that demand, I knew it was over. There comes a time in every financial fraud were the perpetrator makes a similar realization. It's instantly sobering.

"No problem," I lied, stupidly. "Give me until Wednesday or Thursday of next week, and you'll have every address of every job."

They all smiled, thinking that their problems were solved.

It took only a few minutes to get back on the freeway and head toward the softball tournament. My heart was beating rapidly as I planned how and when I would leave the company. *The press is going to jump all over this*, I thought. I would need a good criminal lawyer and as much cash as I could get my hands on. I would spend the first part of the week secretly withdrawing funds from the company. Then on Thursday or Friday, I would tender my resignation.

◇

Several of the girls on my team ran up to greet me as I climbed out of my car. I was a hero to them. Boy, are they going to be disappointed when they find out that ZZZZ Best was a fraud. Then I thought about Byron Buckley, David Lundy, Vera Hojecki, Mike, my mom, and all the other employees who would shortly be out of work. I had failed them as well.

And then I thought about prison.

◇

"I'll be happy to represent you," my attorney John Pearson said. "You look awful, Barry. Why don't you go home and get some rest. I'll prepare the resignation letters and make sure they get to all the board members and Lundy by tomorrow morning."

It felt good to know I had at least one friend in the world, even though his friendship was costing me several hundred thousand dollars. But I was confident that he could defend me against any future prosecution. On July 1, I left his office at 7:30 p.m. and headed for home.

Although I knew I was soon to become known as one of the most notorious con men in the United States, I felt a weird sense of relief. The fraud was about to be revealed. I no longer had to fear a call at 2:00 in the morning from some reporter saying, "We found out about the phony restoration business." It was ending. Financial ruin, even prison lie ahead.

Still, deep down in my heart, I was glad it was over.

SECOND CHANCE

11 STARTING WITH AN "A"

"Mr. Minkow, where do you go from here?" one reporter asked. Before I could answer another jumped in, "What about this God thing? Now that you are out of prison, are you still a 'born again'?" The reporter quickly jabbed the microphone in my face. I remember thinking his question sounded like I had some disease, "born again," that I could somehow shake upon my release.

"Are you going back into business?" another asked. I knew I would have to deal with one or two reporters upon my release from Lompoc Prison to a Los Angeles-based halfway house since it was on the news wires. But I never thought there would be wall-to-wall reporters hurling questions at me from all directions.

"Is there going to be a movie about your life?" questioned a particularly annoying reporter that came within inches of my face. Just a few hours earlier I was saying good-bye to all my friends at Lompoc. Now I was face-to-face with the media. I felt safer back in prison.

"A movie on my life? What are they going to call it? *Don't Let This Happen to You*?" I quipped.

"No," the reporter exclaimed, "this could be a great comeback story. Kid goes into business at sixteen, gets involved with the Mafia, and then comes out of prison and does good." I suppose if you were going to summarize my life in as few words as possible that would be it.

"Well, I will get back to you when I start doing some good for some people." With that, most of the reporters laughed. I remember that comment being replayed later on that evening on the news. I pondered my statement, *What possible good could I do that would ever make up for the evil I was responsible for causing?* This was not the first time I had considered the question. I used to walk the track in prison and contemplate what possible good I could do upon my release to help people.

My motives to do this were not always pure. Like many, I cared about what other people thought of me. You would be surprised at how many people in prison still care about what people think of them, which motivates many of us to want to come out of prison and make a positive impact on the same people we once victimized. But how could *I* possibly help anyone? What endeavor could I be involved in that would both put money back into the pockets of my victims and do good to the financial community that I had hurt? Being a pastor of a church was certainly a start, but there was a real potential that people would think I was hiding behind the church in order to avoid paying back victims. There was something else that I would need to do to meet this two-fold goal. I just needed to figure out what.

⌒

The room was just as I had left it eighty-seven months earlier. Sure, a few faces were different, but the principle players were the same—especially one. My mind's eye had captured what my dreams wouldn't let me forget. He sat down at the head of the table and motioned for me to sit beside him. I glanced down at the marble floors that led from the entryway to the dining area. I saw my muddy reflection in that spotless flooring and thought back to the countless floors I had waxed to a similar sheen in prison.

I drew in a deep breath and could feel multiple pairs of eyes on me. I sat down to his right and peered at a briefcase that was lying on the table opposite of me. It was locked, allowing me the opportunity to wonder what was inside. Somehow, I knew better than to ask.

"You look good, Barry. Prison has preserved you well," he stated flatly. The onlookers nodded their approval. Everyone was focused on him, since he was still clearly in charge.

"How's your dad doing?" he asked, with mock sincerity.

"He's just had his third stroke," I said softly. "He's at the Corbin Care Facility in the Valley and he hates it. He wants to be at home with my mom but he can't walk."

"And full-time, in-home nursing care is expensive, I hear," he said as he puffed from a freshly-lit cigar. "Look, Kid, I know what you are thinking so I'll get right to the point."

I know I should have been scared, but for some reason I wasn't. Initially, I had agreed to the meeting because I knew I couldn't hide. But I didn't want to hide anymore. I had to face him. *Fear is a liar*, I kept muttering to myself. But I will tell you it was no longer a nightmare that held my imagination.

"You passed the test, Barry. By going to trial and not the Witness Protection Program you proved yourself to me . . . to us. You are a stand-up guy who can be trusted," he said as he rose from the chair, stood behind the briefcase, and leaned his two fists on it.

"My sources tell me that you handled yourself well on the inside," he said proudly. I just stared blankly and waited. "Two degrees, one a master's degree, the star quarterback of the football team, active in the church, a perfect conduct record—you even served on the suicide prevention team. Amazing." He paused and smiled. He wanted me to know he had done his homework.

"It doesn't surprise me. You were always destined for greatness," he said with another wide-toothed grin. He backed away from the case, folded his arms, and looked down at me. I was fidgeting with the placemat . . . never could sit still.

"I know you think that we abandoned you during your stint in prison, but we had to know for sure that you were a stand-up guy. And that meant no communication. None."

I said nothing because I had nothing to say. The facts were clear. I received a twenty-five-year sentence and a twenty-six-million-dollar restitution order that was in itself a financial life sentence while he, along with his friends, sold seven hundred fifty thousand shares of ZZZZ Best common stock at an average price of fourteen dollars per share. He was never indicted, nor were his accomplices. Everyone kept his or her profits except me.

Initially I had resented him for it. When my parents struggled financially after my father's first stroke, I was sure an envelope would appear on my mother's doorstep, or in the front seat of her car. Perhaps money would be anonymously deposited into her bank account. "We always take care of our own," he always used to say. I remembered those words as if they were spoken yesterday. But there was never an envelope. Just silence. Seven years and four months of silence—until now.

"So by the look on your face I can see that you don't believe me," he said. "That's okay, I can respect that. After all, wasn't I the one who always told you to let your actions do the talking?" He grabbed the bottom of the briefcase and slid it gently across the glass table.

"What's this?" I asked as I examined the outside of the leather case. "It's whatever you want it to be, Kid. It's my welcome home present to you. It's my way of making up for almost eight years of silence. It's the seed money for whatever business you want to start. And I'm your silent, minority partner . . ." he let his voice fade into silence.

I could feel my heart rate quicken. Seven years and four months of making less than a dollar an hour as a prison baker gave me a new respect for money. And with the reality check of freedom came the necessary demand for money. I thought of my father, who so desperately wanted out of the convalescent home, and my mom, who needed money as it had been over a year since Dad could hold down a job. In the very least, I owed it to them for all I had put them through.

What kind of son doesn't take care of his own parents who were there for him through years of prison? I thought. Then there were my personal needs, too numerous to count. I needed to afford an apartment so I could get out of the halfway house. I needed to cover expenses associated with my past crimes— like restitution. And I had no money for a social life. I set my hands gingerly upon the briefcase and drew a deep breath. This was my answer.

"Go ahead Kid, open it. I think you will be happily surprised," he said as he returned to his seat at the head of the table. He must have been watching me with mild amusement at this point, wondering if my heart and head were currently at war.

The combination was set at "000" on both sides. I wanted to show restraint but like a kid at Christmas I hastily clicked the locks and the case sprung open. It was filled with rubberbanded hundred-dollar bills stacked in several columns. I did not touch the money but had difficulty taking my eyes off it. All the pain of prison, all the missed birthdays and Christmases, all the demeaning looks from the prison staff, all the inadequate medical care, all the lonely nights and bad meals were suddenly a blur. Money had always intoxicated me. With money I could say *I can* instead of *I wish*.

"That money is my way of reestablishing our relationship, Barry. I'll be your partner behind the scenes. But it's your show. And there's enough money in there for you to buy an existing business or to start a new one of your own. I have complete confidence that whatever you do, you will prosper . . . we will prosper." His voice had dropped to a whisper; he reached over and gently tugged at my arm. He wanted me to look him in the eye. I wanted to continue staring at the money and try to guess how much the briefcase contained. Instead I looked up.

As I lifted my eyes to meet his, he said, "And this is my way of saying I believe in you. Now take the money and go do what you were born to do . . . earn!"

Though I hadn't noticed, the crowd had assembled in the room. They were loitering around the table, carefully watching me. I smiled. They smiled. I laughed lightly, and they laughed with me. I gently patted him on his shoulder. I looked down at the money. Time was standing still.

All those people who said I would never amount to anything were about to be proven wrong. All the doubters were about to be silenced. The seed money I needed to start the business of my dreams was at my fingertips. Common business sense dictated that it was always easier to negotiate from a position of strength. The briefcase contained all the strength I needed.

With a wince, I closed the briefcase and secured the locks. My fingers wrapped around the handle tightly. It would take just thirty-two seconds to walk from where I was seated out the front door and begin a new life. Sure, there were some strings attached to the briefcase. Payments would need to be made, but I was going to be successful, and there would be plenty of money to go around. And there would be a few late-night meetings to explain decisions, but I had proven myself trustworthy. The sweat beaded up on my forehead. My pulse raced. My face was flushed. All eyes were on me. The room took on an eerie silence. It was decision time. I knew what I would do in the next five minutes would dictate the rest of my life. Once again, my destination would be chosen.

And then I remembered Peanut.

~

He was my cellmate and best friend in prison. That they called him "Peanut" was ironic because he was 6'4" and about 255 pounds of pure muscle. He was African American, which earned us the name "salt and pepper," and we were inseparable. In 1991, we played in the annual football game, the east side versus the west side. It was the one time of year that the prison guards allowed the inmates to play tackle football without pads. FCI Englewood was a medium security facility, but at the time it was called "Gladiator School" because of the rampant violence.

It was near the end of the first half, and the east side (our team) was down by a touchdown. The sidelines were filled with inmates cheering as if it were the Super Bowl. In a way it was. Bragging rights for a whole year were on the line.

I was the quarterback and remember one certain play vividly. I dropped back to throw a simple out pattern to our fullback. I turned my back to the right side of the field (my first mistake) and prepared to dump the ball in the flat. However, a 6'6" defensive end, nicknamed "Shotgun" (don't ask), broke through the blocking scheme and dove for my body just as I was releasing the ball. His momentum combined with a couple hundred pounds hammered me into the ground.

There was an ugly sound that came from my stomach as my lungs released what little air was left in them, and then things went dark. The next thing I remember was hearing someone say, "Grab a towel. I think his nose is broken."

Peanut and a few of my other teammates managed to drag me off the field to the sidelines. I was given cold water and some ice for my bleeding nose. Within minutes, halftime began and the team assembled around me.

"I think we can take 'em," someone said with startling conviction.

"Yeah, they ain't so bad," another man sneered, "but we've got to double-team Shotgun." *Now they think of it.*

"How do you feel, Barry?" Peanut asked.

"I'll be okay. The bleeding has stopped," I said as I slowly stood up. My eyes uncrossed as the cold air hit me. The thin prison-issue socks and the worn out cleats were doing a lousy job of protecting the tips of my toes from freezing. While playing I had not realized how cold it was, but now that I was stationary the mountain breeze seemed to go right through me. I grabbed my jacket.

"Great, then you can finish the game," Peanut declared.

"No, I don't think so. After that hit I'm lucky to be alive. I think I will just sit the rest of the game out and root for you guys. Ricky can take my place," I said as I painfully worked my arms into the overcoat.

No one said anything. A few guys took that as a cue to grab some water and mentally prepare for the second half. Peanut had other plans. He took me by the arm and dragged me away from the team.

"You got to finish the game," he stated as he looked me directly in the eyes.

"In case you haven't noticed, I'm a little banged up here, Peanut."

"We're all a little banged up. You can't quit on us now," he said. "And don't worry about Shotgun anymore. I can handle him." He was serious. This was more than a game to Peanut. He had an agenda, and I was part of it.

"Two minutes until halftime is over. Two minutes!" the inmate referee yelled as he approached our sideline.

"Barry, do you know why you got twenty-five years?" he asked. I didn't respond. I wasn't in the mood for lectures or sermons. I moved my legs up and down trying to escape the numbing feeling that was quickly overcoming my toes. *Why couldn't I have been sent to a California prison?* I thought.

"It wasn't brains you lacked," he said. "It wasn't your upbringing, and it wasn't the economy. You got a twenty-five-year sentence because you're a quitter. When things got tough, earnings were down, and money was tight at ZZZZ Best, you just did what came naturally, you took shortcuts and quit. Instead of doing the right thing and taking responsibility for whatever that company did good or bad, you took your brilliance, your charisma, your powers of persuasion, and every other gift God gave you and quit. That wasn't a mistake; it was a pattern. You've never broken that pattern. This whole God thing is nothing more than another Barry Minkow fraud. And do you know why? Because you ain't got no heart, man." He now commanded my full attention, but I couldn't look him in the eye any longer. He was right. Suddenly, staying warm was not my top priority.

"When times get tough, you'll do the two things that caused you to end up in here—you'll take shortcuts and quit." He paused, looked around at the guards who were closely watching our conversation, and continued. "But today is your chance to break the pattern. You get back out on that field, and don't worry about the score, the cold, or the pain because this game has nothing to do with prison bragging rights. This game is the one time in Barry Minkow's life that he won't quit or take a shortcut," Peanut vowed.

I nervously blew air into my hands. I turned toward the field and saw Shotgun doing some last minute toe touches before the half ended. Peanut was right. It wasn't the cold, or a swollen nose, that was keeping me out of the game. It was fear. I was afraid of getting hurt, afraid of publicly failing in front of all those inmates and guards, and I was willing to quit rather than face those fears. My life was one long series of shortcuts strung together. I was good at justifying them. There was always a "bloody nose" rationalization I could point to. I needed to break the pattern.

"All right, I'll play," I said.

〜

I snapped back to the present—the room, the mob, the money.

I got up from the table. He was staring at me. I gently pushed in the dining room chair. The briefcase was still on the table as I walked toward the door. I smiled to myself as I remembered that cold day in 1991 in Englewood, Colorado. A day when I faced Shotgun and lived to tell about it. A day when Peanut carved character into my life. A day when I finally faced fear instead of running from it.

"You'll never make it without me, Kid," he yelled as I walked back over the marble floors and approached the entryway. This time when I looked down at the shining, well-maintained marble, I swore I saw Peanut in the reflection smiling up at me.

"I hope you know that. You need this money . . . you need me. No one will ever trust a convicted felon. This is your only chance, you stupid, self-righteous son of a b—! This offer is only good one time."

Not all of my decisions after prison would be good, but this one was one of the best.

⌇

I was in desperate need of a job. The halfway house required full-time work so I could pay "rent" there. And of course, I had the mundane tasks of acquiring clothes and getting a driver's license to do. Most important, I needed to do a lot of family reuniting. My father had just suffered his third stroke. Before I was incarcerated my dad and I were playing tennis; now he was permanently confined to a wheelchair.

People have the wrong impression about prison. They think that spending time in a prison camp is different from spending time in maximum security. Having done time in both types of facilities (mostly in maximum and medium security prisons), I can understand their reasoning. However, I came to the conclusion that prison is not where you *are* (camp versus maximum security). It is where you are *not* (with your family and loved ones).

David Kenner, the criminal defense lawyer who represented me in the ZZZZ Best trial, stayed in close communication with me throughout my time in custody. Most lawyers forget about their clients once the case is lost and they are carted off to prison. Not Kenner. He always believed in me and wanted to help me reintegrate into society. Within days of my placement in the halfway house, Kenner gave me a job as a law clerk at his San Fernando-based law firm. I reported to his office, located in the back of his ten-thousand-square-foot custom home. My duties and responsibilities included making bank deposits, picking up and delivering important legal documents, and performing basic introductory case research.

Much to my surprise, when I reported to work I found out Kenner was heavily involved in representing people like Snoop Dogg, Suge Knight, and even their record label, Death Row Records. I soon learned that Kenner was not only representing Snoop in his upcoming murder trial, but also that he was primarily responsible for helping found Death Row Records. In 1995, Death Row was the hottest record label in America.

I was often asked to pick up invoices from the Death Row Records offices in Santa Monica and deliver checks to "the studio" located in Tarzana, the heart of the San Fernando Valley and not far from Kenner's home. Although I did not speak too often with Snoop Dogg, Nate Dogg, or some of the other rappers, I did have an amenable relationship with Suge Knight. He and David at the time were inseparable, so if you worked for David Kenner, you knew Suge Knight. I was even invited on his yacht one time— the *P Funk* as I remember it—where we shared ding-dongs on the deck of the ship! Call it a law firm perk.

My duties at the law firm also included being Kenner's personal trainer (which I loved) and helping out the office staff in any way I could. They treated me with love and respect, and I thoroughly enjoyed the lawyers and the secretarial staff who worked with David. The irony of my life was that at the very same time I was working for a law firm that represented gangsta rappers, the likes of Snoop Dogg and Nate Dogg, I was also working part-time as an intern at the Church at Rocky Peak in Chatsworth. I was attempting to complete my second master's degree from Liberty University and needed the experience to help complete my degree program.

Dr. David Miller, the senior pastor of Rocky Peak, wrote regularly to me while I was in prison, and his was the first and only church I went to upon my release. Dr. Miller even gave me the opportunity to preach on occasion. Additionally, every Friday morning he personally mentored me. We would meet at Carrows restaurant in Chatsworth and discuss the challenges involved in juggling a life in the ministry and a life working for a firm inundated with gangsta rappers.

"Only you, Barry, could be out of jail three weeks and find himself in the middle of such a situation," Dr. Miller said, shaking his head from side to side.

༓

"I've been a probation officer for over twenty years," Frank Gulla stated as I sat in his office waiting patiently for whatever instructions he was prepared to give me. Frank Gulla was the probation officer I was required to report to within days of my release. He was in his late fifties and clearly the probation officer with the most seniority in the Granada Hills office. He was always assigned the high-profile cases, which caused our paths to collide.

In prison, guys always made the probation officers out to be the villains. Of course, these same guys were always on the wrong side of a probation violation. Oftentimes it was a drug test or a new criminal enterprise, but the truth was easily brushed aside in favor of blaming a probation officer that was "out to get me." I had been in the system too long to believe the hype about bad probation officers. Even so, I was still a little nervous that January day in 1995 when I sat in Gulla's office.

A probation officer could make a newly released inmate's life miserable by inundating him with paperwork, requiring frequent random drug testing, phoning work to check up on attendance, and repeatedly searching his home unannounced. So even though there were valid reasons for concern, Gulla's first statement quickly suppressed them. He flipped through the thick file in front of him, the file that contained all the records from my eighty-seven-month incarceration.

"I'll tell you what I'm going to do with you, Mr. Minkow. Considering that you made it through prison with a perfect record, I'm going to start you off with an 'A'," he said.

"An 'A' sir? I don't think I quite understand."

"What I mean by an 'A' is that I will let you travel as long as you give me notice, and I will give you as much freedom as you want. That's what I give 'A' students." I cracked a wide grin. "But if you do anything to embarrass me or this office, you lose your 'A' and the freedom that comes with it," he added.

One of my greatest fears in prison was how long it would take me to earn people's trust in order to get the second chance I so desperately needed. Now my probation officer, who was the one person trained to be cynical and skeptical, was starting me with an "A," which meant he trusted me. I really did not know what to say, but I needed to respond.

"Thank you, Mr. Gulla. You won't be sorry for believing in me," I exclaimed. He smiled and asked how my father was feeling and how I liked my job. I never expected my parole officer to genuinely care about me, and to this day I have never forgotten it. Frank Gulla was a gift from God that I did not deserve. After this first meeting I called Gulla more than I was required to because he gave me a second chance. Although relieved, I still worked very hard not to lose my "A" rating.

Before our first meeting ended I remember him telling me that the FBI had contacted him about an upcoming Bank Fraud Day seminar that they were putting together and they wanted me to speak. Although I was stupid enough to end up in prison, I was smart enough to want to stay on the good side of the FBI. I accepted the engagement.

Although I did not know it then, accepting this one speech would change the course of my life forever.

∽

There was a lot of pressure at the law firm as Snoop Dogg's murder trial approached. David Kenner knew that if he did not win the case, revenues at Death Row Records would be significantly impacted. Jimmy Ivy and other senior management from Interscope Records, the distributor for Death Row products, called David every day. The consequences of losing were painfully obvious: Snoop could not cut records in prison. But David was a brilliant lawyer and had assimilated a great team of lawyers. I tried to stay out of the way while the lawyers prepared for the trial and simply did what I was told.

During the rare moments David and I were alone, I did not preach to him (he had made it very clear it was not allowed), but I was a friend to him. We had a special kinship. I remember him asking me to go cash a check at City National Bank in Encino for close to eight thousand dollars. I brought the cash to him and I said proudly, "Go ahead, count it. It's all there!"

What he said next nearly brought me to tears. "I know it's all there Barry. I trust you implicitly."

First Gulla and now David. It had been years since anyone had said they trusted me with their money. David was a true friend and an outstanding lawyer, living proof against the crooked lawyer stereotype.

The murder case involved Snoop's bodyguard, Molique, who allegedly pulled out a gun and shot Philip Woldemariam. The defense was simple. Snoop's bodyguard acted in self-defense because Woldemariam pulled a gun first. I remember one day in court at a preliminary motion hearing where

Kenner was arguing this very point. I was sitting quietly, a very hard task for me, next to Suge Knight.

We both looked at Snoop in the defense chair next to David, and Suge whispered to me, "Barry, aren't you glad that it isn't you or me in that chair?" We both smiled. Both he and I shared the experience of being in the defense chair at one time in our lives, and he knew I clearly understood what he meant.

A few days before trial, I went to lunch with Paul Palladino. Paul had worked on my case way back in 1987 and 1988, and we had remained friends through the years. He and his brother Jack are two of the best private investigators in the country with clients ranging from politicians to superstars. He was working the Snoop murder trial on behalf of Kenner and was actually responsible for finding the witness who confirmed that the victim pulled a gun on Snoop first, which led to Snoop's ultimate acquittal.

"Wanna hear something funny?" he asked.

"Sure, Paul," I said.

"You started Death Row Records," he said. I made a goofy face to let him know I thought he was kidding. But he wasn't. "I'm serious, Barry."

"I don't even listen to gangsta rap," I protested.

"You didn't put up the money or start the company intentionally nor do you reap any profits from the enterprise, but there is no Death Row Records without Barry Minkow." I knew Paul well enough to know that he was not kidding. I motioned for him to continue. "I'm going to tell you what even the media doesn't know," he said.

"Go ahead, I'm all ears."

"Do you remember back in 1988 when you were in the hole in Terminal Island in maximum security?"

I nodded. *How could I forget?*

"And do you remember David Kenner encouraging you to refer clients to him?" I nodded again. "One of those clients you referred to David was Brian 'Bo' Bennett. Do you remember Bo?" he asked.

"Oh, yeah. He was arrested for drug dealing in a two-million-dollar-per-week cocaine operation with the Colombians. He was from the Valley like I was, and we immediately hit it off."

"That's right. And you and he met in the hole in Terminal Island in the summer of 1988 shortly after he was arrested. Then you introduced him to David. And then David took the case."

"I appreciate the history lesson, Paul, but what's this got to do with Death Row Records?" I interrupted.

"I'm getting to it," he said. "You see, Brian 'Bo' Bennett also had two co-defendants, Mike 'Harry O' Harris and Mario Villabono."

"Yes, Paul, I remember both of them. We all were in Terminal Island together and were the first prisoners to be shipped from Terminal Island to the new Metropolitan Detention Center in Los Angeles."

"Right again. And David brought in Don Re and David Chesknoff to represent Mike Harris and Mario Villabono." I nodded again. Where was he going with this?

"Well, David and 'Harry O' (Mike Harris) became friends. Good friends. And after you were shipped off to Colorado, Mike Harris, who was good friends with Suge Knight, introduced David to Suge." I just shook my head in disbelief. "Admittedly there is now a debate between the three of them about who owns what in Death Row Records, but there is no debate as to how the players came to know one another—through you Barry."

I didn't know whether to feel guilty or to ask for a royalty!

ॐ

"Of the 1.5 million people that occupy our federal and state prisons across the nation, all of us have one thing in common." I paused for effect. "None of us ever planned on being there," I declared as I stood in front of five hundred bankers and FBI agents.

This was my first "fraud talk" since my release from prison and I was nervous. I paced back and forth across the stage to help alleviate the stress. I knew I had to be original. I had to deliver a talk that not only capitalized on my personal experiences but also couldn't be duplicated by any other speaker.

I had to prove that only someone who has been a CEO of a public company, committed fraud, and been to prison could speak authoritatively about the why behind the crime. And there was one more reason I had to do well. My probation officer was there, watching my every move and cheering me on. He was not fulfilling a requirement; he came because he wanted to.

"Listen," I continued loudly, "do you think Jose Gomez, the brilliant accounting partner at Grant Thornton who compromised his integrity and went on the take in the three-hundred-million-dollar ESM Government Securities fraud originally intended on ending up in prison when he was studying to be a CPA or working his way up the Grant Thornton ladder? Do you think Mickey Monus from the huge, billion-dollar Ohio-based drug store chain Phar Mor, who was recently sentenced to eighteen years in federal prison, ever thought when he took the job as CEO of that company that he would end up lying to the auditors and going to jail?

"And in like manner I did not start ZZZZ Best to perpetrate a fraud on Wall Street and be involved with organized crime before I was legally allowed to drink. Let me tell you why I started ZZZZ Best, and please note carefully that it was not to go to prison."

From there, I gave them the whole story. Growing up in Reseda, the girl situation, the Bomb, the credit card, the carpet cleaning, the fraud. Professional speakers rely on nonverbal communication as the key indicator to assess whether or not a particular presentation is going well. I saw people in the crowd nodding their heads in agreement. They were not only listening to the talk, they were relating to it.

"I had learned a valuable truth," I told them, "*money imputed respect.*" If you had it, whatever else you lacked hardly mattered. "Money became a narcotic that repressed my ability to reason clearly. And so *right* was defined early on in my business career as forward motion and *wrong* was anything that got in my way of achieving.

"And as a CEO of a three-hundred-million-dollar public company I did the same thing. When our stock went from twelve dollars to eighty dollars per unit I would get letters from people telling me how great I was and what a business genius I was. The media heralded me as the 'soaring stock wiz kid.' What people thought about me *became the prize* and an end in itself. Money was merely a tool to gain the approval and acceptance of people.

"When it was time to release earnings to Wall Street, every quarter had to be a little better than the quarter before, despite how awful and unprofitable the business really was, because my worth as a person was tied up in the performance of my stock. What I did, my achievement, was far more important than who I was as a person. No auditor, investment banker, or board of directors was going to get in my way!"

When I finished the talk many people stood up and clapped. I couldn't believe it. Agents who had arrested me eight years earlier were now clapping for me. People surrounded me before I could even step off the stage. They were shouting questions to me about availability and what I charge for these kinds of talks. I collected their cards and promised I would call and make arrangements for future speeches.

Within days of the Bank Fraud Day talk, the FBI had me booked for three days in Quantico, Virginia, for fraud training. They were actually letting me sleep on the premises while I trained agents about why people fall into the trap of white-collar crime. I found that if you begin your speaking résumé with "FBI," other opportunities present themselves. One was filming a video series entitled *Fraudo Dynamics,* a three-part video series that taught auditors the techniques perpetrators use to deceive them. I also spoke to various state CPA societies around the country about the psychology of fraud and received between $1,500 and $2,500 per speech.

The fact that I relished speaking in front of audiences made it enjoyable. A material percentage of the money I earned from these engagements went into a trust fund and was dispersed to the U.S. District Court against the twenty-six-million-dollar restitution order and to Union Bank—the single biggest victim of the ZZZZ Best fraud. Gary Zuene, a CPA and the man who organized and arranged all of my speaking engagements across the country for state CPA societies, was kind enough to make sure my restitution was paid after each engagement. Together, Gary and I got the highest evaluations after each seminar. We were a good team.

༄

"Barry, you have a call on line two," Penny said. Penny (who I always referred to as "Monny Penny" after the James Bond flicks) worked with me at Kenner's law firm. It was late 1995 and I was rarely at the law firm anymore. Between school, the internship at the church, and the frequent speaking engagements, my law clerking was coming to an end. But Kenner gave me a flexible schedule. He only wanted what was best for me and knew I was not going to be working for him much longer.

"Hi, this is Barry."

"Mr. Minkow, my name is Jaak Olesk, and I am a CPA in Beverly Hills. I just wanted to thank you for your video series *Fraudo Dynamics*."

"You're welcome and I appreciate the call. I hope it helps you in your practice." I had a standard response for these kinds of conversations, which luckily came often enough to call it standard.

"It already has helped me in my practice," he said.

"Really? How so?" I asked.

"I am the auditor for a public company, Home Theater Products International Inc. (symbol HTPI), and in doing their audit I got suspicious about a certain accounts receivable." It was not common for a sole practitioner (as opposed to one of the big national firms) to be the outside auditor for a public company, but it was not unheard of.

"So I remembered from your video when you were telling CPAs that during the confirmation process not to just accept a letter from a company that confirms a certain sales figure but to go the extra mile and make sure that the company who sent the letter actually exists."

One of the ways people fool the auditors is by anticipating the procedures they will use during the audit. Nowhere is this better illustrated than in the area of confirmations or what auditors call the "confirmation process." Basically, when the auditor needs to confirm independently from the company that Company X paid them three million last quarter, they send a letter from the accounting firm directly to Company X with an envelope and a return address back to the accounting firm asking Company X to "confirm" independently from the company being audited that, in fact, they paid the company three million. By keeping the company being audited out of the process, this preserves or constitutes what accountants refer to as *independence* for the auditor. There's only one problem. At ZZZZ Best (and we were not the first and time has proved we were not the last), we created a phony company with bogus owners with a PO Box as an address knowing that the auditors would not check to see if that company was real or not.

"That's right—I remember that part of the video," I interjected. I was impressed he could quote that much and decided to give him my full attention.

"So I followed your advice and found out that Home Theater Products International Inc.'s biggest customer was nothing more than a Mail Boxes Etc. P.O. Box. I reported them to the SEC." I almost fell out of my chair. Had I actually helped someone *uncover* a fraud?

"How much are we talking about?"

"They are a relatively small company with a market value of about one hundred and fifty million," Jaak responded. This was like a dream come true! Someone followed my advice and uncovered a fraud *proactively* in a public company. I could barely think clearly in my elation.

"Mr. Olesk, would you please write a letter to Mr. Frank Gulla at the U.S. Probation Office and confirm what you have just told me?"

"Of course I would," he said warmly. And he did. I still have a copy of the letter he sent to Frank Gulla in care of the U.S. Probation Office. Now let me be crystal clear about this. Jaak Olesk uncovered this fraud, and he probably gave me far more credit than I deserved. But this event changed my thinking. *Instead of just teaching about why people perpetrate white-collar crime, why didn't I figure out a way to identify financial crimes in progress, shut them down, and bring them to justice to prevent people from becoming victimized? Maybe there was a way to identify points of similarity between my fraud at ZZZZ Best and fraud being perpetrated by others.* Sure, I had heard of former car thieves creating theftproof vehicles by revealing how they used to steal cars. Or former burglars designing secure homes by drawing upon their experiences in robbing them. But could those techniques translate into the arenas of white-collar crime and financial fraud? Clearly, in the case of Home Theater Products International Inc., a technique I had used to defraud the auditors (confirmations) was being utilized by that company to defraud their auditors. This point of similarity between my fraud at ZZZZ Best and a current, ongoing fraud could be the beginning of something.

I thought back to the reporter who had said: kid goes into business at sixteen, gets involved with the Mafia, *and then comes out of prison and does good.* Maybe proactively stopping millions of dollars in fraud, far more than I had ever perpetrated as the CEO of ZZZZ Best, would be the "does good" part of my story. Maybe, just maybe.

12 | CHOICES

When you are an ex-convict, you can only go for short stretches of time without being reminded of your past. It could be a serendipitous encounter with a former victim or even co-conspirator while at a restaurant. While at an amusement park, you could run into the officer that arrested you. Your past may even come looking for you—intentionally. Whatever the case, no matter how hard you may work to leave the past behind you, there will always be an incident that makes your past a present tense problem. The key is to be prepared for such an occurrence. I was not.

It was early 1996 and I was well pleased with my progress on the speaking circuit. Because of the time I had served (more than most first time, white-collar, nonviolent offenders) and because of the restitution I was consistently paying to Union Bank and to the U.S. District Court, the audiences I spoke to were intrigued, kind, and attentive. They admired me for facing members of the profession I had defrauded (CPA's) and offering whatever help I could to ensure they did not become victims of fraud. My work at the law firm had carried on sluggishly but finally ceased. When I was not on the road speaking, I was spending much of my time at the Church at Rocky Peak, studying to finish my second master's degree and learning how to be a pastor.

If there was one place I felt truly safe, it was at the church. It was easy for me to let my guard down at Rocky Peak. I should have known better.

My weekend job at Rocky Peak was to sit in the information booth and help navigate first-time visitors. The booth was located just outside of the main sanctuary so people coming to the church or leaving the service could easily find it. I helped first-time visitors to locate children's Sunday school classes, to find where the bathrooms were, or to know where the singles group met. The questions varied. When the service let out, people would stop by the booth to get information on upcoming church events.

Normally, once the service started I had free time until it let out. To keep from getting bored, I hooked up a television set in the information booth so I could watch Sunday morning football. When questioned by Dr. Miller, the senior pastor, about how a television set ended up in the information booth, I told him that a *true* information booth had information men wanted, like the scores of their favorite football teams. He did what he normally did when confronted with my shenanigans. He shook his head, mumbled something about patience, and let the television stay in the booth.

One Sunday morning during one of the services, while I was watching television comfortably in the booth, a young lady and her mother rushed out of the service. The lady was about twenty-two years old, and I recognized her mother as a staff member who worked at the Rocky Peak Christian Day School. The daughter was clutching her stomach in excruciating pain. She was in tears and her mother was understandably panicking. I rushed to their aid and the mother told me to call 911. I yelled to another staff person to call 911 and decided to stay with the daughter who was writhing now on the ground. A small crowd of mostly staff members had gathered around the young woman. I knelt down and took her hand and told her help was on the way. I was trying to comfort and soothe her with a calm steady voice. Suddenly I felt the pressure of someone's hand roughly snatching my left shoulder and yanking me to my feet.

"Get away from my daughter!" the voice exclaimed gruffly. There was no mistaking that he was talking to me because the words were accompanied by the assault. *Maybe he's confused and thinks I am trying to hurt her*, I thought, trying to give him the benefit of the doubt. His grip on my shirt was released with the force of my upward momentum. The aggressor was a stocky man about fifty years old with short-clipped dark hair. His wife tried to explain that I was actually helping their daughter, but he was clearly not listening.

"I know who you are mister, and you better get away from my daughter," he threatened. He stepped closer to make eye contact with me. "I'm a retired Simi Valley Police officer and I know all about you. Stay the hell away from my daughter!"

The shockwave of his threats in church created an endless moment of utter silence. The few people who witnessed the event stared at me with a combination of wonder and mild fear. They were probably apprehensive from imagining how I might defend myself. I felt the hair stand up on the back of my neck as my body was pumped with adrenaline. My fists clenched out of habit and reaction but not intentionally. I bent my knees slightly preparing to launch a sidekick to the guy's upper thigh. Then I could pounce on him once he was down. This is how the two Nation of Islam Muslims in prison who taught me karate trained me to react. "Mass times velocity equals momentum, Barry. And it's the momentum that will hurt 'em, so use your hips to generate speed with all your kicks," they had explained.

There was nothing to talk about or negotiate. This was not a case of mistaken identity. This man put his hands on me while I was trying to help his daughter and then called me out in front of my co-workers. In the prisons where I served most of my time, you would die for that, no questions asked and no explanations offered. My mind rushed in a mechanical fashion trying to absorb the situation. I didn't deserve this. I was doing so well, working hard, paying back my victims. Seconds seemed like hours. If I physically assaulted the man while on probation it could be a huge problem. But I didn't care at the time. People were watching, and I did not want them to think I was weak.

But on the other hand, there was the issue of ministry. A troublesome verse in the Bible regarding the requirements for a pastor states a pastor must not be prone to violence. Reacting violently to this man as a staff member on a Sunday was grounds for termination and permanent disqualification from ministry. *Too bad*, I hastily thought. *There may be pastors who can turn the other cheek after someone has grabbed them and called them out in front of other people—I'm just not one of them!* Just as I was ready to strike, by God's grace or divine intervention (to this day I still cannot explain it), I again remembered my best friend Peanut.

⸙

"Peanut, you've got to come quick. Your roadie just got jacked in the bathroom by some L.A. sect!" the man exclaimed in between huffs, half out of breath. He had barged into our cell unannounced. By this point in my stint, I was pretty good at understanding prison lingo. The term "roadie" referred to a friend Peanut had from Washington, D.C., and the term "jacked" meant he was beaten up. I could only assume it was someone from a West Coast gang.

In federal prisons oftentimes the gangs will re-prioritize their affiliations. Usually that meant that the Los Angeles-based Crips and Bloods, although enemies in the outside world, would become allies when placed together in an out-of-state federal prison. The reason? The presence of East Coast gangs. In federal prisons it is not a battle between the city gangs but a battle between coasts.

Before Peanut had become a Christian, he was an active leader in a Washington, D.C., street gang. In prison, your former title imputed both credibility and the assumption of the leadership of people from your area. Peanut was constantly approached about getting involved in the inner workings of gang life in prison but always rejected the offers. Because of his size and strength (he benched about 450 and was 6'4" of solid muscle), rival gang members viewed him as a threat. This fear was despite his constant reaffirmation that he was out of that lifestyle and the love he showed to people from both coasts.

However, whenever there was tension between the East Coast and the West Coast, both sides wanted to know where Peanut stood. Would he get drawn into any one of the countless conflicts and tip the scales of power to the East Coast? His answer was always the same, "I'm out of the lifestyle, fellas. I serve one Master, and it ain't a geographical sect." No one was confused by what he meant.

In this case, however, some West Coast bangers had beaten up a close friend of Peanut who was still active in the gang life. (Peanut had been trying to persuade the man to disassociate himself from the gang altogether.) This was too close to home for him to simply ignore. He grabbed his coat and followed the man who had come into the cell.

"Where are you going?" I asked in surprise as he was leaving.

"I gotta go see if he's okay," Peanut said with a mix of concern and sternness. I thought momentarily about whether or not I should follow him. If the situation were reversed, I knew Peanut would be there for me, so I hopped off the bunk, set my theology book down, and went after him. When we got to the yard I could hear people talking as Peanut scanned the area for his friend—the friend they knew had just been beaten up.

"I knew you would come out of retirement, Peanut!" one person jeered. "Take care of your business," someone else shouted.

That was prison talk from the gang element trying to encourage Peanut to retaliate against the people who had just beaten up his friend. When fights broke out, whether you won or lost, the key was not to let the prison guards know you were in a fight. It was the unwritten rule of prison: get into a fight, and win or lose, you don't squeal or go to the doctor. Peanut's friend was hiding behind the handball courts. When the three of us arrived (Peanut, the guy who brought us, and I), we saw Peanut's friend lying on the ground clutching his side. His shirt was spotted with crimson stains and a little dried blood colored his cheek. Peanut knelt down and spoke to him gently.

"You okay?"

"Yeah," the man whispered. I looked around nervously to make sure no guards were approaching. Fortunately none were.

"What happened?" Peanut asked. His tone of voice let the youngster know only the truth would suffice.

"I shot off my mouth and called these two 8-Treyers punks and they got me in the bathroom."

"So you shot your mouth off?" Peanut asked. The man nodded in agreement. "I told you that you can't do that. These people in here aren't playing and I can't protect you."

"Sure you can, Peanut. Ain't no one in this joint here could whip ya. What do you mean you can't protect me?" the young man asked dejectedly.

"What I mean is that I'm not in this life anymore—"

Before Peanut could finish, four 8-Treyers approached in a loose formation. I did not see them coming until it was too late to warn Peanut. They stopped a few feet from where the young man lay. Two of them were concealing what appeared to be some sort of metal object, like a small pipe, in their jacket sleeves. I surveyed the yard. *Never a guard around when you need one*, I groaned to myself. I did not want to fight these guys. But I had to be there for Peanut. Scared, I rubbed my hands nervously and wiped the sweat from my brow, all the while trying not to look like the sissy I was. Because I bench-pressed over three hundred fifty and played tackle football without pads, they thought I was a legitimate tough guy. Their perception did not give me extra courage, though.

"Why don't we just handle this right now, Peanut, so we do not have to worry about any surprise retaliation later. We know how you East Coasters operate, so let's take care of this here and now," one of them blurted out.

I studied the four men more closely, I decided the one talking was not visibly nervous, but the three that accompanied him were. One of them was openly fidgetedy and wiped sweat from his brow as if mimicking my own actions. I happily concluded that he wasn't carrying a weapon. *Good, I'm not the only one here who is scared,* I thought. My confidence level rose about an inch.

Peanut's reputation for fighting and handling himself had followed him into the prison system. Guys talked about his kind in the chow hall or on the yard during the day and in the dorms at night. They debated who the toughest guy on the street was. Consequently, because of his past, Peanut had their immediate respect. That much was obvious.

I could not help but think that just minutes before this incident I was in my cell quietly reading a theology book. Life was good, or as good as life could be in prison. Now I was about to get beaten up by some gangbangers over some big-mouthed youngster from D.C. Nothing's fair about life in prison.

All eyes were on Peanut, including mine. Whatever he decided, I was resolved to follow. I mentally replayed all my karate sessions, hoping that I would not get hurt too badly. Peanut stood up slowly and casually wiped the dust from his knees. There was no panic in his eyes. Not even a hint of fear.

He was taking his time, and his genuine lack of concern made him more of a threat to the four 8-Treyers, who shifted in place.

"Hey, I just bought some soups from the commissary and was wondering if you guys wanted to come over to my cell so we could kick it together and talk," Peanut stated. The hell-bent quartet exchanged puzzled looks, not knowing how to respond. Peanut continued, "I realize that you were angry at my friend here for popping off. He shouldn't have done that, but now it's over. Can't change the past—and you guys have certainly made your point. And I have this simple philosophy I follow. You want to hear it?" No one spoke, so Peanut took that as an affirmation and continued.

"Never do anything to anyone in prison that would cause them *or you* to stay one day longer in this place. None of us needs a shot for fighting and the loss of any good time. So let's just move on." ("Shot" was prison slang for a discipline report.) No one could argue with that logic. A shot for fighting was an automatic trip to the hole, a loss of good time, and an increase in your security level.

Peanut's friend from D.C. gingerly picked himself up and tried to wipe the dried blood from his cheek. The four men stayed focused on Peanut. However, Peanut could tell that the leader of the bunch needed a little further persuading. That's when he really surprised me by revealing a side of himself that he rarely displayed.

"You know me, Big Larry," Peanut said to the spokesman of the 8-Treyers. "You know I have other options, baby." He said this in a tone that reminded everyone there that he was on the street at one time in his life. "But when I told you that day in the holding cell that I had changed, I meant it. But you know what I am capable of—*you know my work*. I just choose not to resort to that life anymore." Peanut was no pushover, and I watched the group mentally back down. He could fight and had fought successfully many times in the past. Apparently the ringleader knew that all too well.

Big Larry was no economist, but he knew what *opportunity cost* meant. Peanut was giving Big Larry an opportunity not to fight and still save face. It didn't take him long to see that fighting held a much higher risk.

"Other options, huh, Peanut," Big Larry said with a toss of his head. "I like that. What kind of soups y'all got over there?"

"Well, you know I'm on the east side in the projects. We slumming it over there but we can hook you up." Everyone smiled. The tension was gone. Peanut had defused the entire ordeal that we all knew could have turned out much differently. As we walked back to the cell, Peanut turned to me.

"The Bible says a soft answer turns away wrath. Did you know that or did they forget to teach you that in Hebrew school, little Jew Boy?" That was the nickname Peanut had chosen for me. Sounds derogatory, sure, but for Peanut it was a term of endearment.

"No, I missed that one," I murmured as we passed through the education building and got closer to our dorm. The 8-Treyers were following closely behind us, laughing and talking about some girl they all knew back in L.A. It was as if the incident had never taken place.

"When people know you have other options, and yet you choose the more difficult of the two—then and only then will they know that you have changed," Peanut said.

～

I flashed back to church with the angry father. No one knew at that moment what was going on in my mind. But they did see the effect of Peanut's teaching in my actions. I immediately relaxed my stance, apologized to the former police officer, and said I would honor the request to get away from his daughter. I told the small group of people around us that I would make sure the ambulance knew where to come. I turned my back on them and smiled to myself as I dwelled on my best friend Peanut. When the ambulance came I directed them to the girl, who ended up being just fine.

The situation had ended peacefully, but I don't think anyone else watching knew it had the potential to be explosive. The very next morning Dr. Miller called me into his office. He had heard about the confrontation; so had all the staff. He told me how proud he was of me for not reacting violently to the man who grabbed me.

"You exhibited incredible spiritual maturity, and I am honored you are on our staff," he said. I felt like telling him what a fraud I was because of how I really wanted to react. But I said nothing, naturally wanting him to think the best of me.

Then Dr. Miller shared a story with me. He had received letters from people in the congregation back in early 1995 when I was first hired. There were serious complaints about his decision to hire an ex-con right out of prison. He told me that the same people who wrote those letters came to him a year later and apologized because they were convinced after observing me that my conversion was no con.

"Even in Christian circles, Barry, there will be skeptics. Be prepared, don't get caught off guard," he warned, "and always remember: truth plus time equals trust. A lot of truth over a long period of time will regain everyone's trust. Never forget that."

By mid-1996, I was only two classes away from graduating with my second master's degree. I had to travel back and forth to Liberty University in Virginia to fulfill classes that could only be taken on campus. I also continued to do fraud prevention talks. However, I could not get the Jaak Olesk Home Theater fraud case out of my mind. There had to be some way I could be more proactive in the fraud prevention arena. The right opportunity finally presented itself. I was asked to do a daily radio show where consumers could call in and ask questions about business investments or business opportunities *before* they invested.

This way I could prevent fraud or catch fraud in the act, as it were, and "do good" like that reporter had said. The daily radio show aired on the Business News Network for two hours a day, five days a week. I received a modest, monthly salary and, admittedly, was no Rush Limbaugh or Howard Stern, but despite my inadequacies I had fun doing the show. One of my best friends in life, Tony Jaime, was my producer.

Surprisingly, we could actually do the show out of my one-bedroom apartment in Tarzana, California. The network set up an ISDN (Integrated Services Digital Network) line in my apartment, and the connection was so clear no one could tell that I wasn't in a studio. Well, no one except my neighbors who could hear my big mouth and enthusiasm when I was on air.

My motto for the show was simple: "I am an expert at failing. Never ask me what you *should* do in business, because I failed. But I am an expert at showing you what you *should not* do." I was never one for taking myself too seriously. I really enjoyed taking live calls and being put on the spot by people as they questioned me about topics ranging from my past crimes, what prison was really like, or what I believed the next booming business would be. My answer to the latter question was always the same. I will never forget when one caller asked both what the next successful industry in the United States would be and what stock they should purchase based on my advice.

"You want to know the industry that will see the most growth over the next five years?"

"Yeah," the caller said enthusiastically. I was setting him up so I could get on my soap box.

"The privatization of prisons. Private companies who build and run prisons," I stated. There was a long pause, and since I wasn't expecting a reaction, I continued.

"So many people are in a life of crime or headed into a life of crime that there is no way our state and federal governments can build prisons fast enough to keep up with the growth. So they will have to contract with private companies to house inmates. And those private companies will be the stocks that I would buy over the next five years."

"That's a terrible thing to say, Barry! How negative and pessimistic. You should be ashamed of yourself. Not everyone in this country is like you!" he said angrily.

"I never said that everyone in this country is like me, my friend. What I mean is that I can prove to you right now that the same people who complain about crooked CEO's and dishonest business people are sometimes not too different themselves."

"What exactly do you mean?" he asked. I was waiting for that question.

In live entertainment you have to be quick. The rule of thumb is pretty simple: if you are bored talking about a subject then the audience will most likely be bored. That's why in radio you talk about what you know and nothing else. The reasoning? You will be more enthusiastic when you are talking about subjects that you know about. If there was one thing I can safely say I knew, it was prisons and the people who end up serving time in them.

"Here's what I mean. You ever hear of IRS Form 4506?"

"No, can't say I have."

"Form 4506 was created by the IRS for people who lost the tax return that they had filed previously with the IRS. But today that form is used by all mortgage lenders as a proactive tool for fraud prevention. And do you know why that is?

"Because the average consumer, not the average corporate CEO, thinks that it is okay to lie on loan applications about how much they earn annually in order to qualify for their dream home. As long as they make the house payments and nobody gets hurt, and because everyone else is doing it, it's okay to lie to the bank or mortgage company to get that home loan or to refinance. And a whole lot of people were caught lying to qualify for loans, since banks and mortgage companies randomly compared the tax returns submitted to them with the tax returns that were actually filed with the IRS, and they were different. But don't believe me.

"Log on to the Internet and look up Form 4506 and see for yourself how mortgage companies use this form to protect from fraud—not fraud perpetrated by CEOs, but by the average consumer. And what can we learn from all this? Here's what: the average consumer has concluded that the ends—the dream home that we will make the payments on—are justified by the means—lying to qualify for the loan by creating a phony tax return. And my friend, that is the exact same logic I and all my corporate, white-collar crime buddies used to justify our frauds. Yeah, prisons are going to be overcrowded, because once you lie to a bank to qualify for a home loan, the next logical step is lying to a bank to save the company." With that we went to a commercial break.

⌇

I graduated from Liberty University in October of 1996; well, at least that's when I completed my last class. As soon as I had finished the degree program, I had a major decision to make. With a master's of divinity degree from a fully accredited and well-respected Christian university, the opportunity to apply for a job as a senior pastor was a real possibility. However, full-time ministry would mean I would have to significantly cut back on my out-of-town speaking engagements and maybe even the daily radio show.

These were my two primary income generators. I had watched Dr. Miller long enough to know that being a senior pastor was a full-time job.

If I chose to go into full-time ministry I would clearly diminish my earning capacity, which would mean less money to victims. That would certainly not go over well with Frank Gulla or Union Bank. I feared they would think I was hiding behind a church as a pastor so I wouldn't have to pay my victims. Then there was the proactive fraud prevention work I so desperately wanted to do. I felt as if I was being pulled in two different directions.

First, there was the ministry pull. While in prison, Peanut and I had planned on starting a church that was ethnically diverse. I promised him that I would not abandon our goal of working together in a local church, just like we did in prison. Tragically, Peanut would not live to see that dream fulfilled, but I wanted to honor him and go into ministry full time as we had planned. He had invested so much time and effort into helping me grow. But then there was Union Bank and the victim restitution fund and the fraud prevention pull. There were many invitations to speak at various functions around the country.

Perhaps what appealed to me more than the financial benefit of those invitations to speak was the fact that I was actually *wanted*. People were willing to pay money to hear Barry Minkow speak. That appealed to my ego. But this same ego had led me to prison in the first place. I prayed that God would give me wisdom and direction so that I could make the right decision. Money and popularity were tempting, but I had worked hard to complete my degree. The only way I could utilize such a highly specified master's of divinity degree was in the context of being a pastor of a local church.

For a two-week period beginning in mid-October of 1996 I tried to figure out where I could do the most good. I tried to discern where God might be calling me. Don't get me wrong; I was more than thankful that I had career paths to choose from. God had proven He had His hand on my life countless times.

My biggest obstacle was trying to keep the potential for earning a substantial income from influencing my decision. Right when I was sure I could not figure out what to do, I heard Dr. Ravi Zacharias, a famous Christian apologist, on the radio. I had grown to love his show, and that day he told a story I was convinced was meant specifically for my ears.

It was a story about Robert Jaffery of Toronto, Canada. He was the heir to that city's largest newspaper, the *Globe and Mail*. Because he was the heir to the newspaper, he struggled with whether or not to take a job there. But he was fluent in Chinese and decided that God was calling him to be a missionary in China. Since he spoke Chinese, the Standard Oil Company offered him a job to run their operations in China on their behalf. Although the company offered him a huge salary, he turned down the offer. Even after the company promised double the original salary, he still refused. He stated that he wanted to continue his missionary work in China.

Finally, the CEO of the Standard Oil Company sent him a telegram stating: "Dear Mr. Jaffery—at any cost!" Without missing a beat, Robert Jaffery wrote back something that will live on in my mind for years to come. He wrote back: "Your salary is big—your job is too small."

That was my answer! Ministry was the bigger of the two jobs. Why? Because as a pastor I could influence people to live for God and avoid the pain and anguish of a life without God that I had already experienced. I would also have access to businessmen, whom I could meet with privately to encourage and, when appropriate, warn about the pitfalls of even small ethical compromise in business. I could get access to prisons as a pastor which I would not normally have because of my past criminal record. I loved visiting prisons and letting the men know not to give up and that they can turn their lives around and come back from failure—even the failure of prison.

The issue was not revenue and my ability to generate it. This was a calling. As a great thinker once said, *There is a difference between the vital and the important*. It was important that I stopped fraud, but it was vital that I obeyed the calling to be a pastor. Besides, if God wanted me to continue to work in fraud prevention, he would open that door.

Now all I needed was Gulla's approval and a church who would hire a paroled ex-con with a record of fifty-seven felonies, who had been sentenced to twenty-five years in prison and who owed the government over twenty-six million dollars.

I thought I had reached the apex of difficulties by simply making the decision to be a pastor. But with my history, my uphill journey had just begun.

REALITY CHECKS BOUNCE

There's a guy who has locked himself in a motel room and says he's going to kill himself!" Denise blurted out as she ran into my office. She was my secretary at the Church at Rocky Peak. "I think he's on drugs, and he asked for a pastor to come see him. He just looked in the yellow pages in the motel and called us."

"Settle down, Denise. Do you know which motel he's staying at?" I asked calmly.

"Yeah, it's on Sepulveda Boulevard in Mission Hills. Here's the address," she said as she thrust me a piece of paper. "But you're not going there, are you?" Although deeply concerned for the man's welfare, Denise was equally concerned with my safety.

"Of course I am; what's he going to do, shoot me?" I said as I hunched my shoulders. Her lips pressed into a thin line and she sank into the chair in front of my desk. Dean Merrill, who was also a staff pastor and a very close friend, overheard the commotion. Our offices were right next door to one another and he hurried in to join the conversation. Denise quickly explained the situation with the suicidal caller and her concerns about my going.

"Want me to go with you?" Dean asked.

"No, bro, I got this one," I said as I turned towards Denise. "Look, Denise, when you see a house on fire, you don't stop to argue about the cost of the hose. We don't want this guy to die. Maybe I can talk to him, perhaps help him. I've done this before in prison. Trust me." With that, I grabbed my cell phone and ran for the door.

After I was released from prison I developed an entire new approach to life. If I didn't get killed in prison it was highly likely that, if I stayed out of intentional trouble, nothing in the outside world was going to kill me. I reflected on that philosophy as I knocked lightly on the door of the motel. The place was run down and poorly maintained, the kind of place you did not want a church member to see you entering or exiting.

"Who is it?" a gruff voice inquired.

"I'm not a cop. I'm Pastor Barry Minkow from the Church at Rocky Peak. You called us for help about thirty-five minutes ago." I listened carefully for a response but heard none. A face that I could not describe peaked through a window streaked with dirt and seconds later the door opened. The first thing I noticed was that there were no lights on in the room. The second thing I noticed was that the man had pants on and no shirt. The metallic shine of a gun glinted on the bed as daylight poured into the room.

"Come on in, Preacher," the man said. I did not hesitate. I entered the room without fear because I could see the despair clouding his heavily-lidded, blue eyes. I had seen vicious men in prison who preyed upon the weak, and they stared at you like a hawk inspecting a field mouse. This man's eyes were completely void of malice. In fact, he appeared more nervous than I was. He didn't just need help. He was reaching out—he *wanted* help. I thought back to the statement Robert Jaffrey made to the Standard Oil Company, "Your job is too small." Now I truly knew what he meant.

The man asked me to sit down on the edge of the bed. While in prison I worked on the suicide prevention team. The first thing I remember being taught during the mandatory training was to be a good listener. Sometimes people just want to be heard and not given advice. The man grabbed a bottle of what looked like a dark beer, took a long swig, and began to talk. He was from the northern California area. Years earlier he and his father had a booming business in construction. Then the gambling began to take over. At first it was quick, discreet trips to Lake Tahoe. Then it was the daily bets on football, baseball, basketball—the sport didn't matter. Before it was over, he had burned through close to 1.1 million in sixteen months. His wife left him and the company went bankrupt.

When there was no more money to gamble, no family to come home to, and no business to tend, drinking became a daily habit. He cried as he talked. It was a full hour before I said anything.

I wanted him to know that I also had made bad decisions in the past and went to prison. I told him my story and felt obligated to emphasize the fact that I was no better than he—in fact, probably worse because the dollar amount of my crime was far greater than the dollar amount of his. I stood up and placed my hand on his shoulder. He was sitting on the opposite edge of the bed. I asked if I could pray with him, but he said he wasn't ready to pray. I asked him what bothered him most about what he did, and that's when the conversation changed.

"I killed my father," he whispered. "I didn't murder him, but I killed him. He died of a broken heart. A broken heart that his son caused." He paused as the tears began to flow down his cheeks. He took a swig from the beer and wiped his mouth and his eyes with the back of a hairy arm. He stood up from the edge of the bed and paced around the small, unkempt room.

"And the worst part is he died when I was a failure. He will never know me to be anything but a failure. I just could not stop drinking or turn my life around before he passed away. And it kills me every day to know that the father who loved me, gave me the family business and everything else I ever needed, died with nothing because of me. Now my mom barely makes it on Social Security, and I cannot face her because I am so ashamed. But the worst thing, Preacher, is that my father's last memory of me was as a failure."

I had never heard anything so heartfelt. This man's pain was intensely real, and it struck a cord of empathy within me. My own father had died only a few months before this encounter, and I had done what I always do with my feelings: I suppressed them, hoping they would drown with the everyday business of my life. This was a critical survival technique in prison. Despite how many birthdays, anniversaries, Christmases, and other holidays you missed while in custody, you could never cry or express emotion. You put your emotions on lockdown and erected a façade of strength in order to survive. When I was released from prison I continued with that mindset of no visible emotion, purposely avoiding situations where I might be inadvertently confronted with my innermost feelings. This even included my choice of movies. I never went to a movie that I knew could potentially make me cry because I was so uncomfortable expressing my feelings. This self-protection usually worked for me and sadly still often does, but not this day.

As I sat in that ratty motel room I thought back to how proud my father was when I ran ZZZZ Best. He bragged to everyone that Barry Minkow was his son. He had a job as the commercial representative for ZZZZ Best but instead spent most of his time telling potential customers stories about me when I was growing up. The customers loved him for that. Then ZZZZ Best went bankrupt, he lost his job, and I failed. Incredibly, his opinion of me never changed. I proclaimed to be a Christian before I went to prison. Most Jewish fathers would have disowned their children—but not my dad. Even though he clung to his Jewish roots, he respected my choice. He never missed a day of my four and a half-month-long criminal trial. Not even an hour of tedious testimony.

He was also literally right behind me when I got convicted. I was sentenced to twenty-five years, and he wanted me to know that he loved me and that I could turn my life around. He promised to visit me often in prison—even when I got shipped to Englewood, Colorado. He kept his promises. In fact, the first of his strokes happened while he was returning home from a visit to the Englewood prison.

The tender memories of my father hit me full force, and I began to weep. My father died before he could see me turn my life around, too. He had loved me and yet the sad reality was that he died while I was still recovering from my failure. He would never see me truly turn my life around. God had not brought me to that motel to help that man; He had brought me to that motel so the man could help me. He certainly uses the least likely conduits to change our lives.

We spent the rest of the afternoon getting a bite to eat and talking. We even prayed together. As I dropped him off at the local rescue mission, I gave him a hug and thanked him for all he had done for me. He told me that just knowing that someone else knew what it felt like to lose a father who would never know his son as anything else but a failure had truly comforted him.

I never saw that man again after I dropped him off that day. But I was the one who was truly comforted.

ॐ

Community Bible Church had placed a SENIOR PASTOR WANTED ad in the November 1996 edition of *Christianity Today* magazine. They asked all potential candidates to send in a copy of a sermon they had preached to the selection committee. Since San Diego was a beautiful location and only about a two-hour drive from Los Angeles, I decided to send in one of the sermons I had done at the Church at Rocky Peak. There was no annual salary listed in the ad but that did not matter. *The job was big!* However, my concern was that with an ad placed in a national magazine, I did not have a chance against all the other potential applicants. Most graduates from the top seminaries around the country with a master's of divinity degree would die to be a senior pastor at an already established church in Southern California. But just in case there was interest, I had to inform my probation officer, Frank Gulla.

"You okay, Barry?" Gulla asked. I was sitting in his Granada Hills office, which was about to be moved to Woodland Hills. Apparently the U.S. Federal Probation Office had outgrown their facility in the northeast section of the San Fernando Valley. *Business must be good,* I thought. *Lots of people on parole and probation.*

New cardboard boxes littered the room. I sat across the desk and stared dully at the mess that was once Gulla's office.

"This place looks like my old cell," I joked.

"Most of this stuff is from your file," he said with a hint of amusement. "You have the thickest file in the office." He was partly kidding and partly serious. My case was a complicated white-collar fraud coupled with an eighty-seven month incarceration period, which contained my monthly conduct record in the prison.

"Mr. Gulla, I want to go into ministry full time. I don't want to travel around doing fraud seminars anymore," I said apprehensively. He sat quietly and listened. He was never big on showing a lot of emotion because he carefully absorbed information. "I want to be a pastor of a church. I will still train the FBI and other law enforcement agencies for free like I have been, but I just don't want to travel around the country anymore."

"Got any prospects?"

"Yeah, there is a church in San Diego that I applied to, but there will be a lot of competition for that job, so I probably won't get it. But here's the thing. I'm not going to make as much money pastoring as I do speaking."

"And that means less restitution, is that right?" Frank asked.

"That's right," I said, waiting for the other shoe to drop. "And I need you to allow me to do this."

"You give me far too much credit, Barry. You know the U.S. Probation Department cannot give career advice. If you want to take the job, I cannot stop you."

"Yeah, but you can make my life miserable if you think I'm ducking my financial responsibilities," I added.

"Now, if you go buy a Ferrari while you are a pastor and fail to pay your victims, then I would have a problem," he said. "But being a good pastor counts as some kind of restitution. Perhaps not monetary, but you will be doing good for a lot of people. That counts for a lot. When you get the job, we will work out a fair payment schedule."

"*When* I get the job? You mean *if* I get the job, Frank."

"I know what I said," he replied and smiled intuitively. Then he stood up. It was time for his next appointment. He had just thrown open the door for me to enter the ministry full time.

❧

"Your tape was very impressive and so was the sermon you preached this morning," Tony Biondolillo said. "You certainly are a gifted teacher. This search has lasted almost a year and over two hundred people have applied for the job," he said. I concluded I didn't have much of a chance after that statement.

The mass interview was held in room B-2, a Sunday school classroom located on the west side of the church building. I was seated on the proverbial hot seat facing a large circle that included members of the selection committee and the board of elders. Any question was fair game. Community Bible Church had invited me to preach to the entire congregation in January of 1997. There were about one hundred and forty adults in a sanctuary that fit about two hundred and fifty people. Following that, I had to appear before the selection committee and the board of elders for routine questions about my doctrinal positions on certain, potentially divisive, theological issues and anything else that they deemed relevant.

The church's founding pastor was Dr. Gene French. He was sixty-eight years old, and he and his wife, Shirley, were retiring. He was kind and thoughtful and made me feel at home from the first day I visited. There was no animosity or jealousy in his heart. He simply wanted what was best for Community Bible Church.

The questions ranged from what my position on spiritual gifts was to what I enjoyed doing in my spare time. After over two hours of inquiries, the fatigue factor was beginning to become an issue. I politely asked the chairman of the elder board if I could say a few words. He agreed.

"I just want to tell you guys something that may prevent you from hiring me." That caused their ears to perk up a bit. "I just want you to know that I need time to do things other than church work. What I mean is, my testimony is more important than my ministry." A couple of people looked confused, so I tried to explain what I meant.

"You see, according to the Bible a pastor must have credibility from the outside world. Well, I defrauded the outside world and despite having paid a heavy price for that fraud, I have to do what I can to pay back victims. If I don't, I am a bad testimony to non-Christians, so if you want to hire me it must be with the clear understanding that I will also be working on radio a couple hours each day and occasionally will need to do some fraud prevention talks. If that doesn't work for you then I'm not your guy." Although I had expected a revolt, what I got instead completely caught me off guard.

"We've already checked your references and talked to Dr. Miller and he said that you can easily handle your testimony work in fraud education—including the daily radio show—and your ministry responsibilities. That is not a concern for us if we decide to hire you." The meeting concluded quietly, and I drove back to Los Angeles with an inkling of hope.

ᴄ⌇ɔ

The next two weeks passed slowly. I continued working at the Church at Rocky Peak and the radio show. I also spent time preparing my now-widowed mother for the real possibility that I might be moving. I felt guilty about moving because my dad had recently died and because of all the love and support she had given while I was in prison. But she was encouraging as always.

The call from Tony Biondolillo, the chairman of the elder board, came while I was home having a snack. He basically said the job was mine if I wanted it. The pay would be about sixty thousand a year, including benefits. For a guy fresh out of seminary with little experience that was more than fair. If I wanted the job I could begin on March 1, 1997. Elated, I accepted immediately.

ᴄ⌇ɔ

Earlier in this story I mentioned my problem with growing older. I had lived in a world of comparing my age and accomplishments with that of other people my age. If I ever came up short and was not the youngest businessman with the biggest company, the most achievements, and the most money, I felt like a failure. My worth as a person was tied to what I accomplished, not who I was or who I was becoming as a person. When you live on that kind of treadmill, it is only a matter of time before you collapse in exhaustion.

When I became a Christian I was convinced that this type of thinking was behind me. I believed this for two reasons: first, the obvious spiritual implications of being a Christian, and second, the clear fact that I had spent over seven years in prison, was now thirty years old, and pragmatically speaking, there were millions my age who were far ahead of me financially. That is why I was surprised that within weeks of becoming the senior pastor of Community Bible Church this thinking came back to haunt me.

I cannot speak for other pastors, but the first thing I noticed about being a pastor is the similarity that exists between church and the business world. In business, the goal is to grow. In church, I quickly found out that the goal is also to grow. In business, there is competition. In church, there is also competition—other churches in or near your area that are indirectly competing with you. In business, at least for a public company, that growth is often measured by stock price. In church, the equivalent to a good stock price was more people filling the pews.

In business, there are satisfied and dissatisfied customers. In church, a pastor is hired and fired every week. In one week someone can praise you for your talents and in that same week another couple can tell you that they are leaving the church for another church because they don't like you. In business, there is a board of directors that the CEO must be accountable to for success to take place. In church, many congregations opt for a church government system that has a board of elders; the senior pastor's ability to lead and submit to this board is often the one key factor that will lead to success or failure. Then there is the whole money thing. In the business world, a company must stay within well-planned annual budgets. In church, the congregation also establishes well-planned annual budgets. And finally, and perhaps most importantly, in business the CEO often feels he is only as good as his last positive earnings release. And in church, all too often a pastor feels he is only as good as the last sermon he has delivered.

• It is these points of similarities that unlocked something inside me I thought had been dead and buried. Perhaps subconsciously or perhaps much more intentionally, only God really knows, I slowly became in many respects the old Barry Minkow. No, I didn't take the church public or commit investor fraud. It was much more subtle than that. I slowly began to see the world through the eyes of a selfish man who wanted to be the best pastor with the biggest church and the largest budget. I wanted to succeed, and in many instances, all for the wrong reasons. The "numbers" we pulled in every week elicited the same response from me as the stock price of ZZZZ Best once did back when I was a crook. But I was a pastor now, in a position of trust that could not be violated. I had been given a wonderful second chance by a group of godly, committed believers, but there was something seriously wrong with me that began to surface.

I honestly loved the people I pastored. I developed a rhythm of running through the right motions. My sermons were well prepared and delivered with enthusiasm. I used relevant illustrations and personal life experiences grounded in solid theology to come up with new material week in and week out. I was rarely unprepared. I visited prisons, hospitals (and, boy, did I hate the hospitals), tried to save marriages through endless hours of counseling, worked all hours of the night when needed, led people to a saving relationship with Jesus Christ, and even answered everyone's e-mails within two hours of receiving them. As a result, the church grew. Externally, I was, as we said in prison, "the man." I was doing all the right things and avoided all the "S" sins of being a pastor: silver (stealing money), sex (staying morally pure), and sloth (laziness).

For the first eighteen months the church did succeed and nearly doubled in size! We added two more services, one on Saturday night and the other at 10:45 a.m. on Sunday. By October of 1998 we averaged close to three hundred people each weekend. If outsiders observed us, they could easily conclude all was well at Community Bible Church. But internally, something was changing in me. I began to covet the success of other pastors who had larger churches than Community Bible Church. I argued with my elder board, thinking I was smarter than they were and knew better about how to run the church. At times I was even manipulative during meetings with the elder board, attempting to persuade and convince them to do things my way. I was slowly becoming, for lack of a better phrase, the "Christianized version" of the old Barry Minkow. Sure there was no fraud, phony financial statements, or S-1 registration statements with the SEC. So as for repeating a legal offense, I was fine. But from an internal moral perspective I was failing. I had found it easy to hide behind a burgeoning church. "Hey, something must be working—we've grown a hundred percent in a year and a half—so leave me alone" was my standard response to anyone who questioned my motives.

Just as in the days of ZZZZ Best when I did something criminally wrong and then justified my actions, so at Community Bible Church I rationalized being envious, selfish, or manipulative with a new set of excuses.

"It is me versus the world," I would say. "People cannot possibly understand how hard it is for an ex-con to succeed as a senior pastor. If people truly knew my story and struggle, they would see it my way and leave me alone." Such rationalizations and justifications were never spoken publicly but kept close to my heart as constant reminders and convenient excuses to excuse my behavior.

The problem was intensified by the fact that my position in the church encouraged secrecy. The job of a senior pastor could be a very lonely place. I feared I could not really let my guard down around any of the members of the church and disclose my true struggles because of, you guessed it, what others in the church might think of me. My personal pitfall again. I could not simply haul a church member into my office, someone who watched me preach every weekend, and say, "Hey, we need to talk. I am this manipulative person who thinks he's always right and have begun justifying very sinful behavior through rationalizations that I used at ZZZZ Best." If people knew what was really going on in my heart, I would have scared them away.

What I needed was Peanut, someone I could talk to and not worry about what he might think of me no matter what I told him. But I didn't have Peanut here. As a result I began to make mistakes in judgment. I made hiring mistakes. Instead of relying on my board of elders to help me make good hiring decisions, I forced the issue and created discord by thinking I knew best. The irony was that I could leave an elder meeting where I had basically forced the elder board to hire a person against their better judgment and turn right around and truly love and care for people in troubled marriages or with loved ones in custody. There was a neat little compartmentalization going on in my life. At elder meetings I was a self-centered jerk, but then I just put that attitude on a shelf, walked out of the meeting, and became the loving, caring person I was hired to be. The board of elders simply chalked my attitude up to the immaturity of a new pastor and allowed me to continue in my position because they observed how I really did preach with passion, love the people, and meet the congregation's needs. They were able to separate my shortcomings from my strengths, and to this day I am indebted to them.

It is too bad I couldn't see out of one compartment into another to assess who I really was.

～

"Pastor Barry, all I have to do is change the figures on one invoice and then the bank will lend the company the money. And believe me, we need the money," Jim said convincingly from the opposite side of my desk. He was a local businessman who had visited Community Bible Church a handful of times and then asked to meet with me. Jim was the co-owner of a specialty retail product manufacturing and distributing company. "The 1998 Christmas season is right around the corner," he continued. "We need the capital to make sure our product is delivered to the stores in ample time for shelf space. And of course we plan on paying the bank back, so it's not fraud, is it?" he asked.

I wanted to jump across the desk, grab him by the shirt, shake him hard, and say, "Of course it's illegal, Jim! Don't you know our prisons are filled with people with good intentions?"

But I carefully chose my words. I told him how proud I was of him for seeking me out and asking my opinion *before* he made the decision. I told him that if I were half the man that he was, I would have never gone to prison in the first place. That's when I remembered what an old college professor once taught me: truth discovered is a better teacher than truth proclaimed.

So I told Jim an unforgettable story about Bill Spano.

～

"Fidelity American Bank, may I help you?" the operator said.

"Bill Spano, please," said an impatient voice.

"One moment." She quickly transferred the call upstairs.

"Mr. Spano's office, can I help you?"

"Sally, it's Steven Olson from Capital Synergy Corporation."

"Hi, Steven, one moment, I'll get Bill for you." She depressed the intercom button, but Bill did not pick up. He was on the other line. But this was

Mr. Olson, the president of Capital Synergy and one of the bank's biggest depositors and customers. She had to interrupt. After gently rapping on the door, she turned the knob and entered Bill's office. He was still on the line.

"Yeah, Sally. What is it?" Bill whispered, one hand covering the bottom of the phone.

"It's Steven Olson on two."

"Tell him to hold," he said. Sally was used to multitasking. She had been with Bill for the past three years and watched him ascend to the position of Fidelity American Bank's chief lending officer. Since that promotion, Bill never put in less than twelve hours a day and neither did Sally.

"Bill Spano," Bill said, proud that he had cut his previous call short.

"Bill, it's Steven Olson."

"Hi, Steven. You doing okay?" Bill asked.

"I need to see you right away, Bill. Can you meet me at the wharf by 11:00 a.m.?" Olson pleaded.

So much for small talk. Bill checked his watch. It was 10:30 a.m., not much notice. But there was an unusual sense of urgency in Olson's tone. Normally he was laid back and calm. Not today.

Bill thought about his previously scheduled lunch with a prospective bank client. It was a publishing company with a 1.5 million dollar accounts receivable line-of-credit request. *I can push that appointment back to the afternoon*, he reasoned. *After all, I am the chief lending officer, and customers who want to borrow money from Fidelity American Bank have to cater to* my *time. Besides, Affiliated Capital brought the bank a lot of referral business.*

"I can be there," Bill said.

"Great, and please do not be late."

Bill grabbed his coat, barked out rescheduling orders to Sally, and dashed off to the meeting. As he drove towards the wharf, thoughts of a morning argument with his wife played through his mind.

"Bill, before you know it Suzy will be in college. We will not have the money to send her. We can barely afford her ballet lessons. Things are tight," she huffed.

"I understand, sweetie," Bill replied, "but I am sure the bonus stock option program I have with the bank will eventually come through and easily cover Suzy's college expenses."

"The operative word, my dear husband, is 'eventually,'" she said sarcastically. "That's what the bank has been promising you for the last three years. And you keep performing, working seven a.m. to seven p.m., and as far as I am concerned, that bank is behind in the compensation end of the deal." A long pause followed, then she said angrily, "You're a damn CPA, Bill Spano, and you've built that bank's loan portfolio single-handedly! They should be paying you more!"

As Bill placed his arms on her tense shoulders he noticed seven-year-old Suzy had entered the room. Her lip was quivering. Always the sensitive one, she was visibly shaken over their heated discussion.

"What's wrong, Daddy? Why are you and Mommy fighting?" she said in between deep breaths. Bill looked at his wife and gave her an admonishing scowl. He then walked over to Suzy, knelt down, wiped the tears from her eyes, and hugged her.

"Nothing is wrong, dear," Bill said reassuringly. His wife left the room. "Everything is okay. Mommy and I were just having a discussion."

But in the back of his mind Bill knew his wife was right. The bank had made him a lot of empty promises. Promises of performance bonuses, enhancements, and incentives for new business attraction had all but been forgotten. He was working harder than all the loan officers combined and was not getting adequately compensated.

The arrival at the wharf brought him back to reality. Within minutes he had parked his car and was headed to the restaurant. Olson was already seated.

"Thanks for seeing me on short notice," Olson said.

"Everything okay?" Bill asked hesitantly.

"Yeah, but I need your help." He leaned in as the hostess placed two ice waters on the table. He waited for her to leave before continuing. "Mr. Spano, we've been dealing with each other for almost three years now," he paused for effect, "and I admire how you have worked your way up the ladder at Fidelity American. I want to make a deal with you."

Bill surveyed the room. Despite the early hour, the lunch crowd was already picking up. People were being seated. He glanced out the window and noticed the sun gleaming on the calm ocean. He dreamed of being on a boat with Suzy and his wife and not worrying about things like college tuition, unfulfilled promises from bank presidents, and last-minute meetings with bank clients.

"What kind of deal?" Bill asked.

"I need five million by tomorrow to acquire some property," he said.

"That's not much lead time," Bill said. "I don't need to tell you about things like appraisals, escrows, and loan documents, Mike, and these things take time."

"I know, I know," Olson shot back. "That's why I wanted to see you face-to-face." He reached nervously for a small, soft leather carrying case from under his chair and placed it on the table next to Bill.

"There's one hundred thousand in cash there for you, Bill, and another one hundred and fifty thousand upon closing. Now listen to me," he said as he scooted his chair closer to the table.

"You know damn well that I would qualify for this loan anyway. I have a perfect track record with Fidelity American and am one of the bank's largest depositors. And I don't need to tell you how many subcontractors deal with you guys because of me. I know you have a five-million-dollar credit authority on your own signature and if you wanted to you could get me the money."

Bill said nothing. He just sat and listened—half shocked and offended, and half intrigued by the possibilities of the proposition.

"Look, Bill, I'm in a bind. A partner of mine was supposed to contribute to this deal, and he backed out at the last minute. Now I'm stuck, obligated to close escrow without the money. I need your help, and you know I'm good for the money. The cash is for the trouble I am putting you through to help me. Once this deal closes I'll have an income stream I can retire on, and I won't forget you."

Bill leaned back in his chair. He looked out the window again, but suddenly everything was moving slower as his adrenaline hit high gear. His mind raced. *I could never do such a thing,* he thought solemnly. *I know taking kickbacks for loans is wrong. People who involve themselves in such things end up in prison.*

But then he thought of the morning argument with his wife and a debate began within himself. She was right. The bank owed him. *Broken promise after broken promise is my only problem in life and it is all their fault,* he rationalized. And of course there was Suzy. He needed to provide for her. She meant everything to him, and after all, what kind of father couldn't earn enough money to send his daughter to ballet? If only the bank had come through with the money they had promised.

Bill quickly assessed the risk factors—CPAs do that type of thing, especially if they are senior credit officers. The risk in such a deal was not a quick approval of a large loan for a well-known client—as long as use-of-proceeds could be confirmed, that could be overcome. No, the risk was if Olson failed to repay the loan. Since it was a real-estate-secured transaction and considering his past credit history, that was also not a major obstacle. *All bases covered*, Bill determined. *If the bank will not honor my performance, I will get creative and have the bank live up to their commitment to me one way or the other.* His eyes rested on the waiting expression of Steven Olson. *Suzy needs me*, he said to himself and began his path.

"One hundred thousand now, one hundred and fifty thousand when we close, and a hidden stock interest in a few of my other projects," Olson said.

Bill got up from the table and reached for the concealed money. He placed the satchel under his arm and reached out his hand to Steven Olson.

"No time to eat," Bill said, "I've got loan docs to prepare."

Of course the story doesn't end there.

~

The visiting room at Lompoc Federal Prison Camp was a series of four tents set up parallel to one another. Each tent contained wooden floors, chairs, and tables. The sides were rolled up for cross-ventilation. None of this mattered much to me, having spent most of my prison years in maximum and medium security facilities. There, the visiting rooms were closely watched by hidden video cameras in the ceiling, and guards paced up and down the long aisles to monitor physical contact between inmates and their guests.

But I was in a low security camp now. No fences or walls or hidden cameras. Visiting families walked up a steep hill where a uniformed prison guard was seated at a small sign-in table. Then they were free to purchase food, usually popcorn, from vending machines located in a trailer on the opposite side of the tents. Inmates were allowed to walk around the tent area with their visitor and even hold hands! Conditions had changed for the better.

The hard part about visiting in such a relaxed and comfortable atmosphere, though, was saying goodbye. Around 3:15 p.m. every Saturday and Sunday, the following words blared over the speaker, "The visiting room is now closed, the visiting room is now closed." This was our cue as inmates to wrap up our visits, say our goodbyes, and go back to the dorms to prepare for the 4:00 p.m. count.

On this particular Saturday afternoon I did not have a visitor. I was walking around the track when I first noticed her. She appeared to be about nine or ten years old and was walking backward down the steep hill, waving and never taking her eyes off of her father. This was unusual. Most kids hugged their fathers, said their goodbyes, and were gone. By the time they hit the parking lot, it was life as usual. Sure, things were tougher without dad, but most seemed to adapt quickly.

Not this precious little girl. As her right hand waved, her left hand wiped away the tears from her eyes. There was an internal refusal to accept the fact that she was being separated from her father. In my seven years in custody I had seen many children visiting their parents. But this child was different—there was a connection between her and her father that I couldn't help notice. She was special.

Her father stood helplessly by as he watched her vanish into the parking lot. He was new to FPC Lompoc, I could tell. You learn these things instinctively after a while. And prison etiquette (not exactly prescribed in a book) requires that longtime inmates like me help the newcomers adjust. Having seen similar situations many times over the years, I approached with the intention of easing the pain of the end of his first visit.

"That your daughter?" I asked as he stared wistfully down the empty hill.

"Yeah," he said, tears still full in his eyes. He wiped them away. Crying is a sign of weakness in prison. Although he was new, he knew that much. There was an awkward silence.

"She's beautiful. Did her mom come with her to visit you?" I asked.

"Her mom left me and remarried after I got indicted," the man said, "She's having an awful time adjusting with me in here and the divorce. I feel so helpless." I placed a reassuring hand on his shoulder.

"Your first week here?" I asked.

"Yeah, I've got four years, eleven months, and three weeks left," he said.

"I'm sorry to hear that," I said sympathetically. I turned to face him. "My name's Barry," I said as I extended my hand.

"My name is Bill. Bill Spano."

∽

Jim just sat there and stared at me resolutely. A smile came across his face. The truth was discovered, the point was made, and no explanation was necessary. He came around the desk and surprisingly gave me a hug. "Thank you, Barry. If anyone other than you had told me that story I would not have believed it or learned from it. I love you, brother." His eyes misted and he turned to go.

As he left, perhaps for the first time in my year and a half ministry as senior pastor at Community Bible Church, I felt that I had accomplished something. Maybe it was because I was involved in proactive fraud prevention by talking someone out of ever perpetrating fraud in the first place. Maybe it was because I was able to draw on my experiences to help someone not follow in my footsteps. Or perhaps I was learning that ministry is more about others than it is about me. I had finally cashed my reality check.

14 | BORN AGAIN UNTIL YOU'RE OUT AGAIN

And we are here today praying for this building because of the competent leadership of our senior pastor, Barry Minkow," Tony Biondolillo stated confidently. He was the chairman of the elder board at Community Bible Church and my direct boss. Over one hundred people had gathered with hands linked in a circle, praying over the possibility of moving from the facility in an obscure industrial park to a visible location on a main street.

"We have doubled in size over the past year and a half, with our adult attendance pushing close to three hundred. And the reason we are here today is because we need God to open the door for us to buy a bigger building," he continued loudly, "and with Christmas only weeks away, I believe the church will continue to grow beyond our expectations." Tony Biondolillo was a solid, committed Christian man. When I had first applied for the position of senior pastor at Community Bible Church in November of 1996, I remember calling him and disclosing my past crimes with ZZZZ Best. My voice probably sank to a whisper when I mentioned my almost seven and a half years incarcerated in federal prison. The phone almost slid out of my sweaty hand as I waited for his response, which I was sure would be a carefully worded rejection.

"So, I'm a sinner too. You should hear about the things I did when I was younger and before I turned my life over to Christ. They may not have made the newspapers, but they were no less sinful. I can assure you, Mr. Minkow, that this church is more interested in your future than your past," he replied empathically.

The prayer concluded with one hundred voices shouting, "Amen!" I smiled broadly to myself as I drove home because I couldn't help but feel proud. No one had given me much of a chance to succeed in the highly competitive church area of San Diego as a senior pastor fresh out of seminary, but the church was growing. And although my first year and a half had been challenging, I was ahead of the game. I thought about all those media people swarming around me when I was freed from prison. They predicted I would not continue with "the church thing" because I was one of those "born again until you're out again" prison conversion stories. I pictured them racing to their desks to type articles dripping with sarcasm and malice.

Even when I was first released, I knew my faith was real and that Christianity was not another Barry Minkow con, but other people didn't. I had kept myself from committing fraud or any other kind of crime in the three short years since my re-entry to the civil world. Instead, I had become the leader of a growing local church. It was not only growing, but also relocating to a busy street where more people would surely visit. *What an awesome Christmas season this is going to be!* I thought as I barreled down the 15 Freeway toward home.

I thought about all the men still in prison who were cheering me on to succeed. I received letters from several inmates expressing their gratitude for my somehow paving the way for them. Their rationale was simple: the more success stories they could cite to their case managers, wardens, and future employers, the easier it would be for them to get a second chance and rebuild their lives once they were released from prison. I half-grimaced at the memory of spending Christmas away from loved ones for so many years. I quickly pushed that thought aside as I passed the cheerfully lit homes in my neighborhood. I even uncharacteristically tuned into a station playing carols and started singing along, "Rockin' around the Christmas tree . . ."

I pulled into the driveway of our modest, three-bedroom home in Scripps Ranch, looking forward to the best Christmas season that I would ever celebrate. The elation I felt was higher than when I became the youngest man to take a company public on Wall Street. Every puzzle piece of my life was finally starting to fit into a neat pattern, and I was thrilled.

Not for long.

ௐ

"I don't love you anymore and I'm leaving you," Teresa said dully, eyes red and puffy with tears. "You may be a good pastor, but you're a lousy husband!" When I heard those words my stomach was instantaneously nauseous. My legs became weak and I grabbed for the sofa—all the while thinking of how I would respond. I had joyously come home only to see my wife Teresa packing a suitcase.

"You can't leave me. I love you . . . you know I love you. I have been faithful and have never even raised my voice to you," I automatically responded, wracking my brain for a reason why she would want to leave at all.

"That's the problem with you, Barry. No emotion. You're like a damn machine. You never get angry. You never lose your temper. It's like being married to a robot," she said, and coolly went back to packing her clothes. "I've been thinking about this for a long time, hoping things would change, but they never do."

I could not believe this was real. I wanted to march outside and re-enter the house to a different scene. I wanted the idyllic Christmas setting I had just been singing about.

"I didn't even know you were unhappy," I stammered, attempting to defend myself. "Teresa, listen. We can get counseling. We can try to make this work. I'll change. I'll quit the church. I'll do anything but don't leave." She stopped packing long enough to turn around and look me square in the eye.

"Barry, if you were a janitor you would figure out a way to work twelve hours a day." She convicted me with a cold, disassociated stare. I had never seen her eyes set in frigid determination before. This was no bluff. I didn't know how to respond. For the very first time in my life, I was speechless. Her eyes were completely void of warmth, and that let me know her love for me had vanished.

I wiped the perspiration off of my forehead to keep the sweat from mixing with my tears. Teresa was not evil. She was a sweet, Christian young woman I had met while still in prison. Introduced by mutual friends, we immediately hit it off. She visited me periodically, and we wrote each other and talked on the phone all the time. I figured if this woman would love me while I was still in prison, then things would only get better when I got out.

Within two months of my release from prison in April 1995, Teresa and I were married. She was a special woman whom I loved and respected. Although seven years my junior, she was mature enough to deal with reporters and probation officers when they visited our apartment unannounced. I thought back to some of those visits in prison where she would watch me preach with zeal to the other inmates. Both of us were yearning to have a church outside the walls of prison to teach and lead.

"I'm going to my parents' house. Don't follow me; don't call me—" she said icily. I interrupted her.

"What about the church and all the people and, and . . . what about me? We're days away from Christmas. You can't leave now!" I pleaded.

"I don't care about *your* church, and I don't care about you anymore. You'll survive through Christmas. You're the great Barry Minkow, the comeback kid of Wall Street. You'll be just fine without me," she snapped. With that she snatched up her suitcase and charged out the door.

౿

Most men who have been sentenced to federal prison will tell you the lowest point in their lives was the day the judge declared the penalty and slammed down the gavel. The gavel worked like a magic wand that made years of life simply disappear. Not me. The pain I felt when Judge Tevrizian sentenced me to twenty-five years in federal prison was nothing compared to how I felt when Teresa backed out of our driveway. Maybe it was because I was more prepared for the former than I was for the latter. You at least have an inkling that punishment is coming when you know you are guilty of a crime.

For the rest of the night I stared out of the guest bedroom window desperately hoping and praying that Teresa would come back. But she did not. *How could God let this happen!* I cried. I wasn't ripping off Wall Street or investors anymore. I was doing well, working hard at the church, beginning a new life. How could He allow my wife to leave me?

The neatly kept homes on our block all shared identical automatic garage doors with the same distinctive sound. Every time I heard a garage open, I hoped that it was Teresa's car swinging into the driveway. It wasn't. The night dragged on. No call, no Teresa. When the sun rose early the next morning, I knew she was not coming home anytime soon. In the short three years we had been married, she had never stayed out all night without me or without my knowing where she was. I quickly decided to make the next move.

I hopped in my car and drove six hours from San Diego to just west of Phoenix, Arizona, where her parents lived. I replayed our conversation. Heck, I replayed my entire marriage in my mind. *Where had I gone wrong?* I asked myself over and over.

The irony was that as a pastor I had actually counseled many couples through difficult times and here I was on my way to salvage my own marriage. *What a hypocrite I am*, I thought angrily. *I tell others how to stay married and my wife leaves me. Why was God allowing this to happen to me?* I had fought so hard to regain my life and was laying a foundation for the future. My shoulders hunched with the weight of compounded guilt and regret.

As the shock wore off, the harsh implications of her departure coursed through my mind. With Teresa leaving, there was no way I was fit to be a pastor. The Bible is pretty clear on this issue—if a man cannot take care of his own house, how can he be entrusted to handle God's house? The reality that I would be fired from Community Bible Church or have to resign was becoming painfully clear.

How could I ever tell my mother and family that my wife had left? That would not be easy, as they all loved her. And then I thought of the faithful congregation who loved me and looked up to me. They would now lose all respect for me. If I had failed as a husband, then I had failed in everything.

Interstate 8 East offered an appealing solution. Eighteen-wheelers charging along at seventy-five miles per hour were casting shadows over my little car. A quick turn of the steering wheel into one of those large trucks would free me from the pain of telling my family, my church, and even my probation officer that I had failed. But I quickly decided I couldn't die that way—I would still be hurting others in the process of ending my own despair. My heart was pounding. I gripped the steering wheel so tightly it hurt.

I finally allowed a sliver of hope to seep through. *Maybe she will listen to me and come home. I've been good at talking people into things all my life so maybe I had a shot at her changing her mind.* I kept driving and hoped for the best. But I couldn't think straight enough to voice a coherent prayer. The best I could do was keep muttering, "God help me, *please.*"

I finally arrived at Teresa's parents' house. They were kind enough to let me in to talk to Teresa. But she stayed firm in her decision. She was utterly convinced that our relationship was over. "It's better that you leave," she said. "Divorce papers will be arriving soon."

Just like that our conversation was over. And so was our marriage. I had no choice but to go. I did not want her or her parents to see me cry. Call it foolish pride. As I left the house and shakily walked to my car, I prayed to God she would be looking out one of the windows. *If she is, then there's hope,* I thought. I searched every window, but Teresa wasn't looking.

Where was God?

❧

It wasn't long before I was back on I-8 heading west. My stomach was still nauseated. I looked in the rearview mirror and saw dark bags forming under my eyes. My head began to ache from lack of food. Bright sunshine burned my red eyes and the only relief was when eighteen-wheelers passed and blocked the light. I began wishing I were back in prison. At least there life was a little more predictable and in a strange way safer. Not from physical violence, but from unpredictable emotional pain now tearing my heart apart.

The hardest part of all was not having anyone I could call. I was not ready to inform the entire church, two days before Christmas, that their pastor's wife had left him and was planning an immediate divorce. Surely my ministry was over. I had to keep the news to myself for now, which only seemed to make things worse. Hour after hour, I struggled through a downpour of tears.

I stopped for gas at a mini-mart in Yuma, Arizona, the halfway point between Phoenix and San Diego. As I got out of my car, I noticed a family of four making a routine stop to fill the tank and dart into the bathrooms. The kids could not have been more than five years old. I thought about how I wanted children. Teresa and I had talked about it often. Now I was a thirty-two-year-old man without a wife and with no prospect for children. *Prison was easier than this*, I said to myself as I got back in my car.

꿍

I believe it was Cary Grant who once said, "A great actor is someone who does not get caught at it." Con men are actors. They must be able to "perform" and sometimes ad lib in a moment's notice. In my days at ZZZZ Best I was a good actor, and during my four and a half-month trial, prosecutor James Asperger made that very clear to the jury. My style of acting consisted of pouring my heart into a sales presentation for a product or service that I knew to be false. At ZZZZ Best I did this for auditors, bankers, and Wall Street analysts on a daily basis. But that had been years ago, and I was sorely out of practice.

However, when I got up to preach the Christmas Eve candlelight service at Community Bible Church in 1998, I used every ounce of strength to hide my pain. My eyes surveyed the packed sanctuary, noting the smiles covering the faces of happy families and anxious children. If they only knew how I suffered and trembled inside. Trying to preach about the joyous holiday of Christmas when I was hurting so deeply was no easy challenge (especially when I wondered in the back of my mind how God could let this happen to me). I managed though, mostly by increasing the length of singing and decreasing the length of the message—not my usual approach. But being a holiday, it went largely unnoticed.

It was my usual custom to greet people at the door as they exited the church. I forced my facial muscles to smile and told people that Teresa was visiting her parents in Arizona. That was clearly a lie as it only told half the story. I then told them that I was going to Los Angeles to visit my mom and sisters on Christmas Day. Another bold-faced lie. Going to Los Angeles without Teresa would alert my family to the separation. I wasn't prepared to tell the world she was gone. Admitting it would make it more real.

One of the last families to exit the church that evening was Patrick and Debbie Palanski. Their little three-year-old girl Katy had long curly hair and big blue eyes. She was absolutely adorable in her holiday dress. Teresa was Katy's full-time baby sitter during the week. The minute I saw her, my eyes watered. Earlier that week Teresa had taken Katy to the fair, and the recollection made me shudder. How would I ever tell Katy that her "Teesa" was not coming back? I gave them a hug as they left and watched them get into their car and drive off to have a cheerful family Christmas.

Before long the church was empty. Everyone had left for family dinners and special times of joyous celebration. Everyone but me. I was in no hurry to go home but had nowhere else to hide.

⁀

I searched the cupboards looking for something to eat. I thought back to the many Christmas Eves I had spent in prison. *At least there I had a dinner waiting for me on Christmas Eve,* I thought. I opened a can of tuna and sat on the floor against the sofa. Nutritious, if utterly lacking good flavor. Arthur and Molly, my canine companions, came and lay gently next to me. Molly was an Akita and Arthur a husky mix. In some weird, unexplainable way, they could tell that I was hurting. They followed me from the kitchen to the living room and lay down right next to wherever I sat, trying to comfort me.

The dogs were kind enough to help me finish the tuna when I couldn't stomach any more. I surveyed the room and perhaps for the first time it hit me: I was alone, really alone. I was completely alone on Christmas Eve with no one to share the terrible feelings of emptiness that dominated my emotions. Even in prison I had Peanut and others to talk to. *I would give anything to be able to talk to Peanut right now,* I thought. *I am lonelier outside prison than I was inside.* That realization was hard to bear.

I remembered many times when I had told my fellow inmates not to "fail jail." That means do not leave prison the same way you came in. Yet here I was failing real life. Maybe I could have handled Teresa's leaving a little better if I wasn't a pastor. It would have only meant failing at marriage and not at my job. I was crushed by the silence of the house and the reality of the divorce. Nothing I could do would stop me from feeling alone.

I thought about all the people I had tried to encourage in their time of need as a pastor. The family going through the sudden and unexpected death of a loved one, or the wife whose husband left her and four children behind for another woman. God was always how my answer began. I would say things like "God is in control. He can give you the strength to endure" or "God loves you and knows your pain." Now I couldn't think about love without thinking about losing my wife. I couldn't focus on God or His strength when every place I searched in my soul was aching with pain. It was me, Barry, who felt alone and unloved. Me, the guy who always quoted the Bible and helped others in need. That's when I pulled the bottle of Valium from my front pocket.

$\backsim$

I was in a holding cell in 1988 in Los Angeles when a man who had just been sentenced to ten years told me that if he got convicted again he would get a life sentence. As I later found out, this was his "second strike," and if he was released and caught again he would face a life sentence. But it was what he said to me that day that stuck with me.

"Barry, if I get into trouble again, I won't let them take me in and give me life," he said.

"Well then, just don't go back into crime—you're obviously not too good at it," I quipped. "But how will you stop them from giving you life with three strikes?" I asked.

"That's easy. I'll hold court in the middle of the street. No one is going to take me back to jail to do a life sentence. *I can't go out like that . . . too much pain.*"

I knew what he meant. If he was confronted by the police and it was his third strike, he was going to make them take him dead—not alive. But it was the phrase: "I can't go out like that . . . too much pain" that resonated with me. I never forgot it.

Now the tables were turned. It was *me* who did not want to go through the pain of disclosing my failures as a husband. It was *me* who did not want to lose my job as senior pastor in utter disgrace. It was *me* who did not want to face my family and ministry friends with the news of my wrecked home life. *I just couldn't go out like that,* I thought. Suicide was my way of "holding court" in the middle of the street.

⸎

Earlier that day I had researched online how much Valium a man weighing 195 pounds would need to take in order to kill himself. I had also considered getting a gun, but with my luck I was afraid of getting pulled over for a routine traffic stop. Because of my probation status, the car would be searched, the gun would be found before I used it, and I would end up in prison (with a fifteen-year minimum) because I was an "ex-con with a gun." Pills were easier and a lot less messy.

I stared at the bottle. Just a week earlier I was on top of the world. The church was growing, I was not involved in any criminal activity, and I was proving to the skeptics that I was not one of those "born again until you're out again" prison conversion stories. But I was convinced that there was no way people would believe ex-con Barry Minkow over Teresa when it came to explaining that I really tried to be a good husband but simply fell short. I feared the perception would be that Barry Minkow is not the changed man he proclaims to be as evidenced by his wife's leaving him.

I just could not bear the thought of that kind of scrutiny again. The suspicious stares, the under-the-breath comments, the rolling of the eyes, all the other nonverbal gestures that only those of us who have failed can sense. I knew them all too well. Then there were all my ministry friends. People would now lose respect for me because Teresa had left. I had earned their respect after a long time and much worthwhile effort.

Where did I go wrong? I thought for probably the hundredth time that day. My forehead beaded with perspiration. I clung to the pill bottle like it was a safety blanket. My palms were so sweaty I wiped them on my pants and tightened my grip on the bottle. Hot tears slid down my face, staining my white shirt. God had abandoned me. Worse yet, He had forgotten about me. He was going to let me die of a broken heart. I opened the bottle. No time for a note, I started pouring out the pills. Suddenly, a shrill sound in the background made me jump.

⋞

There is something strange about me. Call it being compulsive, call it being a perfectionist, but if I misspell a word while writing I must spell it correctly before I continue. I check my e-mails a hundred times a day in fear that I will get behind. I cannot relax if someone has called me and I have not yet returned the call. That's probably why I answered the phone when it rang that dreary holiday evening.

I decided I could lie one last time. I picked up the phone hesitantly and prayed that it wasn't my mother. I felt a little relief when a male voice spoke on the other end of the line.

"Barry, this is Bob Shank. How ya doing, my friend?" Bob Shank was the last person I expected to hear from. There was no one I respected more in the world than this man.

Bob is primarily known for hosting the Franklin Graham and Greg Laurie crusades. We met while I was working my way through seminary back in 1995 at the Church at Rocky Peak in Chatsworth, California. He was also known for having a special kind of grace and compassion for people like me. People with a past.

At that moment I had to make a choice. It was no coincidence that Bob Shank had called me when one hand held the phone receiver while the other held thirty-two ten-milligram tablets of Valium. My mind raced through the scenarios. *What if I tell him the truth about Teresa and he shuns me for being a bad husband?* I thought. Then I considered how God may be trying to help me through Bob. I had to make a choice . . . a choice that would either save or cost me my life. Before I could open my mouth, a particular memory surfaced that had taught me one of my most valuable lessons. One I had almost forgotten.

⋞

"Barry Minkow, report to the lieutenant's office. Barry Minkow, report to the lieutenant's office," the voice over the prison loudspeaker commanded.

Getting called to the lieutenant's office in prison was never good news. The reasons for such a summons varied. If there were a dirty drug test, for example, the inmate would be called into the "LT's" office and carted off to the hole for sixty days. Or an inmate could be called for paraphernalia found during a random search of his cell. All eyes followed me as I walked across the courtyard of FCI Englewood into the lieutenant's office. Since I was one of the most visible (though not most spiritually mature) Christians in the prison, this was clearly an opportunity for skeptics to scream "hypocrite"—a favorite expression on the inside for those of us who looked to Jesus to turn our lives around.

My mind raced through the possibilities of why I was being called into the LT's office. I had been in custody at that time for almost five years with a perfect conduct record. When I arrived, the lieutenant on duty wasted no time.

"Minkow, you've got to sign this piece of paper acknowledging that you were served with this judgment," he said. Since inmates cannot officially be served while in custody, these types of procedures went through the lieutenant's office. I signed for the papers, received the package, and walked back to my cell (much to the chagrin of certain onlookers who were hoping to catch me being escorted to the hole). When I arrived at the cell, I plopped on the bunk bed and read the document. I was stunned to see an eighteen-million-dollar judgment from Union Bank against Barry Minkow.

It was a lien against all my real property at 9595 West Quincy, Littleton, Colorado, because that was the address of the prison. The bank was even free to lien the one dollar an hour I was earning working in Unicore repairing radio mounts for the M-1 tank. But I also knew what the document really meant: it was the equivalent of a financial life sentence. Union Bank had lent ZZZZ Best seven million dollars and lost it all. And unlike other victims who received much of their investment back because of a class action lawsuit, Union Bank received no monetary repayment from those suits. That is why I did not contest their lawsuit against me, which paved the way for their judgment.

But now reality hit. An eighteen-million-dollar judgment, which could not be dismissed in bankruptcy, would loom over me for the rest of my life. As the reality of that was setting in, Peanut entered our cell.

"What did the LT want from you?" he asked.

"Gambling debts caught up with me," I said without looking up. I just kept reading.

"And I thought it was drugs," he said. "What they want?" he asked. I had learned that true intimacy in a friendship is the ability to share your heart without the fear of judgment or ridicule. But for some reason I was reluctant, perhaps ashamed, of telling Peanut about the financial life sentence I just received. He sensed something was truly wrong and turned his attention toward me.

"Hey, you know you can't keep anything from me. What is that?" he asked as he pointed to the documents. I made the decision and handed him the papers.

"'All real property at 9595 West Quincy.' Does that mean they're going to take away our cell?" he joked. We both laughed, which helped me a lot. He kept reading, "Eighteen million. Hmm . . . lotta money. Okay, let's go workout before count time," he said as if ignoring the issue at hand.

"You know what that is, Peanut?" I asked. "It is a financial life sentence. When I get out of here I can never own a house, I can never get a job, and I can never own anything. This is a life sentence," I argued. "You would think that a twenty-five-year prison sentence and probation would be enough. When do I stop paying for the mistakes I made at ZZZZ Best?" I asked.

"You never do, Barry," he answered, "but let me show you something." He grabbed his Bible and flipped the well-worn pages to Romans 8:31. "Read this out loud."

"If God be for us, who can be against us," I intoned.

"And do you know what that means?" he asked rhetorically. "It means that the only thing Barry Minkow needs to do is stay right with God and no matter what happens in life or who turns against you, God will see you through. Even an eighteen-million-dollar judgment." He paused for a moment. "There will be more setbacks like this, you know, and you've got to be ready for them. And remember one thing. Don't ever quit on me, Barry. I believe in you. Promise me you will never quit!" he ordered as he held his fist out to me.

I glanced back at the text I had never noticed until that day and smiled.

Peanut was right. He usually was. "I promise," I said. "I promise," I repeated again and hit my fist on top of his, a prison oath.

∽

The memory of that prison promise loosened my tongue, and I told Bob Shank what had happened to my marriage. Peanut may have been dead by that fateful night, but his teachings and his memory lived on in my heart and ultimately saved my life. Bob Shank listened attentively as I told him the story. He was unfazed, calm, and loving. He refused to judge me but instead empathized with what I was going through. He gently inquired as to my marital faithfulness to Teresa and if I had ever abused her physically in any way.

"Of course not, Bob. And to Teresa's credit she is not making any of those accusations," I said.

He then shared some examples of other pastors who were not unfaithful to their wives but went through similar circumstances. Suddenly I did not feel so alone. Not only was I relieved to share this burden with someone, but I also was relieved to know that I was not the only pastor to go through such a painful event. Bob also told me I wasn't the first one to seriously consider suicide. "But that is never the answer," he added quickly.

"Barry, I want to share something with you," Bob said. "At ZZZZ Best you lied to Wall Street and the auditors in a blatant, premeditated way. That was wrong, and you paid a heavy price for those mistakes and in some ways are still paying. But not disclosing to people, to those who are closest to you, the pain and struggles you are going through is another kind of material misrepresentation. It is what I call a material nondisclosure, and although not as bad as a premeditated lie, it can be just as damaging. I know you want to be the guy who has all the answers and helps everyone, but right now you need help. God's mechanism to help you is the special people He has put in your life. I'm just glad to be one of them. But you must become more transparent and that must begin now."

I thought about what Bob said. Caring about what other people thought was rearing its ugly head again in my decision-making process, and Bob had spotted it. Admitting that I was hurting and failing and needed help was mostly hard because of my pride. Bob was right. When would I ever learn to stop caring so much about what others think?

When I hung up the phone, I went to the bathroom and flushed the Valium down the toilet. I washed my face, which was caked with a combination of dried sweat and tears. I looked in the mirror and saw my dogs, Arthur and Molly, staring at me. They had followed me to the bathroom, never taking their eyes off of me. They knew what was happening. Nothing could ever convince me otherwise.

I thanked God for Bob's call and for the memory of Peanut's encouragement. He had not abandoned me after all. Now I had hope again, perhaps not for Teresa coming home, but for a life I would not quit in the midst of failure. My failure. The phone rang, again.

"Hello?" The most comforting voice in my life answered back with the same greeting. "Hi, Mom. I'm glad you called. I need to talk to you about something important."

15 LIVING IN A FISHBOWL

"I don't know the formula for success, but I know the formula for failure: trying to please everyone."

CLYDE COOK,
president of Talbot School of Theology

Tom Lewis had heard and seen everything in his twenty years as a divorce lawyer. I met Tom while I was the associate pastor at the Church at Rocky Peak and never expected to call on him professionally. I sat quietly in his office with a pained expression clouding my face as he read through the divorce papers. He would occasionally glance up pensively and ask me about income, the exact date Teresa left, and other details like where we were married. Then he would input those answers into his computer. During the long pauses between providing answers to questions I never thought would be asked, I surveyed the room. The walls were covered with plaques honoring Tom for his various accomplishments. As divorce lawyers go, he was one of the best.

Tom explained that because I was the primary wage-earner of the home, I would have to pay Teresa twelve hundred per month beginning immediately for eighteen months, half the length of the marriage. This would be added on top of the monthly payments I was already making to Union Bank and the U.S. District Court for restitution. There was not a high likelihood that they would reduce my monthly payments just because my wife abandoned me.

I tried to explain to Tom that my total earnings from jobs as a pastor, part-time radio show host, and occasional fraud prevention speaker did not equal the alimony payments. I still had the right to eat! But the formula for spousal support for primary wage earners was pretty simple. Income is plugged into a preset equation, and out spits the number I would have to pay for half the length of the marriage. It all seemed so cold and calculated.

Debt was also a problem. Not only did I have the twenty-six-million-dollar restitution order, I had also allowed our family to ring up another thirty thousand in credit card debt (all my fault). I never was too good at handling money. Then there was the ten thousand Teresa's father had lent us to buy our first home in Scripps Ranch. My mother had also lent us ten thousand, and I still had the mortgage on the home to consider. Since it was early in 1999, the housing market in San Diego had not yet skyrocketed, so there was little equity in the home.

Tom also added one more caveat. He explained that under California law a couple split the debt of the marriage. However, he suggested that I pay *all* the debt of the marriage and pay back both my mother and her father for the loans we received to buy the house. He also insisted that I give her whatever furniture or property she wanted from the home without contesting it. His reasoning was simple. I was a pastor of a church, and I should accept full responsibility for the marriage and the debts, and go above and beyond what the law requires. He believed this would be a good "testimony" to my church and to Teresa and her parents.

It was then that Tom told me I would probably need to get another job for at least eighteen months in addition to my job at the church in order to pay my ever-growing list of debtors. "This is the only honorable way out of this mess, Barry. I wish I had better news for you."

I was initially reluctant. *What have I done to deserve all this*, I thought, still in the denial stage. But I had to trust Tom—even though it made no sense to me at the time. Why would I want to pay the tab for her leaving me? I wanted to fight back. That was how men handled difficulties in prison. But I wasn't in prison anymore.

As I drove home from Tom's office in Los Angeles to San Diego, I thought through his rationale. He was right. I had to deal with this in the most loving way I could, despite my feelings of anger and frustration. There would be no bitter divorce, no complaining about asset division or debt repayment—I would give her anything she wanted. It would take getting used to, but it was the right thing to do. There was only one small problem. How would I pay for it all? I needed another job.

∽

As I said earlier, pastors get hired and fired every week. With the constant influx of people, it is a real up-and-down kind of profession. People who decided to leave the church always broke my heart. Not those who left because of relocation, but those who left because of my failures or lack of good leadership. I hated "getting fired" and took it personally. To some extent, I still do.

When the news about my divorce became public, surprisingly few families left Community Bible Church. Most stuck by me and voted to keep me as their pastor. I had insisted the elder board hold a meeting and have a vote from the entire congregation whether or not they wanted to keep an ex-convict on probation with a twenty-six-million-dollar restitution order against him and who was now going through a divorce. The vote was 198 to 2 to keep me. I remember leaving the meeting that Sunday evening and driving home reflecting on the love and grace that I had just experienced. My eyes watered as I thought about how God had not forsaken me. Peanut and Bob Shank were right!

To help me heal, the elder board arranged for me to go to counseling which they paid for twice weekly. There I could grieve the loss of the marriage and get the strength I would need to help others. Then the church hired an assistant pastor, Jim Robeson, to perform marital counseling and the administrative duties of the church. Jim was about twenty years my senior, married, and had three children. He was stable and felt like he could help the church through this crisis. And he did. Basically, my job for the entire year of 1999 at Community Bible Church was to preach on the weekends and to work at either restoring my marriage or, if Teresa was not willing, to heal from the breakup. I really wasn't surprised when it ended up being the latter.

The final step the church took was to cancel the building program as they decided it would not be fair for me to lead us through a demanding building program while going through the divorce. We had to let the land on the busy street be sold to someone else.

ᔐ

After the church issues were resolved, I began to notice a subtle change in my heart. Call it grief, call it anger, call it being wrongly motivated, but something inside me began to stir.

For some reason I had an insatiable desire to succeed in something that would not only overcome my current failure but also show Teresa, her parents, those who left the church, and anyone else that Barry Minkow was a survivor and a winner and that "they" were wrong for not believing in me.

These feelings were rooted in the fact that I was now back in the fishbowl looking out. Church members and others in the community who found out about the divorce were looking at me again. I was intimately familiar with the feeling of living in a fishbowl. In a fishbowl, everyone could see you clearly, but looking out through the water your vision is a little blurred.

Although I tried to deny it, deep down I knew what the root cause of these feelings were: I was completely fixated on what other people were thinking of me. I was sure people were staring at me and thinking negatively about me. Sure they were cordial and sometimes even sympathetic, but what were they really thinking? My mind always conjured up the worst scenarios. The hardest part about failing publicly (and at this point of my life I was an expert at failing—first with ZZZZ Best, and now with marriage) had become my perception of what others thought about me. My pride and ego, the two things that caused me to end up in prison twelve years earlier, were making me paranoid.

I did whatever I could to escape the pain of these feelings and overcome the fishbowl effect. After work each day I went to the gym. I stayed there as long as I could because I dreaded coming home to an empty house. A good friend took care of the house chores and the dogs while I was busy avoiding the loneliness of home. When I did finally come home, I spent hours worrying about money and how I would meet all of my new financial goals. My appetite decreased and I lost weight, the stress of the situation clearly taking its physical toll. I told myself over and over again, *You survived seven years and four months in a federal prison in maximum and medium security facilities— you can make it through this*. I did my best to mask my true feelings—I was still a pretty good actor.

But no matter where I turned, I found people who I was convinced had lost all respect for me. When I came home it was the people on my block who knew Teresa had left. I could just hear what they were thinking: *There goes the loser, ex-con pastor whose wife left him*. At work I was sure that the people I was preaching to each weekend were looking at me differently. Sure they appeared to be behind me, *but what were they really thinking?* Why was I so obsessed with what other people thought of me? I should have already learned . . .

࿔

It was the day before Thanksgiving 1988 and I was in maximum security in Terminal Island. My cell was approximately five-by-seven feet and consisted of a bunk bed, a toilet with an accompanying sink, and a small two-foot-high locker to store things like books and my toothbrush. My cellmate was John Hensley, a fifty-four-year-old bank robber with spider web tattoos on his elbows.

I asked my attorney, David Kenner, to visit me in the morning that day because we were in the middle of a criminal trial and every second counted, even if it was the day before the Thanksgiving holiday. The guard's voice echoed down the long corridor, "Minkow, you have a lawyer's visit."

I hopped off the top bunk and grabbed my legal paper work that consisted mostly of transcripts from witness testimony from the previous day.

"Get some cigarettes," Hensley mumbled.

"Now would I forget you, my friend?" Hensley just smiled. He had no family or friends in the outside world to send him the miniscule pleasures of prison life, like batteries for a transistor radio or cigarettes. But I always took care of him and he knew that.

The guard approached, and I placed my hands through the ten-by-twelve-inch steel trap door that was cut into the middle of the cell door. This allowed the guards to handcuff those of us in maximum security before opening the cell door. *So much for white-collar criminals being catered to at golf-course-type prison camps*, I chuckled to myself.

As the guard escorted me down the corridor toward the lawyer room, a few inmates stuck their heads through the trap doors and provided me their usual greeting, "What's up, Mink?"

I walked with my chest out and always spoke in the deepest voice possible. Many of the inmates were in for life for violent crimes, and I did not want them to think I was weak. By then I had spent the past few years of my life perfecting how to impress others. "Just going to see my lawyer, man. You know how it is," I stated as I passed by. They nodded in agreement.

Just before I reached the end of the corridor, a man popped his head through the trap door and said, "Hey Mink, I like those shoes. Can I have them?"

He was referring to the new tennis shoes I bought through the prison commissary. I thought he was kidding.

"Sure, man," I said, not even thinking twice. The guard opened the lawyer room door, I stepped in, and he unlocked the trap door so I could stick my hands through and get the cuffs off. After an uneventful two-hour visit I was escorted back to my cell.

Within a few minutes of my return, Bobby Viani, an inmate orderly, approached my cell trap door and said, "Hey Mink, dude down the hall said you got some shoes for him." I thought for a moment and remembered the encounter. Then I thought about the repercussions of giving my shoes to a guy I barely knew. That could make me look weak. Besides, I did not think he was serious when he asked. Hensley looked at me and waited for my reply. My pride kicked in.

"I ain't giving nobody my shoes," I snapped.

"Hey, I'm not in this, Mink. I'm just the messenger." He left and returned within three minutes. I was on the top bunk reading through paperwork.

"Mink, I think you should know this. That dude down the hall with the shoe . . ." he whispered, glancing both ways to make sure a guard was not within earshot, "He's going to kill you. Says you punked him with the shoes. Watch your back, baby, watch your back." And with that he was gone.

My stomach felt nauseated. Color drained from my face. My palms began to sweat. My mind raced. *This isn't the way conflict was resolved on Wall Street*, I thought. I had been in prison for eleven months and this was my first death threat. I didn't know what to do. Hensley said nothing. He was too busy smoking.

"He can try to kill me," I boasted so that Hensley could hear, "but I'll be ready." Hensley wasn't convinced. Neither was I. The rest of the day dragged by.

It did not take me long to learn that the threat came from a man with a ninety-nine-year sentence who was on his way to Marion, Illinois, an underground maximum security prison for the rest of his life. He had nothing to lose. When I went to bed that night I noticed that Hensley had placed a note on the front of our bunk which faced the cell door. "Minkow's bunk is up there," the sign said, with an arrow pointing upward. I wasn't laughing.

I tossed and turned all night; every sound had my full attention. I could hear the guards' radios as count times were announced and normal evening prison business was conducted. When morning came I had made up my mind. Dying, or even the threat of dying, over a pair of tennis shoes was not worth it. After all it was Thanksgiving Day, and I did not want this to be my last Thanksgiving. At this point, I was looking for something to be thankful for. Anything would do.

I immediately called the morning orderly over to my cell as he passed out breakfast, handed the shoes through the trap door, and instructed him on the delivery. He came back and informed me that the shoes were delivered. I gave him a pack of cigarettes (to Hensley's dismay) and that was that. The only person more relieved than I was Hensley.

An hour later I was called for another lawyer visit. Although unexpected, any visit on a holiday was worth getting. The guard escorted me down the hall, opened the door, and locked me in the room. However, this time, he had forgotten to open the trap door and undo my handcuffs. So there I was, in the lawyer room with my hands cuffed behind my back. At least I knew that when my lawyer was escorted to the room, the guard would help me.

And then, out of the corner of my eye I recognized something as I looked down: my shoes. I looked up and saw that the man who had threatened to kill me was five feet away from me and slowly closing the gap.

Apparently our lawyer visits crossed, and his attorney was being escorted out while mine was waiting to come in. So we were alone in the room. The first thing I thought was this was how my life would end, in the lawyer visiting room of the maximum-security wing of Terminal Island. He was coming closer.

If I thought that screaming for help would have made a difference, I would have hollered like a teenage girl. But by the time help could feasibly get to me, I would be dead. He came right up to my face.

"Mink, I don't like you. I never will. But I want to teach you something about doing time," he said. I said nothing and tried to stay calm. My hands fidgeted behind my back. I blinked repeatedly. He continued, "You're going to do a lot of time. So let me tell you something that I don't want you to ever forget. In here when you give someone your word or promise them something, no matter how trivial it may seem to you, just do what you say you are going to do *no matter what anyone may think.*" And with that he walked away, kicking the door to alert the guard that his visit was finished and that he needed to be escorted back to his cell. Sixty seconds later he was gone. I finally exhaled; it had felt more like sixty minutes.

I stood there and thought about what he said. Alone, hands cuffed behind my back in a dirty visiting room, the words "no matter what anyone may think" haunted me. That is precisely why I was in prison. Why I almost got killed. I was so concerned with caring about what other people thought of me, whether it was Hensley or Wall Street, that I had made decisions that cost me my freedom and almost my life.

By the time I went back to the cell it was Thanksgiving mealtime. The only problem with that was the kitchen was so far from the maximum-security part of the prison I occupied that by the time our meals arrived they were cold.

But not to worry. The kitchen always placed our meals in Styrofoam containers, and as soon as they were received, they were placed into the microwave ovens and reheated. The problem then became that our salads, desserts (often pudding), bread, and in this instance turkey, were all zapped together.

So I sat there on the bottom bunk on Thanksgiving Day of 1988, and took in my surroundings. I looked down at my microwaved salad, over to

Hensley and his spider-webbed tattoos, to the toilet that was inches from my eating area; I looked behind me to a door that was locked and finally down to the old pair of tennis shoes I was now wearing. I finally had the courage to admit, *Maybe it's me. Maybe I am in a place like this prison not because of how I was raised or where I grew up or how many people were testifying against me, not because the economy stunk and I had the best of intentions. Maybe I am in a place like this because there is something seriously wrong with me: I cared more about what other people thought of me than I did about doing what's right.*

✍

Our minds do not remember pain too well, especially when we're busy seeking external excuses for internal issues. If they did, no one would get hungover twice in one lifetime. I was becoming convinced that the only relief for me was success. Success in something that would prove to all those who thought of me as a failure that I was not a loser or a quitter. Now the only thing that was missing was the proper vehicle to get me from Point A (failure) to Point B (success). I went on the hunt, not for a job this time but to get back into business. Barry Minkow was coming out of retirement!

✍

In January of 1999, the Internet boom was in full swing. Every day I would watch CNBC or Bloomberg and see another company raise millions of dollars with pro forma earnings. Pro forma earnings are those that the company raising money did not yet have, but expected to have if the investment community gave them millions of dollars. This system really bothered me because back in the mid-1980s, a company could not attract an investment bank to take them public on Wall Street until they had been profitable for at least three years.

ZZZZ Best was not profitable, so I had lied to make the company attractive enough to raise money. Fourteen years later, companies were raising millions without any earnings at all! I remember joking to a group of accountants one day that my only mistake was timing. I could have taken

"ZZZZBest.com" public with no earnings, no lies, raised millions, and avoided jail. They laughed heartily at the comment, noting the irony.

Upon my release from prison I received several offers to go into business, but my standard response was to refuse. Some people would minimize my fraudulent activities and say things like, "But you were a brilliant business genius. You did things that no one your age ever did. Sure you made a few mistakes, but that's because you were involved with the wrong people."

I don't know about you, but for me a mistake is when I am figuring out my monthly bills and add something incorrectly. Or when I choose the wrong tie for a certain suit. Those are mistakes. A mistake is not a fifty-seven-count indictment resulting from a multimillion-dollar intentional Ponzi scheme. A sophisticated, ongoing, white-collar crime is not a mistake; it is a grievous *sin*!

Nevertheless, I was always flattered and surprised that someone, anyone, would trust me as a business partner. But for the same reason that as a pastor, I advise recovering alcoholics not to take jobs as bartenders, I did not feel I should run any company. I feared the temptation to compromise. I gave fraud prevention speeches monthly and even hosted a radio show that focused on consumer fraud prevention. But those jobs were nothing like running a company.

One fateful afternoon during this precarious time a radio caller suggested something.

"Let's go to Alan in Tifton, Georgia," I said as I swerved around in my chair.

"Hey, Barry. I need your help in convincing my mom not to go into the mail-stuffing home business opportunity. She read an ad that said you can earn $1,845 per week by simply stuffing envelopes from home."

"Oh yeah, I know the one," I quickly interrupted. "That's where they say you can earn that kind of money, but to 'make sure you are serious' you must first send them $49.95. Is that what is being offered here?" I asked.

"Exactly, Barry. And I've tried to tell her this is a scam, but she won't listen. What advice do you have?" he asked. I could hear the concern in his voice.

"Here's what you do," I said. "Tell your mom to do the deal, go into the business under one condition." There was a stunned silence on the other end of the phone. "Tell her to call the people and have them take the $49.95 up-front fee out of her first $1,845 check. Then she will know if they are serious." My producer and best friend Tony Jaime gave me a big thumbs up along with a knowing smile.

"Great advice. Why didn't I think of that?" the caller exclaimed. I was ready to give my standard "thank you for the call" and move on to my next caller when Alan spoke again.

"Hey Barry, one more thing." I said nothing and waited. "You should go into business to take your mind off of this whole divorce situation." There had been a recent article in a national magazine highlighting an update on the story of my life. It had referenced that I was going through a divorce. I decided to flush this out a little bit.

"And what business would you have me go into?" I asked half-jokingly.

"Barry, if you went into the online tire and wheel business you would be a success," he gushed. "It wouldn't matter what industry you chose, you would make millions. I'd invest in you!" The phone line clicked and he was gone. I was so caught up in the moment that I had entirely forgotten another invaluable lesson I had learned in prison.

༄

It was January of 1988 at Terminal Island Federal Prison in Long Beach, California, when a friend sent me a book entitled *When Smart People Fail*. Although the fact I was in prison may have argued against my being a qualified owner of this particular book, I enjoyed reading it. The one point that stuck with me from the book was the writer's warning about the decision-making process after a person fails. The author warned against making any major decisions for at least six months after failing. A person's judgment is impaired, and inevitably one will end up regretting long-term decisions made from a position of pain. This was great advice I would regret not following eleven years later.

༄

Call it superstition (another on my long list of sins), but while driving home from the radio station that day I became convinced that the caller from

Tifton, Georgia, had not contacted me by accident. I had been toying with the idea of going back into the business world and helping expand and run a company instead of applying for a job. I just could not think of the industry.

The only thing I knew for sure was that the carpet cleaning business was not an option! Any other business was fair game, including selling tires and wheels online in the new and ever-expanding world of online shopping. My mounting debt was never far from my mind and was a primary motivation. But the upside was promising. If things went well with the new business venture, I could pay off my alimony, the debt from the marriage, and once and for all prove to all those who I was convinced thought badly of me that I was no loser. This was my way out—I was convinced of it.

That call, combined with my ever-ready impulsiveness, had me racing home to look through the business opportunity section of the newspaper. I was looking for tire and wheel stores that were for sale. Of course, in doing that I was breaking the number one rule of business fundamentals: know the business. I knew nothing about the tire industry unless you count purchasing cars and making sure they have four of them. Going into a business that I knew nothing about was a mistake, but no one could have told me that at the time. I had something to prove.

〜

"You know the United States Probation Office cannot advise you on what to do and what not to do, Barry. You are on parole. You cannot commit a new crime, but you are entitled to earn a legitimate living," Phil Hendley said. Hendley was my probation officer after I had gotten off parole. Each month I was required to fill out a report disclosing my financial transactions, which was designed to confirm that I was not living above my means while still owing my victims. Every other month I actually went in to meet with Hendley.

It wasn't that I needed his permission to go into business again, but it would have been unwise if I had not disclosed it to him. Hendley was about my age, but his experience in the probation office had given him a discerning, healthy skepticism about released inmates. Although Phil Hendley was no Frank Gulla, he was still fair, and when you are an ex-con on probation, that's all you can ask for. I had come armed with a large file and a letter from Tom Lewis, my divorce lawyer, explaining our approach with the divorce (I pay all the debt) and the court-ordered alimony and debt repayment schedule. Hendley was already familiar with the restitution payments I was making so it didn't take long for him to see that my church salary and occasional speaking engagements nowhere near covered my new expenses.

I disclosed to Hendley the plan that I had spent a month putting together. While learning as much as I could about the tire and wheel business, I also created a business plan. The goal of the new company was simple. First, I had to raise enough money from a few friends (no banks and no public offerings, obviously) to purchase three retail tire stores in the Los Angeles and San Diego areas. That would provide immediate cash flow for the company and fund the construction of a state-of-the-art Web site that allowed customers to purchase tires and wheels online. My concept even included an interactive preview so customers could see what their new wheels would look like on their particular make of car. Finally, all I had to do was land a big contract with a large, up-and-coming online retailer to drive traffic to the Web site. I had it all planned out. Hendley didn't see it that way.

"Look, I can see what you are up against," he said as he thumbed through the large file in front of him. "I know you are going through an awful time personally and now financially. And I am very impressed at how you have not quit and keep pushing on." It was obvious that he was trying to say something. On the one hand, he was required to keep his professional distance from me. After all, I was the notorious ex-con who at any moment would lie to his own mother to get ahead. At least that's what his training classes told him. But on the other hand, Phil Hendley was a good man who genuinely cared about me and felt bad for the pain I was going through. He saw something that I did not see.

He raised his eyes to look at me directly before continuing. "Barry, you've had a perfect record from the day you were arrested until now. No disciplinary actions for the entire seven years and four months you spent in custody and not one blemish on your record for the last four or so years since your release. You've never even missed a restitution payment, and you are not yet legally compelled to make them," he pointed out. What he meant was that because my crime was committed before November of 1987, when the law changed, I was considered an "old law" case. That meant when I was released from prison and on parole, the court-ordered restitution order (in my case twenty-six million dollars) did not kick in until I was off parole and on probation. So technically from April 1995, my release date, to April 2000 I could not be legally compelled to pay the court-ordered restitution. However, I immediately began making restitution payments upon my release from prison because I was convinced that being a Christian, if it meant anything, meant paying back the people from whom I stole. Or at least attempting to.

"But I fear for you to get involved in the business world at the expense of your church duties and responsibilities. The church has been growing and it seems like such a good fit for you there," Hendley argued.

"But Mr. Hendley, I am still going to be a pastor," I protested.

"I know you are. But your work may suffer greatly because of the many distractions involved in running a new company. You remember how stressful it is to run a business," he said flatly.

I tried to block out what he was saying. He was wrong. The business world was much different than when I was in it years earlier. *Nowadays you just need to put a dot-com after your company name and you will succeed*, I thought. *I can still be a pastor and a good businessman.*

"Look, Barry. What I am trying to say is that I like you. I even respect you for all you've accomplished these past years. I see guys come in and out of here everyday that I violate for one reason or another. But not you. You are one of the bright sides to this job," he said reassuringly.

I said nothing as he recaptured my attention. It was not often that a probation officer complimented a probationee. I was as shocked as I was flattered.

"But I do not think this business thing is a good idea. I can't stop you from doing it. You've disclosed it and will continue to keep me updated. But on a personal level, I do not want to see you revert back to your old ways."

I took that as my cue to interject, "I won't let you down, Mr. Hendley. No bank loans, no public stock offerings. I've really thought this through." I stood up from my chair. "And I really do not have too many other options right now," I said, pointing to the folder which contained my financial obligations. He glanced down and then looked at me as I headed for the door.

"One more thing, Barry," he said as he stood up. "You're not motivated to do this to prove anything, are you?" he asked. The names of those who had left the church quickly flashed through my mind. So did the expression on Teresa's face the last time I saw her. I pictured my house minus most of the furniture lost in the divorce. The pain of lonely nights, staying home watching videos resurfaced. Hendley was not in the fishbowl looking out. I was.

"Of course not, Mr. Hendley," I smoothly retorted as I grabbed the handle to his office door. "I've got nothing to prove to anyone."

16 | FAILURE, AGAIN

"You only have to do a very few things right in life so long as you don't do too many things wrong . . ."

WARREN BUFFETT

By early 1999 depression was setting in. Not a good state of mind for a senior pastor of a church. I detested walking to the mailbox and finding a letter from Tom Lewis. Receiving correspondence about the divorce and just knowing that Teresa was involved on the opposing side brought on feelings of anxiety and sadness, the perfect cocktail mix for depression. The letter also reminded me of my new financial obligations, which were daunting.

What seemed to make me feel better was constantly staying occupied. The busier I was, the better I felt. I dodged emotions by guarding my life from free time. Quiet time meant the opportunity to reflect, and I wanted to avoid coming to terms with my broken life.

Nettires.com, like most companies, was started with the best of intentions. For the investment capital needed to jumpstart the company, I went to Tony Jaime, my best friend and producer of the radio show. He believed in me and even mortgaged his house to help fund the company. I explained the risks of opening the company and the possibility we could all lose our money. But being the consummate salesman, I painted a pretty rosy picture about our likelihood of success. I assured Tony that I would be able to secure a large Internet retail account that, for a percentage of our sales, would drive traffic to our Web site. I pointed out how owning three retail tire stores would help fund the Internet business and provide us with better purchasing discounts with our suppliers. Finally, I assured him that another investor, who was also a longtime friend, would fund the three retail tire stores. To protect Tony's interest, he would still be a majority owner in the company.

"I figure we can build this company up to a certain level and sell it within eighteen months to one of the big tire chains and make a ton of money," I declared.

"Sounds great to me," Tony agreed. I quickly secured his commitment to invest.

Tony based his investment decision solely upon his trust in me and his desire to see me continue to pay my victims and the debt from the marriage. Unfortunately, it indirectly put additional pressure on me to succeed. Upon my release from prison I quickly learned that when people gave me a second chance, like probation officer Frank Gulla and attorney David Kenner, I never wanted to let them down or make them ever sorry for giving me a second chance. The fact that Tony Jaime trusted me enough in a business context gave me even more motivation to succeed.

But there were also other less pure motivations. If I could build this company, earn a lot of money, pay off the debt from the marriage, and make it big in the dot-com era, then Teresa was sure to come back. I began to believe that somehow, through success in business, I would earn a second chance with Teresa. Then, of course, there were the many skeptics who I was convinced thought I was a failure. I had to prove them wrong. Once again, armed with powerful rationalized motivations, I continued raising money.

Next on the list was my mom, an easy sell. She also agreed to cosign on supplier credit applications to help establish more favorable terms. Her only condition for the money was that my business involvement would not get in the way of my ministry. She understood my involvement in the tire and wheel business was more of a necessity than a future career move. Feeling a bit like a teenager promising to do my homework after I took out the trash, I agreed to the terms and assured her that I would still preach every weekend and diligently perform my duties as senior pastor.

The third and final investor was an old friend, and in exchange for a minority percentage of the company, he agreed to contribute the money necessary to purchase the three tire stores. Much like my mother, his concern was that the business would be a distraction from the full-time position with the church. As I did with Tony and my mother, I disclosed that I would work on a small salary, just enough to pay for the extra monthly alimony and debt that had arisen out of the divorce. He agreed to the terms. Now, with the investment group assembled, the pressure was on me to execute. So there I was—back in the one arena that I swore in prison that I would never return to—the business world.

⌇

I worked long, hard hours between March of 1999 and June of 2000. My schedule was to drive from San Diego to Los Angeles late Sunday night and then return to San Diego late Thursday night to prepare for the weekend. Pastor Jim ran the church during the week, and the elder board supported me with the understanding that it was for a finite length of time. They also were impressed with the fact that I was keeping current with my restitution payments to Union Bank and the U.S. District Court.

When I stayed in Los Angeles I lived with Paul and Teri Mann, a couple I had befriended while working at the Church at Rocky Peak. They were good friends and were more than happy to open their home to me. In the mornings I worked out with Paul, and the rest of the day I ran various errands associated with the tire and wheel company. They even allowed me to install an ISDN line in their home so I could continue my daily radio show in the late afternoons. Everything went smoothly for the first month, and I felt like I was on the right road.

Late one evening I received a disturbing call from my third investor. He said he needed to meet with me right away. Now where have I heard that before? It was my experience from both business and ministry that when people need to see you right away it is not because things are going well.

I made the thirty-minute drive from Chatsworth to the Jeri's Deli in Encino, the heart of the San Fernando Valley. When I arrived the third investor looked distressed. After conversing with him for a while, I understood the reason for his grave concern. Apparently, the partner in his primary business had died and as a result, he had to file bankruptcy. He did not offer too many details, and I respectfully did not push, but this much was clear: his former partner had been putting together an investment group to help their company, and just days before funding was to take place, the man died. As did the financing he had carefully pieced together.

My friend announced with a furrowed brow that there was no way he would have enough money to invest in three retail stores like we had planned. In fact, he could only invest in one retail store and would have to borrow money from three different people to do that!

As I sat placidly at the restaurant, a wave of familiar emotions struck me. It was the same feeling I had felt at ZZZZ Best when confronted with unexpected bad news. I had carefully planned for things to work out a certain way and then—Bam! The unknown variable knocks you off your feet, and you're stuck sitting there scratching your head. I was shocked at how clearly I was able to recall similar predicaments that had occurred fifteen years earlier at ZZZZ Best.

The predictable temptation to do the expedient thing and not necessarily the right thing jerked my thought process out of whack. When confronted with discouraging sales news at ZZZZ Best, I would simply increase the sales figures so that they were no longer disappointing. Back in the mid-1980s, a little whiteout bottle could do wonders for a balance sheet. In this instance there was no temptation to do something illegal, but I did consider taking a shortcut, which would violate a promise I had made to myself before I ever went into this venture.

In this country there is no crime in raising money for a business venture with full disclosure to the investor and then failing in that business opportunity. It happens every day, and as long as the investor knew the risks up front, no crime has been committed. Disappointment maybe, but no prosecutable crime.

However, when you are Barry Minkow, a convicted felon who defrauded investors in the past, there is zero room for failure. Why? Ask any ex-con, and he will tell you. Even if you fail honestly, an investor can scream "fraud," and if you're the one with the sordid history, you lose. That was especially applicable now that I was a senior pastor and vulnerable to even the appearance of wrongdoing. Even though this entire business deal was disclosed to the

United States Probation Office and my church elder board, any risk of fraud accusation was ominous.

This is the primary reason that I swore to myself I would not borrow money for the tire company from people who I did not know. If things failed, I just could not risk the accusation of fraud. The minute the third investor said that he could not fulfill his original commitment because of the death of his partner, I should have thanked him for trying and not gone any further. Cut my losses, so to speak, and not violate the solemn oath I took before entering the tire venture.

But that's not what I did. I reverted back to the old Barry Minkow way of doing things.

I began rationalizing that I could still make the company work. After all, Tony had already invested and the Web site was almost completed. There was a large online retailer, who would most certainly provide us with more business than we could handle. Of course I also had to consider all those people I knew were thinking of me as a failure. I *needed* this company to succeed. And there was that one last motivation: maybe Teresa would come back to me! I shifted uncomfortably in the vinyl booth at the restaurant, and as I watched a woman in the booth next to us snuggle closer to her husband, I was painfully reminded how lonely I was. This company had to succeed and there were no other options. Before I swung out of the cramped parking lot that night, I instructed the third investor to get the money from whoever he could so we could purchase at least one retail store.

∽

To my extreme disappointment, the tire company failed. By mid-May of 2000, the Internet bubble had begun to burst, and our cost overruns had finally caught up with us. Despite working eighty hours a week, driving back and forth from San Diego to L.A., and mortgaging my house four times to raise additional funds, it failed. In the end failure really isn't all that complicated.

The only silver lining in the deal had been the rapid appreciation of real estate values in San Diego, which had allowed me to come up with more and more funds. Also, I somehow still managed to work on the radio show and earn money, which, along with my modest church salary, helped keep me current with the restitution and alimony payments.

One single decision, which was mine alone, was the primary reason why the tire company failed. I had made a deal with the Internet retailer to give them 30% of our sales in exchange for their prominently placing us on their Web site. Why did I offer such an outrageous percentage? The best I can remember is I offered that percentage because I had promised everyone that our company would be the tire and wheel business that this Internet retailer would choose to place on their highly trafficked Web site. The only way I could make sure that we got the account was to make an offer they could not refuse. However, it turned out to be a rotten business decision made out of desperation which ultimately buried the company.

No matter how hard I tried to salvage the company or how much money Tony, the third investor, or I poured into it, it was an uphill battle and a losing proposition. I thought back to what a good friend and extremely successful businessman and church member told me one day after watching me juggle church life with the tire business. "Barry, if God isn't in something, you will never succeed no matter how hard you work." How right he was. It truly seemed that no matter how hard I fought, worked, and sold, this tire company was divinely doomed. Even the one retail tire store we had purchased was operating in the red every month. In fact, if the original owner of that store had not allowed us to utilize a business credit line that he had established in his name, the store would have gone broke six months earlier. I finally met with Tony Jaime and the third investor, and we concluded that the only right thing to do was to turn the one retail tire store that we had bought back over to the original owner, close down the Web site, and cut our losses. Barry Minkow had once again failed in business.

Life was a good teacher; I was simply a poor student.

⌁

As I contemplated how I could somehow avoid what looked to be an imminent business failure with the tire venture, I retrieved an e-mail from Melissa

Koen, a young thirteen-year-old seventh grader who attended the church. The subject line was titled "Help."

How in the world can I help a seventh grader? Doesn't she realize I'm busy? Better yet, why doesn't she go to her mom and dad or our junior high pastor? I'm busy trying to figure out how to save this company! I angrily double clicked on the e-mail. What I read caused my heart to skip a beat.

> Dear Pastor Barry,
>
> My life is empty and I want to commit suicide. I have tried to pray these feelings away, but nothing seems to work. I talked to my parents and they asked that I write you directly. I am in so much pain, and I do not know what to do or where to turn. Can you please help me?
>
> Love,
> Melissa

That's when it hit me. With my head in my hands, I read the e-mail three more times, not knowing what to do or how to respond. After the initial feelings of guilt for complaining about the e-mail subsided, I began to do some serious thinking.

What the hell am I doing! I thought bitterly. I am so caught up, distracted, and involved in this awful business world that I am missing what is really important in life. I wondered how many other Melissa's were out there who may have wanted to e-mail me with similar struggles but did not because I was so preoccupied with making money that I was not accessible to them and therefore not meeting their needs. The guilt finally disconnected my thoughts from the disease of rationalization. I kept repeating to myself over and over again, *What am I doing in Los Angeles trying to make some tire company succeed when I am needed in San Diego?*

For the first time in months, I took an inventory of myself. I was running away, and the escape vehicle from my San Diego pain was a tire business in Los Angeles. Instead of going through the normal process of healing, I had chosen to run. Run to the security of a pot of gold at the end of the Internet rainbow. Sure, I needed money to pay off the debt of the marriage, the alimony, and the restitution, but I did not have to start another business to pay off that debt. Instead, I could have scheduled more fraud speeches, expanded the radio show, or even worked nights at a supermarket. But those outlets had been less attractive because they required no geographical relocation. Melissa's e-mail forced me to examine my real motives for starting the tire company. Those rationalizations shadowed the overwhelming desire to run away. *Same old Barry.*

I immediately rang Melissa. I remember pacing back and forth in that office as I talked to her. I told her that I loved her and was concerned about her thoughts of suicide. I asked why she believed that suicide was her only option. She explained that she struggled with feelings of guilt and living up to the expectations of others. She felt lonely and isolated and despite her many prayers, those feelings did not subside. Then there was the pressure of being a Christian and having those kinds of feelings. After all, Christians are supposed to be joyful, not entertain thoughts of suicide.

As I listened to her ruminate I realized she and I had a lot in common. Both of us were in emotional pain, and both of us sought unhealthy outlets to deal with that pain. I was counting on a business endeavor in another town to overcome my feelings of loneliness while Melissa was seeking a permanent escape. I decided to take a chance and openly shared with her the pain that I was going through and the mistakes I had made. We talked for almost an hour, and as was the case with the man in the motel years earlier, I was the one who benefited the most from the intervention. I then spoke with her parents about some professional counseling and thanked them for allowing me to speak directly with their daughter.

I remember how appreciative they were for my taking so much time with Melissa. If they only knew it was really me who needed the help! As it turned out, a thirteen-year-old girl revealed to me more about myself than I ever could have known without her. I had some decisions to make that involved tires and not a vehicle of escape. It was time to pay the piper.

~

With the decision to close down the tire venture, I knew I would need money to pay back the handful of investors and suppliers. At least the tire store was not a publicly held company. Admittedly, our original plan was to build up the tire store's online presence over eighteen months to become an attractive takeover or merger possibility for a current publicly-traded company. (As usual, I had been busy looking at the end result and not focusing on what needed to be done day-by-day.) Mercifully, that did not happen or I would have faced stockholder lawsuits.

The other good news was that there was no bank debt aside from the credit line in the name of the tire store owner. But a few of the people who had lost money I did not personally know, and if I did not pay them back, fraud accusations would fly. I needed to make a lot of money very quickly, by the summer of 2000. The one place I could do that was the fraud prevention speaking circuit.

During the eighteen months I spent working on the tire deal, I had received countless invitations to speak. I had politely declined, asking to be kept in mind for future speaking engagements. Without hesitation, I went back to all those e-mails and blasted out an "I'm available" message in hopes of securing immediate engagements. I received so many positive replies I was forced to quit the radio show, which had run for four years. There was no way I could lead a church, speak at fraud seminars, and host the radio show, and the fraud seminars paid better. I also refinanced my house again, using the proceeds to settle debts from the tire venture.

The third investor and I decided to split the remaining debt between us. After about six months of flying all over the country performing speaking engagements and earning as much money as I could while keeping current with my restitution payments, I was finally able to secure notarized paid-in-full releases from the final three investors. Only one of them had threatened to sue me for—that's right—fraud!

While in the midst of trying to juggle the various demands on my time, I found out that Teresa had remarried. There would be no reconciliation or a second chance. The irony was I had started the business in part to win Teresa back.

To combat the pain from the news of Teresa's remarriage, I decided to reestablish some kind of personal life for myself. I met a very nice and beautiful Christian woman and began a relationship with her. But I was not ready. While she was looking for a good man she could respect, I was just the opposite. I was a selfish, angry, and manipulative man rebounding from a disastrous marriage. I was not surprised when the relationship ended.

Strain from my business and personal failures began to spill over into my leadership at the church. I made several poor decisions, some of which even embarrassed our entire church.

Finally, the one area that I thought I could count on, my health, became an issue. The overwhelming stress from eighty-hour workweeks and constant trips back and forth from San Diego to L.A. caught up with me: I began to suffer from panic attacks. Barry Minkow, the guy who could speak in front of thousands of people without blinking an eye, was afraid to appear in front of my own congregation. Terrified, I sought the help of a professional. I spent several hours with a psychopharmacologist who told me that I had experienced more stress and emotional devastation in the last three years than most people do in a lifetime. He prescribed Ativan, a rigid diet and exercise program, and some time off.

I tried to take comfort from that great Winston Churchill quote: "Success is going from failure to failure without losing enthusiasm." I wisely followed the doctor's advice and took some time off. Taking a long drive to the Miramar Hotel in Santa Barbara where my father used to take us on vacation as children, I checked into the hotel and walked down the familiar sloped driveway that ran from my room to the pool area. I thought back to when I walked that very path when I was little and did not have the problems I now faced. How good life was then! I longed to return to the days when social security meant I was having dinner with my family and childhood friends.

I lay by the pool and replayed the events from early 1999 to June of 2001. I had failed in a marriage, failed in a new relationship, failed in business . . . again, and was currently in the process of failing as a senior pastor. My health was terrible. I thought about Melissa Koen, the guy from the motel, and my failed relationships. I glanced over at what appeared to be a happy family splashing and laughing in the pool. The father had his daughter in his arms, teaching her to swim, while the mother watched protectively. Here I was with no wife, no children, virtually no money, and perhaps even no career. For the first time since prison, I began to seriously doubt my ability to do anything right. I needed help but was too proud to ask.

Where was Peanut when I needed him?

～

In prison we kill our wounded. Some of the toughest opponents to change are not the skeptics who await us upon our release, but the cynics who work, eat, and sleep with us while we are doing time. Instead of coming together as a group and believing in one another, many inmates resort to tearing one another down. If you were an inmate who was trying to turn your life around for the better, you were fair game.

One memorable target was Ron Jordan, a.k.a. "Big Ron." Ron's cell was two down and on the same side of the hallway as the cell I shared with Peanut. Ron was about 6'3" tall and very strong. He grew up in the projects on Gorman Street in Watts and was as tough as anyone I ever met. On Sunday evenings he would come over to our "house" and listen to Dr. Tony Evans, an African American Bible teacher from Dallas, Texas. Ron and Peanut shared more in common than they cared to admit. Both were big, strong men who at one time were leaders in the gang world. Both were looked up to and respected by *all* inmates—black or white. Ron, like Peanut, had turned to Christianity to change the direction of his life and, as he added, "the direction of his eternity."

If Ron had one Achilles heel it was his temper on the playing field. He simply did not like to lose and rarely did because he was an exceptional athlete. Ron, Peanut, and I often talked about how best to control our tempers when we were playing sports. In prison, the best way to get labeled a hypocrite was to go to church on Sunday evening and cuss out another player in the softball game the next day.

On Monday evening there was a highly competitive softball game. Big Ron's team, which consisted primarily of all black men, was pitted against an all white team. The teams were tied for first place in our prison league. These kinds of square-offs always ended in some kind of fight, and this evening was no different. While Big Ron was playing catcher, an opponent tried to make it home from second base on a shallow single hit to leftfield. The leftfielder threw it right to Ron, who was covering homeplate. It was clear that the man was going to be tagged out. But rather than go peacefully, the man came in at full stride and tried to take Ron out. To this day I do not know what that guy was thinking, because hitting Ron was like slamming into a telephone pole while riding a moped!

Ron, angered by the man trying to take out his knees, retaliated. One punch knocked the man out. Instead of letting it end at that point, the other team rushed off the bench to challenge Ron—as if they needed to stick up for their buddy. It was truly like a scene from a movie. As each guy came to attack him with fists blazing, Ron promptly knocked him clean out!

After about five bodies littered home plate, the guards came to restore order. The most amazing thing of all was the guards did not take Ron to the hole for fighting! One of the perimeter drivers witnessed the entire incident from his truck and confirmed that Ron was defending himself and the attacks against him were unprovoked. Instead, they took the guys who cleared the bench to the hole along with the still-unconscious man who dove into Ron in his futile attempt to reach home plate. FCI Englewood had two trucks armed with shotguns that circled the prison twenty-four hours a day just to make sure no one thought of escaping, and thankfully for Ron, one of the drivers had saved him from a sure trip to solitary confinement.

That night after count the dorm was buzzing with what had happened on the softball field. Ron was clearly distraught as more than one person pointed out beating up five players was inconsistent with the Bible passage that says to turn the other cheek. Peanut wanted me to visit Ron's cell and encourage him.

"Why should I?" I halfheartedly complained.

"Because people who fail or make bad decisions need to be encouraged. Now stop being so selfish and get over there and encourage him," Peanut urged. I found Ron lying on the bottom bunk staring at the ceiling.

"Peanut sent you, didn't he?" Ron whispered. *How did he know?*

"Yeah, but I want to be here."

Ron repositioned himself on the bunk so he could sit up. We talked until midnight about everything from his childhood to how he used to use empty coffins to stash large amounts of drug money when he was a dealer. He explained that violence was the way he handled problems his whole life growing up in Watts. When he went into prison, he had promised his mother and his grandmother that he would never resort to violence to handle conflict— no matter what the situation.

His guilt came more from breaking that promise than the "I told you people don't change" criticisms issued by fellow inmates. I explained how I often resorted to my old ways of handling problems when confronted with certain situations. Before I returned to my cell, he actually gave me a quick hug, which is not something Big Ron Jordan was accustomed to doing. Peanut was still awake and reading silently.

"I'm glad you had me go over there, Peanut. It went great, and I learned a lot about Ron. I actually think I helped him. He wants to meet with me regularly for kind of an accountability relationship. I help him with his temper, and he helps me with my selfishness. Thanks." Peanut grinned in response.

"So why did you send *me* over there?" I asked.

"Because Big Ron Jordan is too proud to ask for help. Letting his guard down to someone like me is a lot more difficult than with you." I knew what he meant. Pride would prevent Ron from being vulnerable with Peanut, but not with me. Peanut continued: "The one thing I have learned in my years is that we need encouraging people in our lives after we make a serious mistake. The reason for that is what always accompanies failing is shame, guilt, and disgrace. And that makes reaching out for help all the more difficult. That's why I sent you over there."

Now I finally understood. I nodded my head and jumped onto my bunk. But before I went to bed I had a serious question.

"Hey, Peanut . . ."

"Yeah, what is it, Jew Boy?"

"Promise me when we get out of here that if I fail or make mistakes that you will be there for me. Promise me you won't let me flounder in my failures." Peanut leaned over the top bunk so I could see his face. He had taught me another critical truth—a truth I would need to implement years later. He smiled, looked me in the eye, and held out his fist.

"I promise I'll always be there for you, Barry." He hit the top of my fist as an oath.

⸏

When I strolled out of the pool area at the Miramar Hotel, I knew what I needed to do. There was no Peanut to turn to for help, so I prayed for people to enter my life who would help me. On the way home to San Diego, my cell phone jingled. It was Tony Nevarez, the chairman of the church elder board. He had watched me quietly from a distance the last two years of my life. Frankly, he had seen enough.

He told me that he and Dr. Gene French, the founding pastor of Community Bible Church and the man who years earlier had hired me to take his place, wanted to meet with me as soon as possible. I asked him the obvious: "Am I getting fired as the church pastor because of the mistakes I have made? Is that why you want to see me?" That was a fair question. At that time, a strong case could have been made for firing me as the senior pastor. Witnesses against me would include an ex-wife, an ex-girlfriend, perhaps one or two tire investors, and maybe even a few families who had left the church because of my blatant failures as a leader. I had no energy to defend myself, nor the will to. I quietly prayed for grace, not what I truly deserved—which was to be fired—but for yet another chance to come back from yet another failure. My heart stopped as I awaited Tony's response. What would he do? Grace, which I did not deserve, or justice, which I did. He chose the former.

"No, Barry, we don't want to meet with you to fire you. We want to help you. The only question I have is do you want to be helped?"

I started to breathe again.

I pictured Peanut's broad smile. "You bet I do."

17 THE PERFECT FRAUD STORM

The movie entitled *The Perfect Storm* is based on the true story of the disastrous collision of three separate storms in October of 1991. Although usually one storm cancels another out, this time three converged to give rise to a storm of mammoth proportions, a blockbuster Nor'easter off the New England coast. There is also a perfect storm for fraud. Three united elements can brew a heinous fraud with a giant wave likely to crush hapless investors like tiny toy sailboats in the open ocean. Sophisticated perpetrators of fraudulent schemes are good meteorologists when determining that the timing is right for massive fraud.

When interest rates are low, people are dissatisfied with a 4% annual return from their passbook accounts, and when these same people are watching their homes appreciate in value (while borrowing is made easy and also very inexpensive), conditions for a "perfect fraud storm" exist. People can easily get their hands on a six-figure dollar amount by simply refinancing their home or taking out a second mortgage at a low interest rate. Perpetrators count on this and seize the opportunity for exploiting people's naïveté. Only those of us who have ourselves perpetrated fraud are aware of these conditions. These conditions create once-in-a-lifetime opportunities to raise millions of dollars from unwitting investors.

During the time things had fallen apart in my personal life and business life (mid-2001), the conditions for a perfect fraud storm were subtly forming throughout California and in many other areas in the country.

Interest rates were low, property values were skyrocketing, and many people were dissatisfied with lackluster earnings on Wall Street, not to mention the poor performance of bank certificates of deposit. The three elements were there, but I was too preoccupied recovering from all my bad decisions to be of any use to investors who would pour their life savings into one of these dazzlingly attractive deals.

☙

"Your preaching is outstanding, as evidenced by five hundred people regularly attending each weekend. Your love for people is genuine. Your work at the San Diego Rescue Mission and in the prisons is inspiring to all of us. And the hours you work just so you can pay back Union Bank, the restitution, and all the debt from your marriage is admirable. But your decision making, maturity, and self-control are lacking. You are in desperate need of a life coach," Tony Nevarez counseled. He was seated in the living room of my home next to Dr. Gene French.

He paused and looked over to Dr. French for inspiration before continuing. "Let me put it to you this way: you are at a fork in the road. Right now you can either place yourself under the accountability of Dr. French as your mentor and learn from your past mistakes and from the wisdom a man with a vast amount of experience can offer. Or you can reject wise counsel and end up out of ministry or worse, back in prison. Because that's where you're heading."

His words were harsh but painfully true. I was at a crossroads in my life. At the time of our meeting, Dr. French and I did not know each other well. As a result, I was embarrassed that he was hearing about all my failures in such clear detail.

I was also embarrassed because during the almost four years of my pastorate at Community Bible Church, I had always avoided Dr. French. Not because he did not treat me with love and respect on the few occasions when our paths crossed, but because I felt that in order for me to succeed in the church that he had founded, I had to do things my way and not his.

Dr. French knew the church industry, but more importantly he also knew the real world of business and politics. He had been elected to the San Diego school board of education three times and to the community college board of trustees twice. So he was not some naïve, retired pastor. He sensed that I was slightly uncomfortable by what Tony had said so he jumped into the conversation.

"There is no shame in asking for help. Even the president of the United States has advisors," Dr. French remarked. "And I don't want you to become me, Barry. You have a unique, un-duplicatable style that I want to preserve. I just want to help you make more well-thought-out decisions and to train you how to be a better pastor and maybe even a better person in the process." His smile reflected the warmth and sincerity in his voice. I glanced down at my two faithful dogs, Arthur and Molly, lying quietly next to my feet.

I had always been suspicious of people who wanted to get close to me, stemming back to when I had been desperately hiding the reality of what was going on at ZZZZ Best. After all, no one is lonelier than when trying to conceal the rotten truth from everyone. But even when I had nothing to hide, getting close to people proved difficult—especially as a pastor. Whenever I had let my guard down in the past at the Church at Rocky Peak or at Community Bible Church, it never worked out.

Why? For the same reason people who love hotdogs and sausage should never watch how those foods are prepared, lest they lose their appetite for them entirely. In like manner, most who got close to me as a pastor were quickly disillusioned to find that I had feet of clay. But there was something in Dr. French's eyes, and Tony's for that matter, which told me those suspicions didn't belong here and now. As the chairman of our elder board, Tony was not paid by the church. So he was spending hours of his family time with me for no ulterior motive.

Dr. French certainly did not want his old job back as pastor. He simply wanted me to succeed. And best of all, these guys knew all about the many mistakes I had made and yet they still wanted to help me. I had preached about unconditional love before, but aside from God, family, Peanut, and my two dogs, I had never experienced it—until that evening at my house with Tony Nevarez and Dr. French.

"Tell me when and where you would like to meet, Dr. French. I'll be there. And I cannot thank you enough for giving me this opportunity," I said as I thrust my arm forward to shake his hand. Both men showed visible signs of relief.

∽

We were originally scheduled to meet once a week. Dr. French wanted to meet at my house so that there would be no distractions. If we had tried to meet at the office I would have been pulled in ten different directions in the first five minutes. He always brought an overhead projector and set it on my dining room table. I had no screen for it so we used the freshly painted white wall that separated the kitchen from the dining room. With bachelorhood comes blank walls and empty refrigerators, after all.

In one of our first meetings I remember him telling me something that transformed my life forever. What he said literally changed the way I approached speaking to all audiences.

"Barry, I want you to stop the con," he said. I said nothing as he placed his hands in his pockets, stepped over my Akita, Molly, and walked to the makeshift screen. Two words marred the clean walls like graffiti—*transparency* and *authenticity*.

"These two words represent what will be different about the way you teach. That is, the very next time you get up to speak and are making a point about selfishness, confess to the people in the audience that you are a selfish person who also struggles with that issue. And when they hear that come from your mouth, they will realize that you are preaching *to* them as a peer rather than *at* them from some bully pulpit. The result? They will not only listen, but better apply what they learn."

"Think about how many people have suffered through a painful divorce," he explained. "Instead of feeling sorry for yourself and trying to play the 'poor me' game—use that experience to help others who may be going through exactly what you did." He was picking up steam. My eyes were glued to him as an answer to the "why did God allow this to happen to me?" question was finally addressed—albeit indirectly. "Your problem is that you have spent the last few years trying to selfishly escape your personal pain instead of focusing on others. And it's that kind of selfish, me-centered thinking that brought down ZZZZ Best and will bring you down if it continues."

It was becoming clear to me. He was right. The bad decisions that I had made at the church, the tire company, and in my personal relationships were directly linked to a tunnel vision I had developed. By narrowing my focus, I could make the other painful parts of my life fade from vision and concentrate on me: how do I make *me* feel better, look better, have more, and all the rest? Ouch.

"Now there is one more thing you need to do," he said. I sat up straight and stared at him without blinking. "Just as you need to use your past experiences to help others in the church context, you now have to use your past experiences to help people from becoming victims of fraud. Now, I've talked to your elder board, and they want you to be proactive in the fraud prevention arena. They want you to meet with CEOs and CFOs of public companies and convince them of the real consequences that are associated with white-collar crime that will only be believed when presented by someone who did seven and a half years in federal prison. Who knows, maybe you can talk them out of ever committing fraud.

"Whatever the case, you need to focus on these two areas, because if you really want to contribute something back to society, you need to do what only you can do—help keep people from losing their life savings." He paused to make sure I was still listening before continuing. "You need to remember that you have been uniquely gifted to do two things well: preach and prevent fraud. Not run a tire company or any other business venture. Stick to those two things."

I thought back to the goal I had years before, after the Jaak Olesk Home Theater case, to actually uncover fraud. But because of the divorce, the failed tire business, and the radio show, I had never followed up on that dream. Now it was being presented to me from the mouth of someone I completely respected.

One word can describe how I felt at that moment. *Clarity*. My life was finally developing like a black and white photograph, the images of pain from the past joining with a vision of hope for the future. Dr. French concluded our time together that day by reminding me of a familiar story—a story that has been told for decades. It is a simple, real-life illustration I had spoken about but never applied.

It was the story of Wrong Way Roy Riggles in the 1929 Rose Bowl.

Remember him? He was the defensive back for Cal Berkley who picked up a fumble and ran sixty-five yards the wrong way in front of almost one hundred thousand people. His own teammate, Benny Lum, tackled him just a few feet before he scored for Georgia Tech. Although Cal ultimately lost the game 8 to 7, it was what happened at halftime that was most remembered. Coach Price of Cal waited until a few minutes before halftime was over before he announced that "the same team that started the first half will start the second half." Roy's teammates were stunned into silence as everyone processed what the coach had just said. *He's going to start Roy Riggles?* They grimaced in anger and disbelief. No one said a word. The only sounds that could be heard were the sobs of Roy Riggles. Coach Price approached him as he sat on the locker-room bench.

"Riggles, did you hear me? The same team that started the first half will start the second half. Now get your gear on and get out there!" Riggles looked up with tears in his eyes and said, "Coach, I just ran the wrong way in front of one hundred thousand people. I've embarrassed you; I've embarrassed my family; I've embarrassed this entire football program and this school. I just can't—"

Coach Price quickly interrupted him. "Sure you can, Riggles!" he exclaimed. "Because that mistake you made was in the first half of the game. Now I want you to go out there and play your heart out for me in the second half!" Roy Riggles, according to a few interviews with Georgia Tech players after the game, played with more tenacity in the second half than anyone they had seen in a long time. He didn't run with his second chance, he flew with it.

That day in my living room, my life was redirected. I was Wrong Way Roy Riggles, and Dr. French was Coach Price. I still had a full second half to play. For the next two years, Dr. French and I met every week and sometimes twice a week. People began to see a change in me. Although I tried to give the credit to the influence of Dr. French in my life, he insisted on staying in the background, behind the scenes.

༄

I was never one to believe in the love-at-first-sight theory. Talk about corny! That kind of sappiness is reserved for the chick movies I personally don't watch. Give me action and adventure anytime—I am familiar with that. Despite my disbelief, however, my eyes nearly protruded further than my nose when I met Lisa Palmer. Introduced to me through a mutual friend, Lisa and I had our first date at the Cheesecake Factory in Marina Del Ray in the summer of 2001. Lisa is one of those women you automatically equate with class by her polished composure. She has platinum blond hair, startling blue eyes, and long legs.

I had made the decision not to date any woman who attended Community Bible Church to avoid any conflict of interest. Lisa lived in Los Angeles and attended the same church that my mother had attended for twenty-five years, the Church on the Way in Van Nuys. She was thirty-four years old and worked as a cosmetic sales representative for a high-end line of facial creams. That explained her exquisite complexion. She supported herself with no outside help from family or friends, and in Los Angeles that is no easy task. She had never been married.

After our first date as I was making the now all too familiar drive back from Los Angeles to San Diego, I tried to pinpoint exactly what was attracting me so much to Lisa. I wanted to pick up the phone right then and ask her out again. Sure, she was beautiful, but there was something else that was drawing me to her. I replayed the night over in my head. And then it hit me. For some reason I did not feel the need to impress her. During our three-hour dinner and short walk afterward, we laughed, talked about our families, and just had fun. She was not concerned with how successful I was (or in my case wasn't) or how much money I had. In fact, when I told her I had been in prison and now owed twenty-six million in restitution, she answered by telling me that there were many things in her young life that she had done and was now ashamed of.

This was the first time in my life that I did not feel as though I had to be "better" than any man a woman knew or could possibly meet. She actually seemed to like me just because I was me.

❧

"I think that was the best speech I have ever heard," Steve Austin said. The man standing next to him, Sam Kephart, nodded in agreement. I had just completed an ethics talk for Point Loma Nazarene Business School. Steve and Sam were in the audience and had listened attentively. They asked me to go to lunch with them a few days later, and I accepted the invitation. We met at an upscale, downtown San Diego hotel.

A little background check before the meeting revealed that Steve Austin was a well respected partner in a regional accounting firm in San Diego and Sam Kephart was a technology guru who made a living at taking boring, online training materials and making them interactive and entertaining. During the lunch the two men told me about their vision for what would later become the Fraud Discovery Institute.

Steve was a solid man with quiet but unwavering fortitude. Sam, on the other hand, spoke as if almost each sentence ended with an exclamation point. The two were very different, but somehow balanced each other in conversation. And I immediately took a liking to them.

Sam suggested that he videotape many of my standard fraud prevention and ethics talks and put them on a newly developed Web site for bankers, underwriters, auditors, and executives to watch and learn about the techniques perpetrators utilize to con the innocent. Steve saw another value in the establishment of an institute. He envisioned me actually identifying and stopping what he called "hard fraud" in progress. "No one can spot fraud better than you, and millions of people lose billions of dollars each year and there seems to be no end in sight," Steve said.

First, Dr. French had told me that fraud prevention was how I could best impact the very people I had once hurt, and now a professional CPA was confirming his recommendation.

"I am also aware that you have been making restitution payments and paying Union Bank back these past years—even though in the case of the former you were not required to," Steve added. I nodded in agreement. "To me, that proves that you have learned from your past and provides me a logically compelling reason to work with you in fighting fraud."

"He's right, Barry!" Sam said. "Steve is a very conservative accountant type who is careful about whom he associates with." I was silent but not from disagreement.

"And who knows," Steve pondered. "Maybe this fraud prevention and education venture will make enough money to pay all your victims back."

"Or better yet, maybe it will stop far more fraud than I ever perpetrated," I said. Before we finished our coffee, the Fraud Discovery Institute was born.

֍

Although I knew I wanted to marry Lisa after our first date, it took me eight months to convince her, and in February of 2002 we were married. It was the best day of my life—even better than the day I was released from prison! I still owed twenty-six million dollars in restitution, I still owed Union Bank, and I was still on federal probation, but none of that mattered after I married Lisa. People at the church adored her, and I cannot say I blame them. "You're an answer to prayer," they would always tell her. She *was* an answer to prayer—my prayer!

Lisa and I both wanted to have children, but because of my steroid abuse as a teenager it was not likely that we could have children naturally. I remember fearing her reaction to my confession about this before we were married. Her response only confirmed what I had thought about her. She explained that she was adopted at birth and had no trouble with the possibility of adopting our own children. She told me not to feel bad and that having children naturally or by adoption were equally good options. With Lisa as my wife and Dr. French as my mentor, my life was finally headed in the right direction.

֍

"All rise. This court is now in session. The United States of America versus Barry Minkow. The honorable Judge Dickran Tevrizian now presiding."

Hearing those words brought back bad memories. Only fourteen years earlier Judge Tevrizian had sentenced me to twenty-five years in prison and ordered me to pay back twenty-six million dollars. At that sentencing hearing he had said, on the record, that I had "no conscience." The media never forgot that quote; every time a story was done profiling me, the comment was consistently cited. But at the time, the judge's description fairly depicted my behavior regarding the ZZZZ Best fraud.

However, as I sat in the courtroom on August 2, 2002, I was not there because of something I had done wrong. On the contrary, this time I was there to discuss an early release from my probation and the subsequent dismissal of the twenty-six-million-dollar restitution order. And just like fourteen years earlier, I was represented by David Kenner. However, the prosecution team had changed. Instead of James Asperger, the former chief of the major frauds unit of the Los Angeles United States Attorney's Office sitting across from me, Gregory Weingart was now my adversary.

I had kept in touch with Judge Tevrizian, even when I was released from prison. Every December I would send him a Christmas card and briefly tell him what was happening in my life. When he took the bench that day, he was all smiles. Gone were the scowls and angry tones once directed at me. They were now replaced with genuine concern and applause for a life that he believed had turned around. There was a brief discussion, and then Judge Tevrizian insisted on reading a letter that had been sent to him before the hearing, a letter from none other than my former prosecutor, James Asperger.

In that letter, Asperger asked the judge to release me from probation based on my work with the Fraud Discovery Institute and at the church. He told the judge that he believed that I had truly changed and deserved a second chance. As the judge read the letter, I sat quietly at the defense table with tears in my eyes. Only God could have orchestrated that the same prosecutor who got me convicted at trial and rightfully defamed me with great vigor was now arguing for my early release and a second chance. When the judge finished reading the letter into the record, he made a few of his own comments, which I have taken directly from the official transcript.

Seven years, four months. And based on, you know, some of the other—I call them "robber-barons"—around the country, you did serve a substantial amount of time in custody. We have another problem facing our country now with corporate dishonesty. I hope that maybe you can talk to some of these other people. Go in and investigate some of these frauds, as Mr. Asberger says that you're doing and bring others to justice in this particular matter. . . . I will grant the request for early termination of his probation. I will need an order prepared for my signature, but as far as I'm concerned, he's off probation as of today.

Poof! The twenty-six-million-dollar restitution order was dismissed, and I was off of federal probation three years early. When I drove home from the courthouse that day I focused on when the judge said: "Go in and investigate some of these frauds, as Mr. Asperger says that you're doing, and bring others to justice in this particular matter."

First, Dr. French had told me to pay back society by investigating fraud proactively. Then, Steve Austin and Sam Kephart, after the speech at Point Loma Nazarene, provided the model through which I could actually investigate and stop fraud proactively by forming the Fraud Discovery Institute. But when Judge Tevrizian all but ordered me, on the record, to go and investigate some of these frauds, my life's calling finally sank in.

The drive home seemed quick, but as usual I was using it as a time to reflect. I remembered sitting by the pool in Santa Barbara thinking that my life was over, feeling the pain and consequences of my past decisions and praying that God would send me Peanut—or someone like him—to rescue me. But it was not through one person; it was through three people that prayer was answered.

The first was Tony Nevarez who, instead of firing me, reached out and intervened in my life. The second person was Dr. French, who gave me clarity and vision for the future by spending numerous hours with me. Finally, and most importantly, was Lisa. She provided the one thing I had been searching for in a relationship and had never found. Someone who loved me for me—no matter how many times I failed.

I couldn't help but think during the drive home that if Peanut were here, he would be proud of me. Not because I had done something great, but because I did not quit when I spiraled into failure. I was now ready to take on the world, and as it turns out, I would need to be. That perfect fraud storm was forming and gaining momentum, and I was right in its path. Only now I was ready for it.

18 | THE CURE, PART ONE

The greatest irony in the fraud perpetration business is that those of us who perpetrate fraud are far more gullible than the victims of our schemes. In my experience, no one who has ever perpetrated a material fraud has not first factored a core principle into their thinking. In fact, only those exclusive members of the fraud perpetration club know this principle, and it is a four-letter word: *cure*. We, while in the midst of our criminal activity, do not like to view ourselves as crooks. We also are not naïve enough to believe that we can continue lying and defrauding investors ad infinitum and not get caught.

So we convince ourselves of an even bigger fraud than the one we are perpetrating. The lies we are telling investors, bankers, auditors, or stockholders are justified because they are a means to an end and not an end in themselves. We have a cure that only we know about that will rescue us from our misdeeds by creating enough income to pay back everyone who has invested with us.

For example, the cure for dishonest brokers or traders who have carefully concealed their losses is "that one good trading day" that will result in enough profits to cover the losses they have been hiding. The cure for me at ZZZZ Best was slightly different. My goal was to keep lying to Wall Street, the auditors, the bankers, and the stockholders until my six million shares of ZZZZ Best stock became free-trading. Once they became free-trading, I planned on selling one or two million shares, raising eighteen to thirty million dollars, paying off the mob and all the other investors, and going legit.

Thus the cure accomplishes two critical purposes. First, it helps rationalize illegal behavior based on the fact that it is only temporary. Second, it convinces us that there is redemption, a light at the end of the fraud tunnel, and we simply need to hold on until we can reach that day when all will be made right. That we believe this lie is evidence enough of our gullibility.

No case better illustrates perpetrators' gullibility and the principle of the cure than the one involving Ernest F. Cossey and James Garro. Cossey owned a company called TLC Investments and Trade Company. According to SEC documents he raised $156 million from over twenty-six hundred investors to allegedly purchase distressed real estate, fix it up, and sell it at a profit. However, the SEC alleged that TLC Investments and Trade Company was nothing more than a Ponzi scheme where new investor money was used to pay back old investors.

Cossey realized that time, the enemy of all Ponzi schemes, was his fraud's mortal enemy. He had offered investors in his real estate venture large returns that he was having trouble continuing to pay. Enter James Garro, who himself was running a prime bank scheme offering people an international government bond program that, according to the court-appointed receiver in the TLC Investments and Trade Company case, "would pay returns significantly in excess of those available to other investors in similar instruments."

Cossey needed a cure, something that would rescue him from the cash he needed to pay back his investors in TLC Investments and Trade Company. James Garro told Cossey that if he gave him twenty million dollars, he would receive back forty million dollars in a matter of weeks. Cossey should have known better, but when people are desperate . . .

Cossey knew that these kinds of returns (100%) were not possible as evidenced by the fact that the returns he was offering investors in his deal were not real. No one knew that fact better than he did. Yet because Cossey wanted to believe that a quick cure would rescue him, he gave Garro twenty million dollars in hopes of getting forty million dollars back to pay off his investors in TLC Investments and Trade Company. It is no surprise that Cossey never received the forty million and the court-appointed receiver who took over TLC Investments and Trade Company sued Garro for the twenty million dollars.

The above example proves two points. First, perpetrators are gullible by definition because we believe that our deceit is temporary, and a sure-fire cure will somehow rescue us. Second, this mindset leaves us vulnerable to other frauds as evidenced by Cossey's actually handing over twenty million dollars in hopes of receiving double in return. There is an odd strain of justice woven throughout that irony. The criminals are the ones who believe the bigger lie.

∽

"Come on, Barry. Just take a look at the package. My partner and I want to invest about two hundred thousand in the deal, but we want you to check it out first," Lane urged. "The deal looks fine, but because we do not know the principles involved in the investment, we want to err towards caution."

"All right," I answered reluctantly. I gently tugged the Fed Ex package that Lane had sent me out from under a tower of papers. It was dated May 5, 2003. "I will do some checking and let you know. But remember, my expertise is in training people how to identify fraud, not in finding it myself," I cautioned. As soon as the words left my mouth, I knew I had contradicted myself.

"That's great. You can teach people how to find fraud but you cannot find it yourself!" he quipped. "That doesn't make any sense." Lane had a point.

"Okay, you win," I conceded with a big sigh. "Give me a couple of days, and I will see what I can find."

"Great, Barry—and thanks. And work as quickly as you can, because if this deal is legitimate, I want to invest as quickly as possible," he said.

"You have my word," I promised.

The brochure was a full-color, glossy, custom-created and laser-cut dossier. It was intentionally designed to both impress and impute credibility. Obviously, it was working, as Lane Biggs had explained that the company, MX Factors, LLC of Riverside, California, had raised about fifty million dollars in investor money comprising hundreds of people in at least three states. As I thumbed through the package I soon learned that MX

Factors, LLC claimed to factor receivables for construction companies performing work on government contracts. Further study revealed these companies who were awarded certain lucrative government contracts had no way to finance them because of the tight lending policies of banks and the long period of time they had to wait to get paid by the government.

MX Factors lent the construction company money using their accounts receivable as collateral, which then enabled them to continue performing on more contracts. The promised return to investors was 12% every ninety days, or if you let it roll over, 57% annually.

The company was run by a man named Richard Harkless. His biography indicated that he had years of experience in the collections business, had earned an MBA from a recognized school, and actually taught MBA classes at USC and Pepperdine. The package also listed the Better Business Bureau and Dunn & Bradstreet as references. A long list of satisfied investors and their phone numbers were listed in bold script. There was even a factoring customer included to confirm how the process worked from one of the borrowers.

However, one reference immediately caught my eye: Pam Pallan from Business Bank of Nevada. For a bank officer to be listed as a reference for an investment opportunity was not something I had ever seen before. I remember thinking that to have earned that kind of credibility, Harkless and MX Factors had to be legitimate. On the periphery everything about MX Factors appeared to be in order, and I could easily see, based on the professional presentation contained in the dossier, why people were investing millions of dollars in the company.

Of course the promised returns were high, but I initially rationalized that the receivables factoring business could be risky and therefore lenders might charge a premium to their customers. Further, MX Factors had attracted a large number of investors. If this were not a legitimate deal, surely someone would have found out by now—especially the Business Bank of Nevada. At that point, I determined it was time to perform due diligence and analyze the investment opportunity objectively.

The impressive, high-gloss dossier, the Better Business Bureau membership, the Dunn & Bradstreet reference, the bank official's phone number, and even the many satisfied investors were *not* indicators of authenticity. No one knew that better than I did. Why? Because ZZZZ Best was a member of the Better Business Bureau, had television commercials airing in three states, possessed a high-gloss prospectus, had thousands of happy investors, and even boasted a few bank references. I had to remember my past and set aside the initial subjective impressions and move to the objective methodology of evaluating MX Factors.

I thought back to the Jaak Olesk Home Theater deal and how I had always wanted, since late 1995, the opportunity to proactively uncover a financial crime in progress. But secretly I doubted my own abilities. Who was I to make a judgment call on the authenticity of an investment deal? I certainly did not know more than the hundreds of investors in MX Factors. Giving fraud speeches was one thing, but actually uncovering a fraud in progress was a whole different ballgame. I started to climb up the doubt ladder. I wanted to call Lane back and tell him that I was off MX Factors.

As I reached for the phone I remembered what Dr. French had said: "Barry, you are good at two things: preaching and fraud prevention."

Maybe he was right, I hoped. *Maybe I can be good at identifying investment fraud simply by remembering the techniques I used to deceive the masses and then testing for their presence in other deals.*

I certainly would never know unless I tried. I got up from behind my desk and paced back and forth on a well-worn patch of carpet in my office. I glanced at the picture of Peanut that I had framed below my bookshelf and remembered the lesson he had taught me during the prison football game: "Don't quit, Barry—you've been a quitter all your life."

Then I considered how many victims from the ZZZZ Best fraud were impacted because of my actions; with that case, there had been twenty-six million dollars in total victim impact. If MX Factors turned out to be a fraud, more than double that amount was at stake. For years I had talked about wanting to help people from becoming victims of fraud. Now I had the opportunity to make that dream a reality. The dream was now being compromised by excuses.

My conscience finally won the battle. I convinced myself to thoroughly check out the MX Factors investment opportunity. If the deal was legitimate, no one would ever know I was performing due diligence on the company. If the investment turned out to be fraudulent, I could save future investors from making a devastating mistake.

❦

It was time to get to work. There were four things I needed to do, and I needed to do them quickly. First, I had to independently prove the profitability of MX Factors. Here I had an advantage. At ZZZZ Best I dealt with factors as a way of raising money for my fraudulent restoration jobs. I had approached factors with bogus receivables, and although my success was limited, I managed to raise a few hundred thousand dollars and, more importantly for the challenge I now faced, I learned how the process of factoring receivables worked. Anytime money is lent against a receivable a UCC-1 lien is filed by the lender to publicly record their interest in that receivable—kind of like the deed of trust a lender places on a home. For factors, this is a critical part of the process because if there were no UCC-1 filing system, a company could borrow against the same receivable through different factors multiple times. Thus the UCC-1 process prevents a "double borrowing" from occurring.

I searched the UCC-1 filings for MX Factors as the lien holder and found sixteen companies showing MX Factors as the lien holder. Over a two-day period in between handling church calls and writing a sermon, I tracked each company down and found disconnected phone numbers, out of business companies, contractors whose licenses had been revoked, and in one case a lawsuit that MX Factors had filed because of a client's lack of payment. Additionally, one of the people listed, a chiropractor from Riverside, did not know why he and his wife were listed as debtors as they were currently investors in MX Factors. In the end, of the sixteen companies listed on the UCC-1 public record, only one verified that they used MX Factors.

I was immediately reminded of how ZZZZ Best operated. My fraud fable had involved restoration jobs on behalf of insurance companies. But when anyone ever pressed us for addresses of these job sites, we could never provide them because the restoration jobs did not exist. Now, almost seventeen years later, Harkless was raising money for a factoring business that seemingly had no customers.

I immediately called Don Ray, a public records expert and journalist. If Don did not exist, someone would need to invent him. He is by far the most brilliant person in the field of public record searches while at the same time probably the most unorganized guy I had ever met. I loved and respected Don and appreciated his work. I told him about MX Factors and asked him to recheck my UCC-1 search to see if I missed anyone. I also asked him to perform a complete public records search on Rick Harkless and MX Factors.

Second, I sought an answer to the "who would know" question. If Harkless could pay 12% every three months to investors from the factoring business, then I needed to speak to experts in that industry to see if these kinds of returns were consistent with other factoring companies. After several hours of research, I tracked down three of the biggest government contract-factoring companies in the country, and all of them agreed on one point: the returns MX Factors were offering were way out of line with the industry standard. One of the men I spoke with even said that for a customer to pay MX Factors enough money for MX Factors to make a profit and pay investors 57% annually, that customer would need to pad his government contracts so heavily that he would never be awarded the contract in the first place. I also contacted the International Factoring Association, a trade organization where major players in the factoring industry become members. The IFA had never heard of MX Factors or Richard Harkless. This struck me as odd: if a company were factoring enough receivables to pay hundreds of investors millions of dollars in commissions derived from factoring receivables, wouldn't a major trade organization have heard of them?

Third, I checked their financial statements, which they had submitted to Dunn & Bradstreet. The impression most people have is that Dunn & Bradstreet actually audits the numbers that are submitted to them, but as they often disclose, they do not audit these numbers. Since the average person believes they do, however, perpetrators often encourage those performing due diligence on their company to pull a Dunn & Bradstreet report so investors will see their inflated numbers on Dunn & Bradstreet letterhead. Presto, instant credibility. A cursory examination of the financial statements of MX Factors revealed that the company claimed to have earned almost seventeen million dollars in revenue—and yet I only found one customer.

Finally, Don Ray found through a public records search that the one customer was actually a company partly owned by Richard Harkless. This ownership was not disclosed in the offering materials, but rather the company was made to look like an authentic, independent customer of MX Factors. My preliminary conclusion was finished: MX Factors had fifty million dollars in investor money and was paying those investors 12% every ninety days through a factoring business that had no customers.

Initially, Tim France was reluctant to see me. He is a United States postal inspector located in downtown San Diego. Based on my research of MX Factors, and considering that the fifty-million-dollar fund was growing daily, I believed it was time to inform law enforcement of my preliminary findings.

I chose the postal inspector route because in prison everyone used to say, "Don't mess with the postal inspectors! They will nail you every time." Postal inspectors had the reputation of being aggressive with the prosecution of white-collar crime. But when you are Barry Minkow, phoning your local federal official and telling him that you have just stumbled on to a potential fraud is a little daunting. I expected hesitation and prayed there would not be any insinuation of a prank call.

France had a modest-sized office whose walls appeared to be a shrine devoted to his love of golf. He agreed to see me on short notice but asked that I be prepared at our meeting as his schedule was tight because of an upcoming trial.

"Look, Mr. France," I declared, "I realize I am an ex-con and I have no credibility, but there is a fifty-million-dollar potential Ponzi scheme happening right now in your jurisdiction!" France was responsible for the Riverside and San Diego zones.

"Tell me your story, Mr. Minkow, and do not worry about your past. I am aware that you have helped train law enforcement in the area of fraud prevention. I'll give you the benefit of the doubt. Now tell me what's going on with this MX Factors deal." I remembered that Frank Gulla had made a similar statement to me when I had first been released from prison. Now a federal investigator was giving me a chance, an opportunity to prove that

I could help uncover a financial crime in progress. I did not want to let him down.

I explained how I found out about MX Factors and what my preliminary due diligence had uncovered. I gave him a packet of information that included the UCC-1 searches, which proved there were no customers, and the high-gloss offering materials given to Lane to persuade him to invest. I also told him that the financial statements appeared inconsistent, and that no one in the factoring industry could see how Harkless could offer investors a 12% return every ninety days. I provided him with the phone numbers of each factoring industry expert.

"Very impressive, Mr. Minkow. Have you gone to the SEC with this information?" he asked.

"No sir, I haven't. The people at the SEC don't like me very much. Something about a securities fraud I perpetrated about seventeen years ago," I mumbled. He smiled.

"I've got contacts in the L.A. office of the SEC, and they need to see this right away."

"So you're going to shut them down?" I asked.

"No, I'm not going to shut them down, Barry. There are no victims screaming that they haven't received their money back yet, and just because you say it is a fraud doesn't mean it is a fraud. In this country we still need to give people the benefit of the doubt."

His answer was not what I expected. How much more evidence did he need? Surely he realized that perpetrators keep investors happy for a reason. Just because no one was screaming for their money back did not mean MX Factors was legitimate. Either MX Factors had customers or they did not. If they did not, then it was an obvious Ponzi scheme because the company had no way of earning the money to pay the returns they were promising their investors.

Nevertheless, France was right. The government needed time to independently confirm my findings before they could act. France realized that I was taken aback by his comment.

"Listen, Mr. Minkow. I appreciate this information very much. You have done a great job with almost no resources at your disposal. And whatever other information you may uncover, please get it to me ASAP, okay?"

"Sure, Mr. France," I said as I stood up to shake his hand to leave. "I will keep you posted."

༄

"You're on another fraud case, aren't you?" Barbara Brown asked. I ignored her and continued typing on the keyboard with my eyes glued to the screen.

"You realize that you are still a pastor." I kept typing. She kept persisting.

"Betty Roy is in the hospital." I stopped typing and met her motherly stare.

"I'm sorry, what did you say?" I asked.

"Betty Roy is in the hospital, and she wants you to go visit her when she gets out of surgery tomorrow." Barbara knew Betty Roy was special to me. Betty was an elderly black lady who was like my second mother. She called me "Boy" and always made sure I was spending enough time with my wife, Lisa. Everyone at the church loved Betty Roy, and I was so absorbed in the MX Factors case that I did not know she was having surgery.

"Is it serious?" I inquired.

"Whenever you are in your seventies and have surgery it is serious, Barry," Barbara replied in a serious tone. "Are you going to visit her?"

"Of course I am," I snapped. "It will take me until tomorrow to finish this letter and then I will go visit Betty."

"What are you writing?"

"I am writing about what I think is a fifty-million-dollar fraud," I answered somberly.

"Sounds like a lot of money. You sure about this?"

"Yeah, I'm sure. But only because I have been there and done that." Of course I got a jumpsuit, not a T-shirt.

༄

No longer impressed by the high-gloss dossier or the affiliation with the bank or Better Business Bureau, I addressed a five-page letter to Richard Harkless, the founder of MX Factors, and copied his lawyer of record, George Gonzales from the San Diego-based law firm of Gordon and Rees, whose name I found from the lawsuit filed by MX Factors when I was tracking down the sixteen companies that appeared in the UCC-1 search. In the letter, I explained that I was an ex-convict and that I had been asked to look into the MX Factors business opportunity.

I noted that experts in the receivables factoring industry had said the return on investment being offered by MX Factors was unheard of in the factoring business. Next, I disclosed how I ran extensive public record searches and found only one customer—and that customer was partly owned by Harkless. I pointed out the clear inconsistencies with the financial statements that had been submitted by Harkless to Dunn & Bradstreet. I also qualified all my points by stating, "I could be wrong here but . . ."

I sent a copy of my letter to the Better Business Bureau in Riverside because they were listed as a reference for MX Factors. After reading the letter, Gary Almond, the general manager of that office and a longtime friend, wasted no time and immediately revoked MX Factors from the Better Business Bureau's membership. He then placed them on "unsatisfactory" status. Almond also forwarded my letter about MX Factors to the California Department of Corporations enforcement division.

In like manner, upon receiving the letter, Harkless wasted no time in calling me. He explained that my information was not considering all the facts and that my conclusions were wrong. He claimed to have many factoring customers in Mexico. He also said that his company was currently going through an audit, and he assured me that when the audit was done, all my questions would be answered. He told me to "hold off a month or so before I showed my letter to anyone else" and then he would gladly sit down with me and explain where I was wrong. Our call ended without time for me to ask questions.

I knew that Harkless would not meet with me. He was buying time, just like I used to do when my back was pressed against the wall. Guilty people do that when they are faced with possible exposure. The fact that he called me almost immediately after receiving the letter proved to me that I had hit a nerve.

Two days later his lawyer, George Gonzales, sent a Federal Express letter to my home threatening me with libel, insulting me based on the fact that I was a convicted felon, and stating that my motives were less than pure for checking into Harkless in the first place. He told me if I sent that letter to anyone else I would be slapped with a lawsuit claiming slander and libel for millions of dollars.

Lisa read the letter and was visibly upset. She asked me if I was sure about MX Factors being a fraud. When I told her I was positive she added, "Are you willing to bet our house on it? Because this lawyer is going to sue us for everything we own if you are wrong." I understood her frustration.

"Trust me on this, honey," I said firmly. "I know I am right."

"If you are right then why didn't law enforcement close this guy down after you explained to them what was going on?" she asked.

"They will, honey. Trust me," I said as I wrapped my arms around her.

"Okay, I believe in you, Barry," she said as she returned the squeeze. The pressure was mounting.

꿈

As a pastor it was not uncommon for the phone to ring at 1:30 a.m. I searched for the receiver, still half-asleep and squinted at the clock. *This better be good,* I thought.

"Barry Minkow?" the voice asked on the other end.

"Yes, this is Barry Minkow."

"If you continue causing problems for MX Factors you will not live to preach another day," said a menacing voice.

"I'm sorry—I think I missed that," I said as I sat up in the bed.

"You heard me. You're gonna die if you keep writing letters about MX Factors. If you even so much as make another phone call and mention that company's name—I'll kill you! You will get no further warning." The dial tone buzzed in my ear.

꿈

The next day Lane called me at the office. He had also received a threatening letter from George Gonzales stating that he would sue Lane because Lane was the one who had asked me to look into MX Factors. *These guys play dirty,* I thought grimly. The letter explained that Lane was indirectly involved in getting the Better Business Bureau to remove MX Factors from "good standing" and placing them on "unsatisfactory" because he brought me into the picture. Lane was angry and explained that he did not have the time or the money to defend himself in a lawsuit and that I needed to drop the whole thing.

After I hung up the phone, I buried my head in my hands. I did not know what to do next. I mentally reviewed what had transpired in the last twenty-four hours. First, I was threatened with a lawsuit and my wife was scared. Then I received a death threat in middle of the night, and now Lane, the man who simply asked me to perform due diligence on his investment opportunity, was being threatened by a multimillion-dollar lawsuit.

"Barry," Barb whispered as she gently opened my door, "you have five counseling appointments today and the first one is here."

"How do I have five counseling appointments in one day?" I responded harshly.

"Because you have been so preoccupied with this MX Factors thing that you told me to hold everyone off as long as I could. And today was as long as I could," she said. "And these people need you. One of them was molested as a child and is struggling."

In all the excitement I had forgotten I was still a pastor. And as a pastor I had to be keenly aware of the fact that there were a lot of hurting people out there who needed help. I could not just turn them away.

"Send them in." I quietly prayed for the ability to take my mind off of my problems long enough to help others.

❦

It was 6:30 before the last appointment left. I was alone in my office as Barbara had left earlier. Five counseling sessions had taken their toll on my emotions. But so had the threats. I was scared. And that was an emotion I had not experienced since my first day in a maximum security cell. I picked up the MX Factors dossier from my desk. I thought back to the expression on Lisa's face when she received the letter from Gonzales. I remembered my earlier conversation with Lane and how distraught he was over being pressured by Gonzales. Then I thought about the late-night death threat. The good news was that because of how busy I was with counseling, I had not made any additional calls on the MX Factors deal. *At least I didn't ignore the threat*, I reasoned to myself.

I felt completely alone. The weight of the world was on my shoulders, and I had no one to help me, no one to protect me. *My life is in danger, I'm facing a multimillion-dollar lawsuit where I could lose my house and everything else I own, and for what?* I thought. *No one believes me anyway, so why even try?* With that, I yanked up the MX Factors dossier off my desk with the intention to toss it in the trash and forget about the whole damn thing. If people wanted to pour their hard earned money into this deal and not do their homework, that was fine with me. *It isn't worth dying for,* I said to myself.

Just as the dossier was leaving my hands for the garbage, I looked up and saw Peanut's picture on the bookcase staring me in the eye. Of all the places for the garbage can to be in my office, it had to be right under Peanut's picture.

Once again, I remembered prison.

19 | THE CURE, PART TWO

I'll be right there. Let me jump in the shower real quick, then I'll meet you on the yard," I screamed to Peanut as he was leaving our upper east unit. I grabbed my shampoo from the small, box-sized locker that sat on top of Peanut's locker next to the door of our cell. I always liked taking showers after the 10:00 a.m. Saturday morning count because they were never crowded during that period. Most inmates showered earlier in the morning or at night.

I wrapped the towel around my waste, grabbed my shampoo container, toothbrush, and toothpaste, and headed for the showers. Looking forward to playing basketball for most of the day, I concluded that my theology studies could wait until the evening. The sun was shining, and I was going to unwind after a long week of term papers and prison work duty.

As I entered the showers, I noticed two fully clothed men to my left in the far corner. They were hovering over a stall. I didn't know what they were up to and quickly deduced that I did not want to know. So I turned and went to the showers. And that's when I heard a muffled "Help." I stopped and turned around. One of the two men saw me pause and said, "This has nothing to do with you, Carpet King. Mind your own business and take your shower." Carpet King was another one of those endearing prison titles I had earned. Preacher Boy, Jew Boy, Mink, Carpet King—need I say more? The man had tattoos that covered both his arms. He was a little chunky in the middle and had a butch-type haircut.

I ignored the advice and moved closer to the activity. Looking under the stall, I could see someone was there, sitting with his back leaned up against the toilet. There was blood on the ground. He appeared dazed.

"What's going on, man?" I asked—as if I didn't know. The second man came out of the stall. I recognized him as someone who was in the last bench-press contest that was held at FCI Englewood. He was two weight classes ahead of me, but I had outbenched him, taking second in the contest.

I had been incarcerated long enough to learn one thing: prisons were ruled by intimidation. Whether by direct threat, by one's association with a particular gang, or just by the way certain men carried themselves, intimidation was the oil of the prison engine. And there were two choices when confronted with the "intimidation test." You either succumbed to the intimidation, were labeled "weak" and suffered accordingly, or you stood up to it. And every inmate who did a stretch of time in a maximum or medium security prison would be tested with a situation that revealed their choice. This was my test.

The first thing I noticed was the man leaning with his back to the toilet was Hispanic. So this was probably one of those prison racial things. The second thing I noticed was that I was naked—except for a towel. Standing up against two men, naked, put me at a clear disadvantage. And it was clear that based on the fact that I was not dressed, they were trying to intimidate me in hopes that I would back down. The last thing I concluded was that screaming for the cops was not an option. No one in prison liked a rat. I set my shampoo and toothbrush down. I rewrapped my towel as tightly as I could around my waist and walked closer to the stall.

"Hey guys, I don't want any trouble. Just let this young man go and no one needs to inform the cops." I bluffed, hoping they would take my advice.

"We're not going anywhere," the second man said. He moved closer to me to prevent me from helping the man out of the stall. He was wearing his prison-issued steel-toed shoes. Not good for me. If used correctly, those shoes could severely damage a shin or break a toe, specifically my shin or toe. My mind surveyed the situation. Because I had moved closer to the point of attack, I could not retreat. I was committed to act, but how? This was not a movie. One person who has taken prison karate for a few years does not magically take on two men—especially naked.

"I don't care how strong you think you are, Carpet King. There are two of us and one of you. And you just put yourself in our business, and I can't have you do that," he said. The intimidation was working. I glanced over at the sink to see if there was anything there that would help me fight these guys. Nothing—just soap. The guy from behind the toilet had crawled out of the stall wanting to see who was coming to his aid. He looked a little disappointed when he saw me.

They were both coming toward me. I backed up slowly. I noticed a guard out of the corner of my eye. He was a white guy with tattoos and had clearly decided to ignore what was going on. That was not particularly unusual. He was watching from just outside the entrance. I made a quick move between the two approaching men and ran to the back of the bathroom where the victim was recovering. I knelt down to help him. I became involved because of him, and I hoped that somehow my concern for him would discourage his attackers from pursuing me. It did not.

"Thanks for helping me," the man on the ground said. But before he finished the first man came at me and attempted to pull me by the elbow. The minute he touched me it was like a shockwave of adrenalin went through my body. I remembered hearing one time that the anticipation of a fight is often worse than the actual fight itself. How true. I quickly pulled my elbow from his grasp and rotated my hips as fast as I knew how and slammed my right fist into his big stomach. I heard a thud and he kind of keeled over, clearly trying to catch his breath. This did not sit well with his friend, and he lunged for me. I slipped back as I tried to avoid him and my back hit the cold, concrete bathroom floor. I lay there, dazed.

This was the end. I had tried to do a good deed and help someone and here I was, on my back without even being hit. There was not much I could do because I was literally cornered. The injured man tried to help me up. It was no use. The second man had paused while I fell but was now ready to kick me. And just before my life passed before my eyes, I heard a familiar voice.

"You know, a guy can't even forget his headphones and leave you alone for five minutes without you getting into some mess." I recognized the voice—it was Peanut's. I picked up my head slowly.

"I really hope I do not see what I am seeing right now," Peanut said rather impassioned. "Because when I see my homie on the ground like that, I think someone is trying to hurt him. And when someone tries to hurt him, they are trying to hurt me. And that just can't happen." He came over and helped me up. No one stopped him. No one got in his way. The man who I hit stumbled over to the other side of the bathroom. I got up and readjusted the towel.

Peanut charged the man who was still standing, grabbed him by the shirt, and threw him up against the sink. It all happened with such speed, it was like I was not there. I had never seen him grab someone before or move so quickly. "I'm going to give you a break today. If you ever even look at Barry again, or if he stubs his toe on this yard, I am coming after you. And you better thank God that I am a Christian, or you would not even be getting this warning." With that he turned him around and pushed him with all his might to the exit. The guy fell backward at the entrance of the bathroom. He got up and said nothing. And it was over—just like that.

I went back to the cell and put some clothes on. The injured man explained that the two men wanted him to bring in drugs through the visiting room to pay off an old debt from the streets. He refused, not wanting to violate the prison rules. He thanked me for "saving his life." Peanut smiled and the guy cleaned himself up and left. As Peanut and I were walking out to the yard, a few people who had heard what happened clapped as we walked by.

"They're clapping for you, Jew Boy. Be proud of yourself. You came to the rescue of the underdog and refused to be intimidated, and that makes you a real man," he said. I smiled and a proud feeling filled my stomach. My back was still a little sore from hitting the concrete.

"How did you know I was in there?" I asked. He put his arm around my shoulder as we walked down the corridor to the exit.

"Because I always got your back, Barry," he said. And whenever Peanut used my first name, he meant business. "We're kindred spirits. When you are in trouble, I will be there. Never forget that. I will always be there for you, so don't be afraid."

⁓

I picked up the picture from the bookcase. I smiled. I could not back down now. I could not just quit and walk away. Somehow, some way, Peanut was going to "have my back" covered. I was ready for anything.

⁓

I called Paul Palladino and Juan Lopez, two licensed private investigators and longtime friends. They both worked on my defense team with David Kenner in the late '80s. I needed to strengthen my case against MX Factors, and to do that I needed their help. I sent Paul to Glendale, Arizona, where a woman was pitching the MX Factors offering to investors. He would pose as an interested investor and gain information about Harkless. Then, I had Juan, who was fluent in Spanish, go to Ensenada, Mexico. When Harkless tried to convince the Better Business Bureau that my report was wrong and he did have customers, he mentioned the name of a customer in Ensenada; the company was called Olocun.

Then I called Tim France from the United States Postal Inspectors office and reported the threat I had received. He told me not to worry and that he gets threatened all the time. "Yeah, but you carry a gun," I protested.

"And you survived over seven years in prison," he shot back. "You'll be fine." With Paul and Juan on the job, I then reviewed all the public records Don Ray had submitted and reread the glossy dossier to see if I missed anything. That's when I decided to contact Pam Pallan from Business Bank of Nevada who was listed as a reference.

"Hi, Pam, this is Barry Minkow. I am performing due diligence on MX Factors and Mr. Harkless," and before I could finish she interrupted.

"Yes, I know Mr. Harkless very well. I can tell you he has been at the bank since the year 2000, and he has two million dollars in his accounts right now." I was slightly taken aback by what appeared to be a well-rehearsed answer. This was not the first time she had divulged this information.

"That's great," I said. "And he is in the factoring of receivables business for government contracts?" I asked.

"Yes, he is. He has also brought a lot of new business into the bank," she added.

"Forgive me if this sounds stupid, Ms. Pallon. I'm not a banker and not the most sophisticated financial guy in the world, but why would Mr. Harkless be willing to pay 12% every ninety days to investors or 57% annually to factor receivables when he could borrow money from the Business Bank of Nevada for a point over prime or about 6% annually?" There was a long pause on the other end. "I mean, after all, if you are giving him a good reference for investors, that means you and the bank believe in him enough, so why don't you guys save him some money and lend him what he needs?"

"Well, Mr. Minkow, to be honest with you he has never asked for a loan." And with that I thanked her for her time and the conversation ended.

There was only one reason why Harkless never asked Business Bank of Nevada for a loan and that was because he knew he could not pass the due diligence process necessary to qualify for a loan. He knew the bank would ask for things like copies of the contracts his customers were performing work on and the names of these contractors. And he knew he had neither. He also knew that banks are not blinded in their due diligence process by the promise of high returns. They make a point or two over prime—that's it—and with those small margins banks cannot afford to make bad loans. That is why they would require MX Factors to go through extensive due diligence—scrutiny that might reveal their fraud. And only someone who had been in a similar situation before would know that.

I then remembered from my initial due diligence a lawsuit that had been filed by Harkless and MX Factors against a "client" for lack of payment. Public records like lawsuits reveal interesting facts and are always worth retrieving.

As I was driving to Riverside, I called my wife and told her not to worry and that I was going to be fine. She reluctantly agreed and was relieved that I had called Tim France. My next call was to Lane, who had been threatened with the lawsuit by George Gonzales. He had calmed down a bit, and I promised him that my lawyer, Tom Lloyd from Higgs, Fletcher & Mack, would represent him at no cost to him if necessary. Tom Lloyd immediately called Lane, got him to sign a conflict of interest waiver, and sent a letter to George Gonzales at Gordon & Rees explaining that he was now counsel for Lane and that any further threats of litigation should be sent to Tom and not Lane directly. Then, with my wife and Lane satisfied, I was ready for the courthouse.

〜

According to the lawsuit filed in the Riverside County court, Harkless and MX Factors sued a large general contracting company, Edge Development, in Riverside. They claimed that Edge had promised to assign money due one of their subcontractors, Team West construction, for twenty-five thousand. Team West apparently factored a twenty-five-thousand-dollar receivable with Harkless, got paid by Edge, and then defaulted on the loan. As I was in the courthouse viewing the file, my cell phone rang.

"You see Betty Roy yet?" Barb asked.

"No, I'm a little busy right now. But I promise to see her later today." I said with an annoyed tone.

"You know that woman loves you."

"I know and I promise to be there. Anyone else call?" I asked.

"Yeah, some new guy who has been coming to the church about a week. He says he needs to see you,"

"Okay, I'll see him. Please call him and set up an appointment. Anything else?"

"Yeah, you have the elder meeting on Thursday night."

"Dang. Already?" Elder meetings were monthly, but it always seemed like they came every week to me. But as Dr. French always reminded me, the elders were not paid employees; they volunteered their time to the church, and therefore I needed to appreciate them. "Okay, no problem."

"You're not going to die are you?" Barb asked. She had talked to Lisa. Barb and Lisa had developed a close relationship. They shared a similar struggle which drew them together: trying to understand me!

"No, I'm not going to die. How would you ever survive without me?" I asked, trying to make light of the situation.

"Oh, I think I could manage. Life would sure be a lot less hectic."

"I'll be fine," I assured her. The lady who lent me the file was giving me a dirty look. Apparently, cell phones were not allowed in the room. I hung up with Barb, apologized, and went back to the file.

It was a simple complaint filed by George Gonzales on behalf of Rick Harkless alleging basically that Edge should have paid MX Factors instead of Team West. Yet the simple places were often where the big breaks lay. For Harkless to file a suit as a lending company, he must have a California lenders license. I gave the file back to the clerk and ran outside to use my cell phone.

I called the California Department of Corporations and asked if MX Factors or Richard Harkless had a lenders license. Under the California Finance Lenders Law, any company that lends recourse money in the state of California—that is money where if the funds are not paid by the borrower then the lender has the right to collect or have recourse against the borrower—needs to have a lenders license. Neither Harkless nor MX Factors possessed a lenders license. And since he was charging the few clients that he did have between 5% and 10% every sixty days, that made Harkless a usurer. And the evidence that he was lending was right in the lawsuit filed by his own attorney!

⁓

"Boy, you ain't no good," Betty Roy said. "I've been in this hospital for three days waiting for you to show up. You're out there doing all these other things when you need to be taking care of your church. Boy! What am I going to do with you?" It was about 9:00 p.m. and the drive from Riverside on the 15 north had been jammed with traffic. I was tired. The truth of the matter was I hated hospital visits. They always reminded me of the last days of my father's life. The sterile smell. The IVs and tubes hanging off of the beds. I avoided these visits as often as possible, but sometimes a pastor had to show up. This was one of those times.

I spent an hour with Betty Roy. She was a dear lady. Her surgery was successful, and she was recovering nicely. In a strange way she reminded me of Peanut. Very direct, firm in her faith, and loving. I gave her a hug. Just as I was about to leave, she grabbed for my hand.

"I am praying that God watches over you," she said and then flashed me a reassuring smile.

"Is it that obvious that I need watching over?" I asked.

She just kept on smiling.

౻

Paul Palladino and Juan Lopez had completed their work and reported back to me. Juan found the articles of incorporation for Olocun (not an easy task in Mexico but he was well connected). According to the corporate records, Richard Harkless and his wife owned 22% of that company. Juan said the company was, of all things, a crab capturing company. What an American factoring company had to do with crab fishing and capturing, I did not know. I knew I needed to find out. One thing was for sure: this crab capturing company was not factoring fifty million in receivables through MX Factors. Juan had brought back pictures of the Olocun offices. It was a small, un-impressive, very rundown operation.

Paul met with one of Harkless's brokers in Glendale, Arizona. The lady was nice and confirmed most of what we already knew about the company. They financed contractors who were awarded government contracts. She said that she received commissions for raising money for MX Factors. Paul Palladino concluded that Harkless was offering a security through un-licensed broker dealers. The evidence was mounting. I forwarded all of our research to the California Department of Corporations and Tim France at the United States Postal Inspector's office.

There was really only one thing left to do—find out the tie-in between the crab fishing operation in Ensenada and Richard Harkless. To do that I pored over the documents again and came across a reference list from an investor package that Paul Palladino received from Arizona that contained a few names of investors as references that I had not yet seen.

One of those names was Randy Harding. I called him a few hours before church on Saturday afternoon. At first I lied and said my name was "Jay" and I was a potential investor for MX Factors. I still feared tipping off the guy who had made the threatening phone call too much to disclose who I really was. But when Randy Harding said he was a Christian, I confessed that my middle name was "Jay" but I was Barry Minkow.

Immediately he knew who I was from Richard Harkless. I had become public enemy number one for MX Factors investors. I was the guy who got the Better Business Bureau to issue an unsatisfactory report against MX Factors which had made raising new funds more difficult. After he got over the initial shock of me lying about who I was, I asked him how much money he had invested in MX Factors. He said twenty-six million. The figure startled me, and I was silent for a minute. Randy Harding explained that through his company, JTL Financial Group, he had raised twenty-six million dollars from mostly "church friends" and invested it with MX Factors.

I then asked him what he knew of the crab fishing operation in Ensenada, Mexico. He said that "Rick was making a financial killing out there." I thought about his comment for a minute and then realized I needed to meet him face-to-face. I asked if he could meet with me on Monday morning in Corona, California, which was where he lived. I assured him that I had evidence that he needed to see and that it was worth his time. He agreed and the meeting was set for 8:00 a.m.

As soon as I hung up I called Tim France and left a message for him that I was meeting with Randy Harding and that Harding had told me he had raised twenty-six million for Harkless. Because Corona was a two-hour drive from San Diego, I decided to drive up Sunday evening after church and stay the night in a hotel near the Ontario Airport—not far from Corona. The city of Corona was in the midst of the greatest housing value appreciation in its history and interest rates were low—the perfect storm setting for fraud.

To prepare for the meeting I stayed up late and reread the materials, trying to figure out the connection between MX Factors and a crab catching operation in Ensenada. I thought back to ZZZZ Best, trying to put myself in the mind of Harkless. At ZZZZ Best I did not have real earnings with the restoration jobs, so I had tried to use my stock as currency to buy another company so that my fraudulent earnings could somehow be legitimized through that profitable company's acquisition. For ZZZZ Best that company was KeyServ, the subsidiary of a company in England that cleaned carpets for Sears nationwide. That's when it hit me. I sat up in my bed as if the lights had just come on: *the crab fishing business in Mexico is Rick Harkless's "cure."*

౿

I woke up with a migraine headache—just my luck. Normally I would go to the hospital and get a shot of Toradohl, a non-narcotic anti-inflammatory, but I had to see Randy Harding. My stomach was nauseated and my face pale, but I had to show Harding the evidence about Rick Harkless and MX Factors. I drove to the parking lot of a Denny's restaurant. Minutes later he pulled in driving a brand-new Lexus. I opened the door to the passenger side of the car and sat down. After introducing myself and trying to conceal the pain and nausea that I was experiencing, I began to present the evidence.

I started with all the UCC-1 searches and showed how MX Factors had no customers to justify the millions of dollars they were raising. I then showed him the lawsuit where Harkless was claiming to be a "lender" yet possessed no lenders license. Then I showed him what other government contracting factors had said about the impossibility of MX Factors being able to pay 12% every ninety days for capital. I told him that the best thing for him to do was call Tim France from the United States Postal Inspectors office and explain how Harkless had made claims to him that were not true. But he was reluctant. Something was wrong.

"Don't believe me, Randy? Check this stuff out yourself," I said, trying to convince him to call France.

"But I have received commissions on the money I have raised. And if people lose their money, they will blame me," he said.

"No, they won't. You are one of many victims here. And what matters now is what you do with the truth once you are aware of it," I said. My head was pounding. I prayed that I could just hold on long enough to finish the meeting. Randy was nervous. He grabbed the steering wheel with both hands and then turned to me.

"Okay, let's say this factoring thing is not what we thought it was. I've got hundreds of people in this deal—many from my church. I even have the captain of the Orange Police Department in MX Factors," he said. "I can't face them and tell them they lost their money." He paused. "Look, Rick is down in Mexico. He owns a ten-million-dollar fishing boat and has the license to fish for crabs in a certain area. He is going to make millions through this crab catching business. He is there right now. All we need is the time for that business to succeed and then Rick can make good on all the money he owes."

I stared out the window at the people entering and exiting the Denny's. The pain in my head intensified. I rubbed my temples trying to eliminate the pain—not just from the headache but from the words Harding had just spoken. That he knew about the crab catching business and its intentions of rescuing MX Factors from investor obligations caused me to question Harding's culpability in this deal.

"Brother," I said as compassionately as I could, "if you think Mr. Harkless is going to somehow make everything right in Ensenada, you are believing a lie—"

"No, I'm not believing a lie," he interrupted. "It's really true . . ." I couldn't hear anymore. It sounded like me sixteen years earlier. Harding's faith in "the cure" had blinded his objectivity.

"Randy," I said as I placed my hand on his shoulder, "you need to call Tim France and come clean with him. Who cares what people may think of you—it's time you did what was right." I knew I wasn't getting through. No more than if someone would have told me the same thing at ZZZZ Best when I was trying to buy KeyServ and was waiting for my stock to become free-trading.

We said our goodbyes. Randy sped off into deception. He never called Tim France. He would later regret it.

⌒

On September 26, 2003, the California Department of Corporations issued a desist-and-refrain order against MX Factors, claiming that they were operating a Ponzi scheme. Hugo Martin, a reporter with the *L.A. Times*, covered the fall of MX Factors and on September 30, 2003, wrote the following:

MX Factors came to the attention of authorities through Barry Minkow, the former Reseda businessman who spent seven years in prison for defrauding investors and banks when he operated ZZZZ Best carpet cleaning.

Minkow is now a pastor and also an investigator for the Fraud Discovery Institute, a private San Diego firm that investigates potential fraud for private clients and insurance companies. . . .

The next day at home Lisa picked up the paper and read the article in the *L.A. Times* and tears came to her eyes. "I always believed in you," she said. She gave me a hug.

Tim France also called that morning and expressed gratitude for the help with the case. "We ex-convicts are good for something," I said. He laughed. And as I hung up the phone with France, I could swear that I saw Peanut out of the corner of my eye, smiling, holding a big "thumbs up" to me. He was still watching over me. I could feel it.

Within days, George Gonzales, the lawyer from Gordon & Rees, resigned as general counsel for MX Factors—which meant neither I nor Lane was in danger of being sued anymore.

Not long after the state of California issued their order, the Securities and Exchange Commission issued a similar order and civilly charged both Rick Harkless and Randy Harding with fraud and selling securities without a license.

While at a lunch meeting with the court-appointed receiver for the MX Factors fraud, Robb Evans and Associates, I asked Brick Kane, the CFO of that company, what ever happened to the crab trapping company in Ensenada. He smirked and said that Harkless poured millions of MX Factor investor money into that operation and there was little to show for it. "The boat he bought that was supposedly worth millions sold for scrap metal," he said.

I asked Kane what the final victim impact of the fraud was, and he said fifty-five million dollars. "That's over twice the victim impact of the ZZZZ Best fraud," someone at the table said.

20 THE GREED BLINDFOLD

"Wealth obtained by fraud dwindles . . ."

PROVERBS 13:11a

Barry, you've got a call on line two," Barbara shouted in a shrill voice. Her voice can cut right through walls and closed doors. The man I was counseling smiled as if giving me the okay to answer the phone.

"It'll just be a minute," I said as I held one finger aloft and darted behind to my desk to answer the phone. "Hi, this is Barry."

"Mr. Minkow, my name is Bruce McKinney and I read about you in the newspapers regarding MX Factors and Financial Advisory Consultants."

"Yes sir, how can I help you?" I said somewhat curtly, while glancing at the man in my office with a half smile.

"I recently attended a seminar at a hotel by the L.A. airport and was given a package where I was promised a 10%-*per-month* return. A good friend of mine has already invested fifty thousand dollars and now she wants me to invest. And this investment fund is supposedly endorsed by the NFL. I was wondering if you could check it out for me?" he inquired.

I don't know which claim was harder for me to process—the 10% per month or the NFL endorsement. Then I thought about the fact that people were starting to view me as a source to help them assess the authenticity of an investment. Just a few years earlier it would have been laughable, and now people were actually calling me before they invested. I did not relish this newfound trust, though—I feared it . . .

My initial response was to refer the man to a certified financial planner or lawyer. I did not want the pressure of another case because if I was forced to arrive at a conclusion and that conclusion was wrong—I was done. *Back to one and done*, I thought. After MX Factors and Financial Advisory Consultants, perhaps it was best to quit while I was ahead. *Nah.*

Then, of course, there was the more obvious question: if this deal was not legitimate, wouldn't the NFL and the people who have already invested in it have figured it out already?

I stared at the man sitting uncomfortably on my sofa. He represented the Pastor Barry side of my life. He did not know or care about the Fraud Discovery Institute or my fears of taking on another case. He wanted to resolve marital issues, and as his pastor I was his first stop for assistance. Then, on the phone was McKinney—a man who needed my help in assessing an investment. He was not interested in the fact that I pastored a church. For the first time my two lives collided at the same moment. Two unique callings—neither of which I could ignore. I told McKinney that I would call him back, and we exchanged numbers.

"Who was that?" asked the husband patiently waiting for my full attention.

"You don't want to know." I smiled and shook my head, then resumed our counseling session.

ᦡ

I called Bruce McKinney back within the hour. He explained that a company out of Florida called Ware Enterprises and Investments Inc. had an "Accredited Investment Firm" that lent short-term money to banks and brokerage firms. According to Ware Enterprises they were able to generate huge profits by performing short-term lending for certain clients.

"That's how they claim to be earning 10% per month," Bruce said with a hint of awe in his voice. I asked him to send me the materials that he was given at the conference held at the hotel. He agreed to forward them by overnight mail. Before I hung up I reminded him not to invest and not to leak any information regarding my participation to Ware Enterprises and Investments Inc. He agreed.

I hung up the phone, leaned back in my chair, and turned to my picture of Peanut. "Here we go again," I told his quiet and comforting likeness.

⁓

Lisa and I desperately wanted to start a family and had agreed to adopt. However, we added the stipulation that the adoption should be based on need. There seemed to be many Americans who wanted to adopt children from Russia or China, but not necessarily from third-world countries like Azerbaijan, Haiti, or Guatemala. After considerable prayer and discussion, Lisa and I decided to focus our efforts on finding children in Guatemala.

But there was one problem. Even though Judge Tevrizian dismissed my probation three years early and dismissed my twenty-six-million-dollar restitution order, I still had the Union Bank debt. That financial liability could easily cripple our future family. I imagined a child's crudely depicted crayon drawing of our family being crumpled up and tossed carelessly into the wastebasket.

Union Bank was represented by a San Diego-based lawyer named Dave Brody. Brody was naturally skeptical of me when he first took over the case involving my debt with Union Bank. Through consistent monthly payments and good communication, however, he had become friendly. I considered that progress because even though the debt was almost twenty years old, it was still seven million dollars which had made me public enemy number one at Union Bank for many years.

But I never worried about the Union Bank debt. The reason? Numerous bank mergers were occurring in the California area. Back in the 1980s the three major banks in southern California were Crocker Bank, Security Pacific Bank, and First Interstate Bank. Every one of these banks merged or was taken over by rival banks. So I wasn't vexed about the large debt I owed Union Bank because I was convinced that they would also be taken over or would merge with a new bank who would "wipe the slate clean" with cases like mine. But something weird happened, or rather *didn't* happen. No matter how many banks merged or were taken over, Union Bank stubbornly remained Union Bank! I couldn't believe it. Every time I opened the business section of the newspaper and some big bank merger was announced I always hoped it would be Union Bank. It certainly never stopped me from making consistent monthly restitution payments to them, but in the back of my mind I was looking for an easy way out. That never happened. It rarely does, and I should know.

With the merger option proving to be an extremely remote possibility, I had to settle for scheduling a meeting with Dave Brody. When we met, I told him that Lisa and I wanted to adopt children from Guatemala. I explained that we had originally wanted one child, but the adoption agency told us that there were twin boys, infants, and if we wanted to adopt them both we could. I told Brody that the adoption agency informed us that if we did not want to adopt both children, there was a high likelihood the boys would be raised separately in various foster homes in Guatemala. "That's one of the reasons why Lisa and I decided to adopt both boys," I said, carefully watching his face for the coming reaction, "and I need Union Bank to release their lien on my property so I can refinance our home and pay the $32,500 fee to adopt both children." His response was not what I expected.

"I will run it by the bank, Barry," he promised, and my heart leapt. "But I am going to recommend that they release the lien so that you can adopt the children." I almost fell out of my chair. To my surprise, he followed through quickly and the bank released the lien.

∽

I think every fraud perpetrator must use the same excessively priced print shop. The slick package from Ware Enterprises reminded me of my own from ZZZZ Best. It was an impressive, high-gloss dossier containing twelve pages of information touting the incredible investment success of Ware Enterprises. Other than the difference in content, the presentation materials closely resembled the MX Factors package. And the promised returns of 10% per month were the most aggressive I had ever seen. *If this guy had a way of actually earning 10% every month he most certainly would not need any investors, considering most investments do not return 10% per year!* I said to myself. I picked up the phone and punched in several digits.

"Don Ray," the voice on the other end answered.

"What are you doing?" I asked, wondering why his end had a distinctive echo.

"I'm naked. In the shower. Why, what do you got?" I shook my head and tried to keep from laughing at his admission. I could have used a little less information.

"Ten percent a month, multimillion-dollar investment deal that supposedly is endorsed by the NFL and has NFL players invested," I answered. "I need everything there is on a Mr. Warren Ware and Ware Enterprises and Investments Inc."

"Hold on, I'm getting a pen," he said. I heard some fumbling, and the sound of running water grew faint.

"Do you need me to check to see if the investment is registered?" he asked.

"No, I can do that. Get me lawsuits, judgments, that kind of thing."

"How long do I have?" Don asked. I decided to be silent and let him answer his own question. "Okay, I will have it for you in the morning," he said. "Why do I ask dumb questions? You need it yesterday blah, blah, blah . . ." I let him ramble and heard the sound of the shower again as the phone clicked.

I went back to work studying the package. *If this deal was not legitimate, how would I structure it?* I asked myself. How I answered that question would determine how I would uncover this fraud. That is because of the second irony to fraud. The first irony, of course, is the irony of the cure and the lies we tell ourselves. The second irony of fraud is that the very greed that we perpetrators count on our marks (potential investors) possessing to drive them to invest and blind their objectivity is the same greed that blinds we perpetrators and makes *us* vulnerable to detection. Greed is a one-size-fits-all blindfold that both perpetrators and investors wear in tandem. Though neither will admit it.

For someone to offer a potential investor a 10% monthly return, as seen in the Ware Enterprises deal, they are clearly relying on the fact that the investor's desire—more appropriately termed greed—for that return will weaken his or her objectivity. The interpretation of the 10% return to me, as a former perpetrator, meant only one thing: the deal could not stand strict scrutiny and had to attract investors who, dazzled by high returns, would not ask tough questions or do much digging into the viability of the investment.

I deduced that the way to uncover the fraud was simply to turn that thinking process on its head. To infiltrate this scheme, if it was in fact a scheme, I would need to pose as a potential investor, dangle a seven-figure investment over their head, and get them to want that investment so badly that they would not check me out! After all, by late December 2003, a simple Google search would reveal my involvement in the Fraud Discovery Institute and my participation in the MX Factors and Financial Advisory Consultants frauds. But if my theory that perpetrators could be snared by their own greed was true, I could offer Ware enough investment money he would in turn provide me with the information law enforcement would need to shut him down without first checking me out. Information like his bank accounts, the offering memorandum which reeled in investors, the list of current investors to see how many millions of dollars were in the fund, or even the smoking-gun evidence which blasts the news, "It's a fraud!"

Time to take the plunge. I picked up the phone and called Ware Enterprises in Orlando, Florida, and asked for an investment package. I spoke to Roderick Ware, the brother of Warren Ware and the senior accounts manager for the Ware Investment firm. I told him my name was Barry Minkow and that I was an ex-con who had served over seven years in prison but was now the senior pastor of a church in San Diego. After the phone conversation with Randy Harding where I had used my middle name to identify myself, I made a decision that when performing due diligence on these kinds of investment deals I would always disclose my real name and disclose that I was an ex-con. Then, I would place my trust to remain undiscovered in the All-Encompassing Greed Blindfold theory.

Roderick Ware informed me that he was also a pastor and that many church people were invested in the Ware Enterprises Fund. I asked him to fax me an investor list so I could call a few references, and, although at first he was reluctant to do that, when I mentioned that I was considering a one-million-dollar investment from our "church building fund," he quickly faxed over the list. The theory was starting to prove itself.

The first person I talked to from the list said that he would only talk to me face-to-face. He lived in L.A., and I agreed to meet him at a lobby restaurant in the Bonaventure Hotel. *If you want to catch financial crimes in progress you cannot be lazy*, I said to myself as I hastily headed for the door. If this deal was a fraud, every second counted since new investors were clearly being actively recruited as evidenced by Bruce McKinney and my call with Roderick Ware. The faster I could provide law enforcement with a roadmap to the fraud, the faster they could act and minimize the number of future investors.

"I gotta go to L.A.," I said as I barged into Barbara's office lugging my bag.

"Not until you give me a title to this week's sermon so I can print the bulletins!" she said perfunctorily.

"Well, it's like this: I don't have a title to my sermon yet so I can't give you one. But I promise to have it to you by tomorrow," I said, giving her my best Boy Scout honest expression.

"You said that yesterday," Barb reprimanded.

"Have I ever not been prepared for a weekend with a message?" I asked, eyes wide with mock surprise.

"No, you are always prepared, but it's easier for us if you would be prepared a little sooner," she said. I set down my bag and encircled her with a big hug and gave her a peck on the cheek. She ignored me and continued to work on her computer, wholly unimpressed with my flattery. "Another fraud case, huh?" she asked without removing her stare from the screen.

"Yeah, but this one will be quick—I promise," I said. She rolled her eyes.

"There are no easy fraud cases, Barry. Or before they make it to you, they would already be uncovered." She had a point, and I had no time to counter.

‿

The Bonaventure Hotel was always busy. People were stacked up like dominoes waiting to check in. The restaurants were overflowing and even the valet had a ten-minute wait. I met Jason at the Ciudad coffee shop right across from the front desk. He was a tall, lanky, middle-aged man who was nicely dressed. He seemed extremely intelligent and was more than happy to answer all my questions. He explained that a friend introduced him to the Ware Investment program and that he had been receiving 10%

returns each month for a year and a half. He was also quick to point out that certain Miami Dolphins and other professional athletes were invested with Ware. When I asked him to explain how Ware was able to generate enough profits to pay these kinds of returns, he pulled out one of the company high-gloss dossiers and urged me to read out loud the following explanation:

> When you make a deposit into your checking or savings account your money is guaranteed with a return. The banks invest your money in whatever ways they deem profitable. They can do this because they have the ability to borrow against your money 15-20 times over. These accounts usually return somewhere between 2-3% annually. However, when you look at the financial reports of these banks, they have profited 250 million to 1 billion in a quarter! We operate under these same guidelines, but we give our clients a greater return on their investment and a real opportunity to have financial freedom.

"You want to tell me what that means?" I asked.

"Yeah, it means that Mr. Ware does what banks do, and instead of hoarding the profits he shares them with his investors," he said levelly. I leaned back in my chair and tried to collect my thoughts. In the distance I could see a man at the front desk who appeared to be arguing over charges on his bill. I turned back to Jason and looked him square in the eye.

"Okay, Jason, so you believe that this investment is legitimate and above-board and that Mr. Ware, by acting like a bank and doing short-term loans, earns enough money to pay out 10% per month plus earn a profit for himself, because he isn't doing all this for free?"

"That's right, that's what I believe," he declared. I was dumbfounded.

What I wanted to say at that point was: "I don't think you truly believe in Mr. Ware, because if you truly believed that this deal was above-board, you would have given me the information I asked for over the phone." People who demanded this kind of rendezvous were usually concerned about something. Maybe he assumed I was a cop or a reporter. Whatever he thought, the fact that he had insisted on a face-to-face meeting was a red flag to me. In his heart he had to know there was something amiss. My job was to find out what was wrong. Evidently, Jason was not going to reveal it to me. I grabbed the check, laid down the money to cover the bill, shook his hand, and began the long journey back to the office.

During the drive home I called Don Ray to see what the public record search had yielded. He explained that Warren Ware had two judgments filed against him totaling almost $70,000. One of the judgments was filed less than a year ago for $54,816.18 and was growing daily because of the 10% annual interest being charged to Ware while the debt remained unpaid. My mind raced: *Why would a guy who earns enough money to pay investors 10% per month allow a judgment to accumulate at a 10% a year interest against him?*

❧

When I returned to my office, I called the Department of Financial Services Office of Financial Regulation in Florida to see if Ware or his investment was registered in any capacity in that state. Neither was. I received the same answer when I called the California Department of Corporations and the National Association of Securities Dealers. I checked to see if Ware Enterprises was a licensed lender in California or Florida because the very business model the company was relying on—lending money short-term to banks and brokerage firms—would require them to be licensed lenders. Even the banks they were comparing themselves to were licensed lenders! But the inquiries revealed that Ware Enterprises was not a licensed lender in any state.

After checking the regulatory issues, it was time to answer the "independent proof of profitability" question. To do that I needed a banking expert, someone with credible industry experience, who would know if Ware had tapped into a certain aspect of banking that could generate these large profits. I contacted Thomas A. Tarter of Andela Consulting Group Inc. Tarter had twenty-five years of experience as a banker and extensive knowledge on how banks and related financial institutions operate. He was often used as an industry expert witness. When I described the returns Ware was offering to investors and how he was generating these profits he told me to "get to the U.S. Attorney's office as quickly as possible." He further explained something that only an authority in the field could easily identify:

he said that the most profitable income generator for the banking industry was consumer credit cards, and even credit cards only averaged a 15% annual return, far less than what Ware would need to generate 10%-per-month returns.

My next step was to contact the other investors. Many were church people who were very complimentary about Ware. But none of them had ever seen an audited financial statement or any other independent confirmation of Ware's business activity. They all pointed to the fact that professional athletes were in the fund and Ware himself had played college football at the University of Pittsburgh, which was how he attracted professional football players and other athletes. Most investors confirmed at least twenty NFL players were currently invested. It also became clear from the interviews that Ware was the main decision maker with all investments. I was left with one last call. I needed to find the cure, so I phoned Roderick Ware again.

I knew that both Roderick and Warren had to have some plan that would somehow bring in millions of dollars and pay off all their investors. That dream or deal would serve as their motivation to keep going each day. After pressing Ware, he told me about a deal Ware Enterprises was investing in involving a man who had invented a device that would go on the gas lines of vehicles to increase gas mileage. This inventor "was very close" to signing a lucrative deal with Federal Express because, as Roderick Ware told me, they have 237,000 trucks. Ware represented that this device could increase the gas mileage on FedEx trucks from 6.5 miles per gallon to 11.5 miles per gallon. The inventor had unfortunately used all of his money in the development of the product and had no money to take it to the next level.

According to Ware, Federal Express had the device on some trucks right now and was "testing the device." Ware added that such a deal had "huge potential," and as soon as Federal Express signed a contract to purchase the device, Ware Enterprises "would be in the position to earn millions for partnering with the inventor." The cure was clearly visible but just beyond reach, as usual.

When I hung up with Roderick Ware it was time to put the pieces of the puzzle together and write the report. I mentally went over the checklist of what I had learned: there was no independent proof of profitability. The business model told to investors by Ware was untenable—the banking expert proved that. Ware was clearly using the imputed credibility of professional athletes in the fund to attract others to the fund. The investment was not registered in any state, nor was Ware a licensed lender.

I sequestered myself in my office and sat down to prepare the report on Ware Enterprises to tip off all the relevant law enforcement agencies. As I flipped through the investor list previously faxed to me by Roderick Ware, I studied the names. These were real people who had invested their life savings with Ware. I thought back to the people I had hurt with the ZZZZ Best fraud. Each of them had a story of how I had devastated them financially. Sadly, so would the people on this list. This was no game. People were going to get hurt, but if I didn't hunker down and start typing, more people would be hurt.

*

"You're investigating fraud without a private investigator's license," the caller exclaimed. I sat mutely with the phone pressed to my ear. This was all I needed in the middle of writing my report on Ware Enterprises: more encouragement from the crowd.

"I read about you in the local paper regarding MX Factors and Financial Advisory Consultants—how you have uncovered these frauds through investigations—and as a licensed private investigator I want you to know that no ex-con can be licensed to do investigations in the state of California." He finally took a breath before continuing with the accusation. "As an ex-con you have no rights, and you should not be investigating."

Forget about the obvious fact that these investigations stopped financial frauds in progress and saved people money. Somehow that had gotten lost in the pettiness of his judgment. Nevertheless, I wanted to be kind.

"Sir, let me please explain," I said calmly. "The Fraud Discovery Institute has private investigators that we use for matters that require licensing. We used two licensed investigators in the MX Factors case as law enforcement can confirm. However, to perform due diligence on investments, you do not need to be licensed. Additionally, most of what I do for the company is training and all you need is knowledge for that."

"You do need a license if you are charging money," he countered. "The law is clear on that issue."

"You are right. Now, may I send you e-mails from the people who hired me for MX Factors and Financial Advisory Consultants which confirm I did not receive a fee for my services in those cases?"

"You didn't receive a fee? How do you guys make money?" he asked in sincere surprise.

"Training," I said. "Insurance companies, CPA's, banks—anyone who wants to know how to identify the techniques perpetrators use to deceive. And please remember that we do use private investigators when the need arises—and charge for it. In fact, one of our partners in the Fraud Discovery Institute, Juan Lopez, is a licensed private investigator."

"Okay, send me the e-mails from the clients and let me confirm directly with Lopez that he is a partner and I'm satisfied," he responded. I immediately complied with his request. Juan Lopez called me later that day and said he talked to the disgruntled investigator and explained his involvement in the Fraud Discovery Institute.

"Don't let these guys get you down, Barry. You're doing a good work and the people in my field who are complaining are mad because you are getting the headlines and they are not. Keep exposing those frauds and I'm right there with you," he said.

"Juan, I'm the only one I know who could get accused of a crime while uncovering crime." We both laughed.

⁒

On January 4, 2004, I submitted my twenty-six page report on Ware Enterprises and Investments Inc. to the Securities and Exchange Commission, the FBI in Miami, the Office of Financial Regulation, the Bureau of Security Regulation for the state of Florida, and the NFL Security office in New York (who themselves were already looking into Ware and had asked for a copy of my report). Additionally, Bruce McKinney received a copy of the report because he was the one who originally asked me to check out the investment.

After reading it, McKinney forwarded a copy to the friend who had brought him to the original meeting at the hotel and another participant in the Ware fund who had four hundred thousand dollars invested. That investor called me at my home late the same evening and was furious! He said my information was inaccurate and that I was just "jealous" of Ware's success. He also accused me of "seeking headlines" for my own gain. I tried to explain to him that I was not the one happily depositing his investment checks! I was also not the one who had misled him. But his misguided anger continued, so I encouraged him to independently confirm my findings. To persuade him to check the facts contained in the report, I told him that since his name was on Ware's investment reference list, people were throwing money into the fund based on his association with Ware.

"And if you are wrong, you are partially responsible for the people you have recommended the fund to who lose their money. You want that on your conscience?" I asked. Silence greeted my question. What amazed me most was that the guy was mad at *me* and not Ware for deceiving him. It was one thing for the perpetrators to hate me and threaten me, even for other investigators to gripe, but to have the participants (victims) to join in the hate parade was unnerving.

This fraud prevention business stinks, I said to myself after spending an hour on the phone with the irate investor. *And this whole deal came to me—I didn't go looking for it.* However, the investor did concede to check out my findings. I hung up and told Lisa the whole fraud prevention business is not worth the trouble. That earned me the Master of the Obvious Award in light of the previous death threats issued during MX Factors.

I had to do something about the investor who refused to believe my report. So the next morning I had our report on Ware Enterprises intentionally leaked to certain media outlets in hopes that an investigative reporter would recognize this was a financial crime in progress and write an article about it before law enforcement acted so that further people would not invest in the company. Also, I figured that if the investor I spoke to did not believe me, perhaps he would believe an investigative reporter when something on Ware Enterprises was published. You can usually rely on people believing what they read in good old black and white type in the newspaper—especially when an ex-con didn't write it.

I also knew one more important fact about investigative reporters from my past criminal activity: all perpetrators fear what we call unknown variables (triggers which can potentially prove to be incriminating) which can neither be planned-for nor prevented during the commission of a crime. Obviously, when we plan our crimes, we follow Plan A, but there are fallback stances. Things happen that are out of our control. For example, the wife of a perpetrator catches her husband having an affair and blows the whistle on the crime; or a sudden and unexpected change in the economy wipes out the cash flow entirely. But by far the number one fear factor is the investigative reporter.

In the case of ZZZZ Best it was a persistent investigative reporter who aided in exposing the fraud. In Watergate it was the duo of Woodward and Bernstein who brought down the president. And in the case of Financial Advisory Consultants, Don Thompson, an investigative reporter with the Associated Press, used our report to break the story weeks before the company was shut down by the FBI, which probably saved potential investors hundreds of thousands of dollars. For those of us who conspire, the greatest unknown variable is the investigative reporter.

Armed with this understanding, I hoped to get someone to write about Ware. I had a track record now of being right a few times and thought, after re-reading the twenty-six-page report, I could convince a media outlet to report on a fund offering 10% per month that is not licensed, has NFL players associated with it, and has an untenable business model. I soon learned that many reporters are slammed simply trying to keep up with daily events. There was little time to dedicate to proactive investigative reporting. To my chagrin, I also received the occasional, "Just because Barry Minkow says it's a fraud does not make it a fraud. Come to me when you have a victim or when the regulatory agencies shut them down."

By then it would be too late for the victims. Two days later another investor called me who had been given the report. Apparently, it was making the rounds within the Ware investment group. The investor calmly pointed out that I was an ex-con who had no idea what a legitimate deal was because every deal I was ever involved in was fraudulent. I rubbed my fingers through my hair and stared blankly at the wall. My track record in uncovering pro-active fraud was perfect, yet no one believed me. Not the media, not the investors, not even other investigators. I did not react angrily to the cutting remarks, but he was not willing to listen to my reasoning. "I guess only time will tell," he said. "And be assured that when Mr. Ware sues you for everything you got for libel, I will be the first witness he calls to the stand." With that he hung up on me.

⸌

On January 27, 2004, the Securities and Exchange Commission obtained a temporary restraining order against Warren Ware and Ware Enterprises and Investments Inc. accusing them of orchestrating a Ponzi scheme which totaled at least $16.5 million. The very next day the Dow Jones Wire carried the story and cited the Fraud Discovery Institute for proactively providing law enforcement information used to shutdown the company. I never heard back from any of the investors who called me, and I wasn't holding my breath. However, the court-appointed receiver for Ware Enterprises, Michael I. Goldberg, called me a few weeks after the SEC shut the company down to thank me for the work I did in the Ware Enterprises case. I gratefully expressed how much his call meant to me.

"Hey Barry, you'll never guess what kind of car Mr. Ware bought with investor money in this Ponzi scheme," Goldberg said. I already knew before he answered. "A Ferrari," he said with a snort.

We perpetrators are so predictable.

NFL WARNS PLAYERS ABOUT FLORIDA INVESTMENT PROGRAM
By Phil McCarty, Dow Jones Newswires
January 28, 2004

WASHINGTON—The National Football League has warned players about investing with Florida-based Ware Enterprises and Investment Inc., which promises a 10% monthly return.

The Florida Office of Financial Regulation uncovered possible criminal activity after looking into Ware Enterprises and turned over its findings to the FBI in September, a person close to the probe said.

NFL spokesman Greg Aiello said the league investigated the Ware Enterprises investment program in response to a request from some of its players last summer. During the probe "we discovered that there are potential problems with the investment program," he said, but didn't provide further details.

As a result, Aiello said the league sent a memo to its teams and players in late July saying that they "developed information regarding possible misrepresentations" with respect to Ware Enterprises.

The memo asked players and teams to contact the NFL security office if any players had invested in the program, Aiello said. As many as 20 NFL players have invested with Ware Enterprises, Aiello said.

The NFL contacted the FBI and the Securities and Exchange Commission last summer about Ware Enterprises. In mid-October, the NFL turned over more specific information to both the FBI and SEC, Aiello said.

Calls to the FBI and SEC office in Miami went unreturned. An SEC enforcement attorney at the agency's headquarters in Washington declined to comment on the case.

Warren Ware, Ware Enterprises' president and chief investment manager, said in a telephone interview that the FBI and SEC "don't have a problem with us."

Asked about allegations of securities fraud and the NFL investigation, Ware said he doesn't have to register the program because he doesn't sell securities or invest in speculative funds. Ware added the NFL is frustrated with him because he will not provide it with information on his program.

He said his investment opportunity known as "Dreamkeeper Program" guarantees a 10% monthly return for the first 10 months, saying Ware Enterprises "has special relationships that allow it to have large returns."

Ware's brother Roderick, a senior accounts manager for Ware Enterprises, declined to say how the program invests client funds.

The head of the NFL Players Association financial advisory program, Kenneth Ballen, said he's heard of Ware Enterprises, but that it is not registered with the players union. The Players Association registers investment advisers and others who offer financial services to players.

Fraud is a real risk for NFL players. The Players Association conducted a survey showing that between 1999 and 2002, 78 players were defrauded of about $42 million. Ballen said he didn't know of any players who had invested with Ware Enterprises.

The Dreamkeeper literature says that the fund has "relationships with some of the nation's largest brokerage firms" that allow it to take part in "major initial public offerings and targets specific companies that may become participants in potential takeovers."

Ware's brother Roderick said, "If we were doing anything wrong, they would have shut us down already."

Federal law lets the SEC regulate investment contracts in addition to conventional stocks and bonds. The Supreme Court has said such contracts include "countless" plans in which people invest in enterprises in exchange for profits. . . .

A San Diego private investigator, the Fraud Discovery Institute, also has investigated Ware Enterprises and Warren Ware, and charged that Ware Enterprises has made "proclamations that the fund is endorsed by the NFL."

The NFL's Aiello and Larry Sweeny, the NFL's director of investigative services, said they have no "firsthand" knowledge that Ware Enterprises is claiming to be endorsed by the NFL. Both were aware of the endorsement claim in the Fraud Discovery report.

"We urge players to consult us about their investments, but ultimately it's up to them," Sweeny said.

The Fraud Discovery report was produced by Barry Minkow, the group's co-founder who was imprisoned for seven years for defrauding investors through his ZZZZ Best carpet cleaning company. Minkow, now an antifraud investigator, in early December uncovered an $800 million Ponzi scheme in Orange County, Calif., involving a firm called Financial Advisory Consultants.

Minkow said he interviewed several investors in Ware Enterprises and that many "immediately knew and could sometimes name NFL players that are participants in the fund."

According to Minkow's report, Ware Enterprises has more than 1,000 investors with a total of at least $100 million invested.

The report also said 15 to 17 NFL players have invested in the program in addition to some players from the National Basketball Association.

Minkow said he also has contacted the FBI and SEC about Ware Enterprises.

Ware declined to comment on Minkow's report, saying he hadn't seen it.

The head of NBA's security, Bernie Tolbert, said he is familiar with Ware Enterprises and said as far as he knows no NBA player has invested in the program.

The NBA provides training to all rookies on financial management and how to detect potential fraudulent investments. The NFL provides a similar service for their players.

The Dreamkeeper Program solicitation materials said it accepts investments ranging from $2,000 to $10 million and guarantees investors a check equaling a 10% return each month for 10 months.

"After the first 10 months are over, payment of 5% of the active account balance will be paid out monthly. That is still 60% per year before taxes," the Ware Enterprises material claims. But later in the material, Ware says the 5% per month is not guaranteed.

"The prospectus contains no independent proof of profitability (and) is clearly an unregistered security being offered in several states (and countries) by a man who is not a registered investment adviser," Minkow's report said. "The offering itself offers returns that clearly convey impropriety."

21 | THE PAST RIDES AGAIN

Special Agent Peter Norell had invited me to Quantico, Virginia. This was not the first time I had been asked to assist the FBI as a speaker. My first visit had been not long after my release from prison in 1995. I stayed three days at Quantico and even spent the night on the premises. Safest I had felt in years! Even then, I couldn't help but think how years earlier the FBI was pursuing me for fraudulent crime, and now I had been tracked down to address agents at their training headquarters.

Years ago the stone-faced crowd had seemed a bit apprehensive about my presentation, so I decided to loosen things up a bit by getting them to laugh—no easy task. While everyone was quiet I stood up, looked around, and pointed a finger at the camera filming the session. I announced in a booming voice: "It is an honor and a privilege to be here to train you today, and I noticed that you are videotaping me so that this session can be used with future classes. I think that's great, and I want to thank the FBI because this is the first time you guys have let me know *in advance* that you are taping me and I appreciate that very much."

Everyone laughed at my remark, and the session ran smoothly from that point forward. Now, in early March of 2004, over nine years and a few multi-million-dollar proactive fraud uncoverings later, I was back at Quantico.

"If I were perpetrating fraud today, here's what I would do," I said to the packed room of FBI agents. "I would simply go offshore—out of the reach of the jurisdiction of the Securities and Exchange Commission—and challenge the already overburdened FBI to come get me." The class tilted their heads and stared at me. "What I mean is that since 9/11 the Bureau has changed its priorities from white-collar crime to terrorism. And I think that an emphasis on keeping the nation safer is good, but perpetrators see the shift and that is why we are seeing a dramatic increase in white-collar crime. It is an opportunity for us," I stated with conviction. My intentions were not to offend any agents but to merely say what most of them already knew. The FBI had reallocated agents who used to work on white-collar crime to counterterrorism, and there was a void, a void that perpetrators were more than glad to see.

"The result? As long as investment fraud can be kept out of the jurisdiction of the SEC, perpetrators feel like they are untouchable. That is because the SEC brings civil cases, not criminal cases, and therefore has limitations outside of the United States.

"And if I were a criminal today, I would go to the Cayman Islands, the Bahamas, or Bermuda, set up shop, and target American investors with promises of 30% to 40% annual returns along with the intrigue of an offshore investment."

I could tell that what I was saying was resonating with the agents. Several heads bobbed in agreement. They were following my argument. Now it was time to drop the bomb on them. I had secured Special Agent Norell's permission beforehand just to make sure.

"And I brought with me one of those very investments." I stopped and passed out to each agent a brief, twelve-page offering memorandum from an offshore fund that claimed to have close to three hundred million dollars "under management" and also promised returns of 40% annually. "I have been covertly gathering information on this company for the last few months. It is my hope that one of you here today will formally initiate an investigation of this fund and put all fraud perpetrators on notice that anyone who targets American investor money through fraud and misrepresentation will be prosecuted. Anyone here have a desire to do that?"

ҩ

Because the Ware Enterprises case involved professional athletes and was carried on the Dow Jones Wire, word began to spread about the Fraud

Discovery Institute. One day I received a call from a man who worked for a local phone company and had been asked to invest in a real estate fund that was paying 18% to 27% every six months. The name of the company was Chicago Development and Planning or Chicago D&P Inc. According to the man who had been solicited, the company claimed to earn these large returns through the purchase of real estate with investor cash which enabled them to buy property without bank financing. Then the company claimed to establish profitable businesses on the properties they had purchased. This was how they generated the high returns.

"Can you check this investment out, Mr. Minkow?" he asked. I agreed to take a preliminary look into it and get back to him. *Here we go again.*

I checked out the company Web site—pretty benign in that the large returns offered to my potential client were nowhere to be found. However, the Web site did reveal that the company was owned and controlled by a woman named Pat Morgen, who began the business in Chicago, Illinois, before moving the offices to Reno, Nevada, and Emeryville, California. The Web site also boasted that Chicago D&P Inc. had made the "honor roll" of the Better Business Bureau for the years 2001 and 2002. I made a mental note of that. What was really confusing was the long list of subsidiary companies posted on the Web site. These included Nasaky Investment Group, Realtpoia Inc., Oroshima Funding Group, and Lifestyles of the Up and Coming—all of which were owned or controlled by Pat Morgen and connected to Chicago D&P Inc.

I sat back and asked the question I always did when evaluating an investment deal: *If this were a fraud, what would I be doing to perpetrate it to attract the most investors who will ask the least amount of questions?"*

That's when I remembered the diversion technique. I reevaluated the Web site with diversion in mind, and it became apparent that Chicago Development and Planning was trying to portray itself as a large corporation with multiple subsidiaries. That fact, along with the prominent display of the Better Business Bureau's honor roll award, made me think perhaps Morgen was attempting to divert attention from something while simultaneously imputing credibility to her operations.

Diversion always has two elements: "from" and "to." At ZZZZ Best I employed the diversion tactic to keep auditors away "from" the fifty million in restoration jobs that did not exist and get them focused "to" the twenty-three carpet cleaning stores that did exist and could withstand scrutiny. The key in investigating Chicago D&P Inc. was to find out what the "from" and "to" were.

When I called the client back and told him I believed there was a high likelihood that Chicago D&P Inc. was a financial crime in progress and that he would need to cooperate with law enforcement and assist me in securing further information from the company, he wobbled. "I do not want to get killed," he said plainly. "I will only cooperate with law enforcement if they do not use my name in any capacity, and I will not contact the company on your behalf. I know what happens to people who uncover these kinds of things involving millions of dollars." I wanted to say that he had no clue as to what happens to people who uncover these kinds of things, but I let it slide.

Once again I was put into the dual role of retrieving the documents by posing as an investor and then analyzing those documents. I spoke with Juan Lopez about an approach to this case, and he agreed that since the client was unwilling it would be necessary to pose as an investor. I then called Peter Norell and explained the situation. He immediately hooked me up with an FBI agent from the Oakland office. Because of past success and the recent presentation to the FBI agents in Quantico, my information was viewed as reliable and worthy of follow-up. That was a breath of fresh air amidst the usual criticisms.

I also contacted Pauline Calande from the Securities and Exchange Commission in San Francisco. Pauline and I had worked together in the Financial Advisory Consultants case, and she too was interested in Chicago D&P Inc. Finally, I phoned Tony Nevarez, the chairman of the church elder board, and explained how I was going to collect information on what seemed to be a financial crime in progress. Once again, based on past successes, he gave me free rein but did remind me to keep him in the loop.

With all my bases covered, I then called Chicago D&P Inc. and spoke with Pat Morgen. I disclosed that I was an ex-con and was currently pastoring a church in San Diego. I told her we were looking to invest two million dollars from our building fund into her company. She never asked how I heard about her company. She never inquired about my past conviction, and she never ran a Google search to find out who she was talking to about investing. She simply visited our church Web site, saw my profile and the building we had just renovated, and promised to FedEx me the paperwork to invest. She also told me that she would use our money to purchase property in Nevada, California, and Utah free and clear and then establish successful businesses on those properties. She confirmed that our church would receive between 18% and 27% every six months.

"I'll send you all this in writing," Ms. Morgen assured me. "We have hundreds of investors around the country right now receiving these returns." But it was how she concluded our conversation that caused alarms to sound in my head. "If you invest two million dollars before April 1, 2004, I will add fifteen thousand dollars to your principle investment." It did not take an MBA degree in finance to see the flaws in this offer. Merrill Lynch, Janus, or any other legitimate fund never gives incentives to new investors by offering to increase the amount of their principle investment. Morgen was obviously desperate for new money, so she implemented the ticking-clock deadline for us to invest.

～

"Don Ray."

"Can't you just answer your phone like normal people and say 'hello'?" I asked.

"There is nothing normal about me," Don confessed. I did not argue.

"We've got another one," I said.

"Good. I'm ready."

"The name of the company is Chicago Development and Planning or simply Chicago D&P Inc.," I said and then spelled out the Web site address. I heard him scribbling quickly. "I want to take a different approach on this one."

"I'm listening," he said emphatically.

"I want you to run property searches in Utah, Nevada, and California on Pat Morgen, Chicago D&P Inc., and every other name, corporate or private, that you find on that Web site." I paused to give him time to catch up with my discourse. "I need to know two things. First, does this company or Ms. Morgen own enough property to generate enough revenue to pay almost 60% annually. And second, does she or the company own these properties free and clear?"

"That's an impossible request. It will take me days to gather all that information," Don complained.

"Quit whining. You're the best in the business at this kind of thing. You train law enforcement how to search public records, and now you have a real life financial crime in progress that you can help shut down by getting me this information quickly. Now I need this all in an hour . . . just kidding. Two days, Don. Two days."

"You got it, Barry. But only for you."

∾

By now I was getting pretty proficient at this fraud detection thing. Within two hours I had called all the regulatory agencies to see if Morgen, her affiliates, or Chicago D&P Inc. were licensed broker dealers or if her offering to the public was a registered security. And, as was the case with the previous high-return investments I had investigated, there was no regulatory licensing or registration in any state. Nevertheless, Pat Morgen was good on at least part of her word and sent via next-day-air the two-million-dollar contract offer with her signature and the additional fifteen thousand principle dollar increase incentive along with an 18% to 27% return every six months. In her desperation to attract new investment dollars, she literally signed the smoking-gun evidence. Enclosed was the glossy, multi-color dossier, which in my opinion now came standard with every fraud! I started to wonder if the general public was completely suckered by pretty brochures.

She also included a critical piece of information, a reference list of other investors. I spent the rest of the day calling each person on the list. The interesting thing about the names on the list was the number of military people who had invested with Morgen. There was also a record label executive who both recruited people to Chicago D&P Inc. and was invested in the fund to the tune of almost one million dollars. And, of course, there were a fair share of church people involved, including a pastor who had just given Morgen three hundred thousand dollars from their church building fund. *I wish he would have talked to me first,* I said forlornly to myself as I hung up with the pastor.

The next day Don Ray called me back and e-mailed me a list of ten properties; all were owned by Chicago D&P Inc. but most had large mortgages. Morgen had represented to me that almost all of her properties were owned free and clear. Additionally, there was no way Morgen could service the debt on these mortgages and pay investors the returns she was offering. Once again I was racing against time to alert both the authorities and the media to this financial transgression. As I plopped down at my disheveled desk to write the report, the phone rang.

"Barry, there is a caller on line one who will not give his name," Barbara said with a hint of anger. I took the call.

"I'm not going to tell you who I am," the man said, "but I have a large investment in Chicago D&P Inc., and I don't want to lose my investment. I know who you are and how you've been sniffing around calling investors. I know what you're up to; I even visited your Fraud Discovery Institute Web site." I immediately felt my stomach pitch but was somewhat happily surprised that someone else had actually performed due diligence. *Another threat,* I thought. I remained silent so he would open his mouth and prove himself stupid.

"I want to make you a deal. I want to deliver you one hundred fifty thousand in cash tomorrow morning at the Delta ticket counter, domestic, terminal B in the San Diego airport. No questions asked. And all I want you to do is drop your investigation. You don't have to lie; you don't have to say the company is legitimate; all you have to do is put the investigation on hold."

"I can't do that. I already informed law enforcement," I shot back, not knowing what else to say because I was completely shocked. What I should have said was: "No, I'm not interested—take a walk!" I could have cut this conversation off in two seconds, but I was intrigued . . . and tempted. People had threatened me, investors hated me, and most would surely blame me for exposing this fraud like they did with Ware Enterprises, and, of course, I was sure the media would respond the same way they had before when presented with a financial crime in progress: "Just because Barry Minkow says it's a fraud doesn't make it a fraud." I had grown wearily used to these responses. But a man who obviously respected my possible influence trying to bribe me was something new—and a bit gratifying.

"I'm not asking you to buy a billboard and promote Chicago D&P Inc. I'm just asking you to put the case on the bottom of the pile for a few months," the man implored. "Delta ticket counter, domestic, terminal B San Diego Airport. My plane gets in at eight a.m., and I will meet you at eight-thirty. Don't be a minute late."

"You got a phone number?" I asked. To this day I do not know why I asked that question. Perhaps it was a subconscious, impulsive reply to the offer of the almighty dollar.

"No phone number. I'm not playing games here. Be there tomorrow, get your money, and do not continue your work on Chicago D&P Inc. That's it." He hung up the phone with a loud click.

⁓

There were three calls I should have made after receiving the hundred-fifty-thousand-dollar offer. The first should have been to my wife, Lisa, who would have predictably yelled, "No way!" The second call should have been to Dr. French who would have lovingly provided reasons why I needed to report the bribe. And finally, to Tony Nevarez, who would have fired me if I even entertained the idea. I made none of those calls. Instead I began to feel sorry for myself. The stress of running a church, uncovering fraud, and writing reports had taken its toll on me. I did not realize how strongly until the temptation came draped in greenbacks. The more I thought about the phone call, the more I rationalized how I deserved the money. No one would know or find out. I wasn't committing a crime because I was a private citizen and not a law enforcement official.

The next morning I left the house like I did any other day. I had played the whole scene in my mind. I would drive to the airport, pick up the money, put it in my trunk, and be gone. I checked my watch—7:30 a.m. The car needed gas so I pulled into the Exxon station before entering the freeway. There was a hearse filling up next to me. As I undid my gas cap, I wondered if there was a body in there. The thought rekindled an unhappy memory.

⁓

"Hey Barry, how ya doing?" the case manager asked chummily as I entered his office. He stuck out his hand and added a friendly smile. I tried to remember if I made my bed that morning. If it was an inspection day and I forgot to make my bed, I could be in for a disciplinary report, which would be a first for me. I had recently been moved from FCI Englewood to the minimum-security facility in Lompoc, California. The Bureau of Prisons, based on a six-year clear conduct record, had lowered my security level and moved me closer to home so I could visit my father who had suffered three strokes.

"That depends on why you called me in here," I said cautiously.

"You're not in trouble," he said. "Can you shut my door please?" I complied as my curiosity escalated. This was certainly out of the ordinary. Normally, case managers and counselors do not have one-on-one, behind closed-door conversations with inmates. I became nervous and started shifting in my chair.

"Barry, your old case manager at FCI Englewood called me today and asked that I speak with you about something." My mind raced through all the possible bad news scenarios. But there really weren't any, so I just shrugged and waited for him to continue.

"Look, there really is no easy way to say this." I could see that he was uncomfortable, which made me even more apprehensive.

"Is it about my dad?" I asked hesitantly. My father had recently had a stroke, and I thought he was trying to tell me something tragic about my dad's health.

"No, it's not about your dad. It's about Peanut," he said, looking me straight in the eye.

"Peanut?" I smiled at the name. "What about him?" Peanut was on work release in Washington, D.C. We stayed in touch through friends and family members who forwarded our letters to one another. The Bureau of Prisons did not allow inmates to communicate with one another, but we ignored the rule. Most inmates did, and the Bureau of Prisons only enforced it when money or drugs was involved, which was not the case with our correspondence. Peanut and I needed to begin gathering the information necessary to start our own church together; since he was released before I was to a work furlough program, that meant he had the greater responsibility.

"I'm afraid he's dead, Barry," he whispered as he handed me a copy of a faxed newspaper article from the *Washington Post*. The case managers at FCI Englewood knew how close Peanut and I were and wanted to make sure I knew what happened. The full weight of gravity hit me, and my limbs turned to stone.

"He was shot in a barbershop while he was giving his eight-year-old son a haircut. . . ." His voice just kind of trailed off.

I do not remember saying goodbye to the case manager. I trudged slowly to my bunk and eased down onto the edge of my bed. It was dorm living in FPC Lompoc, not like the small rooms Peanut and I once shared. I read the article three times. Apparently, Peanut was on his second day of work release, employed as a barber at Prince George's County barbershop inside the Capital Beltway. The article said that two men dressed in dark clothing walked in, asked to use the bathroom, and as they walked through the shop, one pulled a handgun and fired several shots at Peanut.

I had to get out of the dorm. I did not want anyone to see me cry. Convicts don't cry, especially seasoned ones. There was a long walking track that encircled the prison camp. I walked around it several times trying to process the information. I threw up twice. I had to find "Big Ron Jordan" and tell him what happened. I located him as he came back from work detail and pulled him aside. He knew me well enough to know something was terribly wrong. Big Ron had moved to Lompoc camp about the same time I did from Englewood.

I told Ron the news and showed him the article. He was saddened because he knew what I did not. He knew that although Peanut had done nothing to deserve death, the fact that he had left the gang never to return to that kind of life most likely had gotten him killed. Tears streamed down my cheeks and soaked my uniform as I faced Ron and said, "Just imagine being shot and killed in front of your son. Your eight-year-old boy!"

"It's a tough life to get out of," Big Ron said. "Trust me I know, Barry."

I was mortified—stunned into silence—trying to process the information. Ron tried to comfort me. He had seen more than one dear friend die at a young age without good cause. Ron cared that Peanut had died; there was no question about it. But he was clearly not as shocked as I was, having grown up in the streets of Watts and having seen numerous close friends die prematurely.

"Look, man, if Peanut was here right now, what would he tell you?" Ron asked. Frankly, I was not in the mood to play twenty questions.

"I don't know," I replied with disgust. Ron read my face and discerned my bitter attitude. He lightly gripped my shoulder and nudged as if to awaken me.

"Look at me," he said. "You and I both know Peanut would tell you right now to not quit. To not allow his death to stop you from all the great things he knew you were capable of doing. So don't give me the 'I don't know' crap. You know exactly what he would say right now. And if you quit or give up, he dies in vain."

His lecture startled me out of my resentful mood. Ron was right. That is exactly what Peanut would have said. I gave Ron a hug out of respect and made my way back to my bunk. I picked up the last letter I had received from Peanut. After signing "Love, Peanut" he wrote what he always did in the postscript: "Don't quit on me, Jew Boy!"

∽

I squealed out of the gas station determined not go to the airport. I did not pass go, and I did not collect a hundred fifty thousand dollars. I concluded that had I gone to the airport, Peanut would have died in vain. There was no way I was going to allow that to happen.

So I went to the office and quickly finished a forty-two-page report on Chicago D&P Inc. that contained property searches proving Pat Morgen misrepresented to investors that she was buying buildings free and clear with their money. It was a complete road map to the fraud along with all the supporting documentation: banking information so law enforcement could freeze funds; a detailed investor list which included the top record label executive who was actively recruiting people into the fund and who had almost seven figures in the deal himself; the glossy dossier of the company; and the smoking-gun offer to increase my principle investment and pay 27% every six months signed by Pat Morgen personally. I wanted this report to be overflowing with supporting evidence so law enforcement could move quickly and shut down Chicago D&P Inc. for good.

On March 16, 2004, I sent the completed report to the FBI, the SEC, the United States Postal Inspector, and the California Department of Corporations. I then had our public relations people send the report to certain media outlets, hoping they would do an investigative story on the company and that future victims would see the story before investing. Shockingly I was told, "Just because Barry Minkow says it's a fraud does not make it a fraud." I got so angry with one reporter who said that phrase I practically shouted, "That's why all my reports contain corroborating evidence. It's really an either/or proposition. *Either* Ms. Morgen owns these properties free and clear *or* she doesn't. *Either* Ms. Morgen is selling an unregistered security that takes about five minutes to confirm *or* she is not. If she is, shut her down." But my argument came across as an angry rant and was therefore not persuasive. I later apologized to the reporter for my rashness.

By now I had done this enough times to learn that it took the SEC about two months from the submission of a report to the time when they would formulate their own conclusions and act. So on May 3, 2004, while I was getting ready to leave my house to speak at an insurance fraud conference in Bermuda, I was not surprised when Pauline Calande from the SEC in San Francisco called and asked me to sign an affidavit on Chicago D&P Inc. before I departed. "You know, Pauline, it's great to be on the right side of late-night SEC phones calls," I said. "I'll be happy to sign an affidavit for you."

On May 5, 2004, I read on the newswire that the SEC had frozen the accounts of Pat Morgen and Chicago D&P Inc. and accused her of fraud, misrepresentation, and selling unregistered securities. Later the SEC added contempt of court. While I sat in the airport waiting for a return flight home, I vividly recalled the tangible temptation the hundred-fifty-thousand-dollar offer had caused deep within me. My eyes filled with tears. I was still the same old Barry Minkow, one bad decision away from roaming down the path that I swore off years earlier from a prison cell. I wanted to do right but was prepared to do wrong. I hated myself for it. *I'm still a con man*, I thought bitterly.

Right then I wished that Peanut were still alive. I would have told him immediately about the offer because I could tell him anything. Feelings of loneliness were settling in like a thick wool blanket in August. I tried to comfort myself with the old adage: "Temptation is not sin—only acting on the temptation is sin." That worked for about a minute. And then I remembered the great people who had turned my life around just a few years earlier: Dr. French, Tony Nevarez, and, most importantly, Lisa. I hurried to the phone bank and made the call I feared making to Dr. French. I gave him an abridged version of the story and he listened attentively. Two kids were playing next to the payphone I was calling from, and I strained to hear his response.

"I'm very proud of you," he said.

"What was that?" I tried to politely shush the kids. "I didn't hear you, Dr. French."

"I said I'm proud of you and just because you are tempted to resort to your old ways of doing things does not make you a con man. If you were a con man, you would not have called me."

MAN IS SLAIN ON 2ND DAY OF WORK RELEASE
By Jon Jeter, *Washington Post*
November 18, 1993

On his second day of work release from prison, a barber was killed yesterday by a man who casually walked into a Prince George's County barbershop and fired several shots at close range, police said.

Relatives identified the victim as James Allen Long, 25. He started working at the Capitol Heights barbershop Tuesday as part of a D.C. Corrections Department work-release program, said his sister, Peggy Long.

James Long was shot while he worked in the shop in the 4700 block of Marlboro Pike.

Police spokesman Ken Scott said two men dressed in dark clothing walked in shortly after 1 p.m. and asked to use the restroom. As they walked through the shop, one pulled a handgun and fired several shots at Long, who was cutting the hair of a customer in the last chair, Scott said.

Investigators said they had not established a motive for the shooting or identified any suspects. Peggy Long said her brother began work release Tuesday from Lorton Correctional Complex. He served nearly four years there for striking a man with a baseball bat during an argument on a Southeast Washington street. The man later died, she said.

But James Long wanted to turn his life around, his sister said. Under the work-release program, he was freed each morning to work and required to return to prison each night.

Peggy Long said her brother was a religious man who received barber training at Lorton. His first customer at the Capitol Heights shop Tuesday was his 8-year-old son, she said.

"He had just told me yesterday that he just wanted to get on with his life," Long said. "He just wanted to take care of his son. That was his pride and joy."

The barbershop sits in a community inside the Capital Beltway that police say is a hot spot for drugs, prostitution and violence.

Cleveland Williams said he was pulling his car in front of the shop when he heard the shots.

"I was getting ready to call my wife and tell her that I was at the barbershop when I heard 'pop, pop, pop,'" Williams said. "Then I saw two young guys running by, but I really didn't think anything of it at first. Then I walked around and saw the guy's feet lying in the middle of the floor."

22 MATCHES

"No one will ever believe you, Jew Boy," Peanut said half jokingly. I simply listened as I prepared the food for his going-away party. By "food" I meant what we called the "prison special." The prison special was prepared in clean, reinforced, unused plastic trash bags. In those bags I dumped two cases of Cup of Noodles and thinly sliced pepperoni, which was sold in the commissary; three tubs of soft cheese spread and tomatoes, garlic, and onions diced to perfection (I think Big Ron, who worked in the kitchen at the time, smuggled those items out).

I then added boiling hot water to the bags (always double bag if you are preparing this at home) and sealed the bags. I used my hands to massage the outside of the bag to make sure the ingredients heated through evenly. Ten minutes later the prison special was ready for consumption.

The party was being held in honor of Peanut's departure from FCI Englewood to head back to Washington, D.C., for the pre-release program. I was assembling ten of his closest friends for the gathering in one of the upper east card rooms. Peanut was leaving, and I was heartbroken to lose the best friend I had ever had.

These types of going away parties are commonplace in prison. With a population of roughly a thousand inmates, FCI Englewood was always sending someone home or transferring him to another prison or pre-release program. The adjustment for me was mustering up enough sincere joy for those fortunate enough to be going home or moving to a facility closer to home while I was left behind with a twenty-five-year sentence in Colorado. Furthermore, and although I did not know it at the time, this would be the last time Peanut and I would ever talk. He interrupted my thoughts again.

"You hear me, Jew Boy?"

"Well, frankly you are hard to follow. Here I am preparing for your going-away party and out of the blue you come at me with this 'no one is gonna believe you' line, and somehow I am supposed to make a connection? I don't know what you mean." I shrugged and wrinkled my forehead.

Peanut smiled. This was the frustrated reaction he was seeking.

"What I mean is that I have been thinking of the last piece of advice I could give you before I left and that advice is this, *No one is going to believe that you have changed.*"

"Tell me something I don't know," I chuckled. He lightly grabbed my wrist to stop me in the middle of my culinary pursuit.

"No, I'm serious, Barry. And before everyone comes to the party tonight I wanted a chance to talk to you because I leave early in the morning." His grip relaxed as I stopped and turned toward him. "You are destined to do great things when you get out of here. There is no limit to what you will do. I've met a lot of people over these past years in prison, and there are none as talented and gifted as you. Sky is the limit for you, Jew Boy." He paused and searched my eyes for a glint of understanding.

"But despite all that—many people will simply not believe you," he declared. "They will think you are the same old Barry Minkow running another con. Be prepared!"

"That's impossible," I protested. "Once I am out of prison and paying back victims and not being one of those 'born again until you are out again' prison conversion stories, people are going to believe that I have changed. You'll see," I replied with a tone of defiance. Peanut grew quiet. It was as if he was trying to prophetically warn me of something that I was just un-willing to comprehend.

"Okay, Jew Boy. Have it your way. But I want you to remember one thing. Can you do that? Can you remember one thing?" he pleaded.

"Sure I can," I vowed.

"When you are hundreds of miles away from FCI Englewood and your prison years are long behind you, and you run into the reality of people who doubt your sincerity—remember this: I love you and I believe in you. That's all I want you to remember."

Despite our dream of one day opening a church together, we both knew there would be a period of time when we would not be together. Inmates are not allowed to associate with one another, even when released, until they are off probation or parole.

Peanut grabbed from the table some matches that I was going to use to light a few candles. Since inmates were allowed to smoke cigarettes, obtaining matches was not a difficult task. He switched the lights off and lit a match in the dark room. Our faces were barely visible from the light of the match.

"You see all the darkness around us?" Peanut asked.

"Yes," I said softly.

"All that darkness represents all the people who will doubt your motives, sincerity, and ability to change. And that can get pretty dark at times. But this match right here," he pointed out as he focused on the bright flame, "that is me in your life. And all the darkness in the world cannot overcome the power of one light, one person who wholeheartedly loves and believes in you. And I'm that person." He flipped the lights back on and blew out the match.

"Never forget that, Jew Boy. Never forget that."

ᔐ

"Barry, Steve Austin is on line one," Barbara yelled. I grabbed the phone, anxious to speak with my valued associate.

"Hey Steve, thanks for calling."

"I've got bad news," he announced in a somber tone. "Our plans for the trip to Europe are cancelled." He was right. This was not good news. The European trip had promised a high return for nine days. Steve and I were going to team up and do a fraud prevention boot camp for various accounting firms in Europe.

"How can that be?" I stammered with disbelief. "These people begged us to come out and do those four fraud prevention presentations in France,

England, Eindhoven, and Germany. How did they go from begging us to come out to canceling us?"

There was a long pause on the other end of the line. Immediately, I could tell there was something Steve was not telling me so I pressed him further.

"Look, Barry, it's because of you . . . all right?" I could tell this was difficult for Steve. He was a gentle man who never wanted to make someone feel bad. "The members of the fraud association in America refused to participate in the conference with you as the main speaker. I'm truly sorry."

I sank deeper into my chair as the shocking reality of his words filtered through to my brain. After I hung up the phone, I tried to shake off the shackles of my past. Despite having a lot of practice at being disliked, I still wasn't very good at it. Immediately, the phone in my office rang again.

"This is Barry," I said flatly.

"What did you ever do to the editor of *Week in Business* magazine?" Chris Roslan demanded. He was the publicist for the Fraud Discovery Institute who helped bring our fraud reports to the media.

"I haven't done a thing!" I exclaimed. "Don't even know the guy."

"Well, he hates you! I just talked to him about being an outlet for some of these frauds that you are uncovering and he said he did not care if you caught Osama bin Laden—he was never going to write something positive about Barry Minkow."

I struggled to process the two antagonistic calls. The devastating reports from Steve and Chris exploded like shrapnel in my mind, leaving a torrent of pain. To divert my attention, I glanced at incoming e-mails and noticed one that was entitled: "Been looking for you."

Cool, a speaking gig to replace the lost revenue in Europe, I thought. I double-clicked the bold message and it was from a college student in the Midwest who wanted me to speak at her university. As an aside the student also mentioned that to locate me, she went to a reporter who used to cover the ZZZZ Best crime back in the 1980s. The reporter's words of advice for the student trying to contact me? "Don't bother with Barry Minkow, he's still a con man."

Before I had time to sink into a deep depression over the e-mail and phone calls, my 2:00 p.m. appointment strolled in. It was my longtime friend

Rod Bleakley. I thought he needed some spiritual counseling of some kind but instead he wanted investment advice.

"Don't come to me for investment advice, Rod," I moaned. "I have failed in every business I have ever been in."

"I'll take my chances," he responded. Someone from his church had asked him to invest in TC Enterprises—also known as Triple Crown Enterprises. The company sought investor money to purchase broodmares (female horses) that would be impregnated by studs (male horses with good genes) and subsequently sold off the foals to racehorse speculators. The returns being offered were astronomical: 30% to 40% annually.

I tried to explain to Rod that I did not know the horse racing industry and that because we were close friends, I felt uncomfortable looking into the case. Additionally, the church he attended was so close to mine.

"That's exactly why you *should* look into this deal, Barry," Rod urged. "There are lots of people at my church who are already invested in TC Enterprises. And before I invest, I want you to tell me if it is a good deal or not."

"Who runs the company?" I asked.

"His name is Tim Disney," Rod said.

"Tell me he's not related to *the* Disney family," I said as I rolled my eyes. Rod smiled.

"Of course he is," Rod answered perfunctorily. As he rose from the chair he dropped the green glossy dossier from the TC Enterprises investment opportunity on my desk. "If this were some easy task, I would have done it myself."

Mr. Minkow,

Thank you in advance for taking the time to read my email. I found your name in a document that a friend shared with me regarding the MX Factors investigation. My friend forwarded me the document because I have expressed concerns about some investment activities that a close friend of mine is involved in, and the details of MX Factors (government contracts, stock certificates, guaranteed 12% return in 90 days, etc.) sounded very similar.

About a year ago, my dear friend's brother met a "private investment broker" and, since that time, he has been putting his day job aside completely and has been focusing all of his time and energy on recruiting new private investors for this broker.

I am in the entertainment industry, and investment terminology is very new to me. However, I have been skeptical of this deal and the broker since the beginning and, after reading the reports on MX Factors that you issued, I am increasingly nervous and concerned. I'm not going to go into much more detail at this time, because I'm not sure that this is still a current email address. However, I would sincerely appreciate any opportunity to speak with you regarding this broker that my friend is involved with (who is also located in Riverside, CA), and how I would go about hiring you to check this deal out. It seems that there are many "gray areas" when it comes to investments and my concern is how does one find out which investors are on the up-and-up and which ones are crossing the line.

I look forward to hearing from you soon.

Sincerely,

Ken Arnold

The e-mail arrived early Saturday morning in July of 2004. I had my newly-adopted fifteen-month-old son, Dylan, balanced in one hand while I navigated the computer with the other. Lisa and I had gone to Guatemala and picked up Robert Irwin Minkow and Dylan Gene Minkow three months earlier. We spent five days in Guatemala and left with our precious boys for California.

On that long plane ride home, I remembered sitting and thinking that I was finally a father. Steroid abuse had closed one door, but another had opened and I was exceedingly grateful. Robert was sleeping quietly on the chair next to me, and Lisa held Dylan delicately in her arms in the aisle directly across. The moment was surreal. I thought back to how God really did have His hand on me, even during the difficult times.

I remembered back to the night when I had almost committed suicide and Bob Shank called me just in time.

I thought back to Frank Gulla and the kindness he showed me when I first got out of prison—when I needed it most.

I remembered how the church, after my many failures including the tire store debacle, did not fire me but instead gave me the gift of Dr. Gene French. I sincerely wished Peanut could see me flying home with my wife and children. Dylan slapped his hand down on the keyboard, disrupting my flashback.

I shot an e-mail to Ken Arnold and asked him to call me that afternoon. He did. I learned that his friend was involved with a company called Financial Solutions operated by Chris Hashimoto. According to Ken, who was already an investor, Financial Solutions provided financing for a company that had millions of dollars in government contracts. That company was called Gentech and was based in Riverside, California. Gentech apparently made scaffolding for the C-5 aircraft. The company was willing to pay investors 10% per month to finance millions in government contracts.

I told Ken to fax me all the materials relating to the company and copies of the monthly checks he received from Financial Solutions.

෴

By Monday afternoon I had two cases in front of me, TC Enterprises from my friend Rod and Financial Solutions from Ken Arnold. Both totaled millions of dollars, and both needed my immediate attention. However, I still needed to prepare a sermon for the upcoming weekend and perform a wedding in four days.

As I sat in my office and studied the offering memorandums for both investment opportunities, doubt gradually began to creep into my mind. The criticism from the two reporters and the fraud association was taking its toll on my confidence. Although I had been out of prison for ten years, criticism remained my constant companion. I tried to act like people's hatred and the subsequent self-doubt did not bother me, but it rarely worked. After all, my downfall from the corporate world had been intrinsically linked to wanting people to like me. Back in the days of ZZZZ Best, I was convinced that the three "P's" would be the answer to meeting my deepest needs.

Through *position* (CEO of a public company), *possessions* (Ferraris and big houses), and *popularity* (all the publicity that came with the first two P's), I was convinced that I had a sure-fire recipe for being liked by people. Almost twenty years after watching that theory fail, I still struggled with the preoccupation of acceptance—dangerous if you are in the fraud exposure business.

Peanut had been right. No matter how many financial crimes in progress that I uncovered and brought to justice, or how many years I pastored a church, to many I was still Barry Minkow, the con man. I had been out of prison nearly ten years. When was doing good ever going to be good enough?

I thumbed through the two packets of information from TC Enterprises and Financial Solutions. *I don't need this,* I whined silently. *Why keep trying to do good if no one is ever going to believe that you changed?* Barb barged into the office as my self-pity was reaching an apex.

"Here's the matches you will need for the wedding this weekend. They want a unity candle in the service, and if I don't give them to you now, you'll forget later," she said. Barb noticed I was in deep thought, dropped the matches on my desk, and started to leave. Working with me for almost eight years had given her the uncanny ability to read my moods.

"Hey Barb, before you leave, would you turn out that light for a minute?" I asked. She had intelligently stopped asking questions about my unusual requests years ago. She turned the lights out, closed the door, and left. As soon as she was gone, I grabbed a match from the box and lit it. The smell of sulfur ignited my memory of the time Peanut had lit a match to show his belief in me. As the tiny flame extinguished, I was rejuvenated, ready to take on the world no matter what people thought of me.

✍

"The company, Gentech Fabrication Inc., currently has thirteen million in government contracts but has been promised by the Air Force another hundred and five million in contracts if they perform on the original thirteen million in a timely manner," Chris Hashimoto said proudly.

"Gentech builds the scaffolding for the C-5 aircraft," he continued as he showed pictures from a notebook binder of scaffolding surrounding an aircraft. The pictures were laminated and displayed neatly in a three-ring notebook.

The presentation was clearly well rehearsed. I knew because I *was* Chris

Hashimoto years earlier with ZZZZ Best at potential investor meetings. It's almost as if someone presses play and we make a canned presentation delivered with the appropriate enthusiasm and passion regardless of the fact that what we were saying was not true.

I stared at Juan Lopez who was sitting to my left in the small conference room. We had been invited to a potential investor presentation for the Financial Solutions business opportunity. Before I went to the meeting I spent two days doing background homework on Financial Solutions, Chris Hashimoto, and Gentech Fabrication Inc. It was not just the 10% monthly returns that were problematic. Gentech was not registered with the SEC, the California Department of Corporations, or the NASD. Neither was Hashimoto.

There were about ten people at the meeting, including Juan and me. "The more money the company can raise, the more contracts they can perform. That is why they are offering investors a 10%-per-month return," Chris Hashimoto droned.

"Do you have a copy of any of those government contracts?" one of the prospective investors asked. Hashimoto pulled out several copies of a government contract and handed one to each of us at the meeting. He was well prepared. Yet I was skeptical. Why? Because fraud is the skin of the truth stuffed with a lie. Sure Gentech probably had a government contract, but there is no way they had millions in contracts that could possibly be earning them enough money to offer 10% monthly returns to investors. I made a mental note to thoroughly research just how many and what size contracts Gentech had with the government.

"I'm retired Air Force and am now a parole officer for the state of California," a man said after briefly examining the contract. Hashimoto smiled.

"You're a parole officer? I'm a recently retired prison guard," Alex Martinez added with a grin. Martinez was one of the people that had invited Juan and me to the potential investor meeting. Juan flashed me a suppressed smile. The irony was downright laughable. Here I was, an ex-convict working undercover to bring a fraudulent financial crime to justice into which a parole officer and prison guard were investing.

I covertly returned a knowing smile to Juan. But then I thought about

Frank Gulla and what an awesome parole officer he had been to me. There was no way I could let this parole officer invest his life savings in Financial Solutions.

When the meeting was over, Juan and I made sure we got the parole officer's home phone number. We did not tell him that we were investigating the company but rather asked to join forces with him in performing due diligence on Financial Solutions and Gentech as potential investors.

"You go visit the company," we told him, "and we will call the investors currently in the deal to confirm that they are getting their 10% per month. Then we can compare notes, but let's all hold off on investing until we talk." Thankfully, the parole officer agreed.

When I got back to the office I checked out the government contract that Chris Hashimoto had passed out at the meeting. After several calls and faxes to the Defense Contract Management Agency, I was told that the contract given to me at the investor meeting was for $391,424. I also learned that the other contract Gentech had with the government had been terminated; currently, the Gentech Fabrication Inc. had a total of $391,424 in government contracts. Not a penny more. The company and Hashimoto failed the independent proof-of-profitability test.

It took another day to contact all the current investors. These investors ranged in profession from state employees to teachers to small business owners. They were the kind of people that could not afford to lose their principal investment. I realized that I had to act quickly.

I called Peter Delgreco at the Securities and Exchange Commission in Los Angeles. Peter was a staff attorney with the SEC whom I had worked with on a few cases. He was aware of the many cases I had brought to the SEC in the past year. But unlike some of the other lawyers at the SEC, Peter was always appreciative of my work and what I submitted to the SEC. He never doubted me when I made representations about what I thought was behind a certain case. He never held my past against me. As far as he was concerned, ZZZZ Best was a distant memory, and it was what I was doing today that mattered most.

"Peter, it's Barry."

"Hi, Barry."

"I think I've got something that you need to know about," I stated. I told him about Financial Solutions and Gentech and the government contracts. I told him about the 10%-per-month returns and the many investors whom I had talked to that had put hundreds of thousands of dollars into this deal. "It's a financial crime in progress," I alleged.

Peter told me to fax him the government contract I received at the meeting and my report when I had finished writing it.

"I know you will want an affidavit from Juan Lopez about what Mr. Hashimoto said at the investor meeting," I said. The SEC normally and regularly compiles sworn affidavits and includes them in the injunctions with the federal court to strengthen their case. It was a common practice.

"I'm sorry, Barry. I thought you said that you were at the meeting and that you spoke with the investors?" Peter asked.

"That's true, Peter, but I don't look very good on a sworn affidavit. I'm a convicted felon," I said despondently.

"Not as far as I'm concerned," Peter interjected. "As far as I'm concerned you are a reliable source for the commission, and I have no problems with filing a case with your sworn affidavit."

The words sank in slowly, but they sank in. The fraud association may not have believed that I had changed; the reporters may not believe that I had changed but a single SEC attorney in Los Angeles did, a law enforcement official of all people. I relished the moment and glanced over to the picture of Peanut before responding to Peter.

"Thanks, Peter," I said hoarsely, masking the tears I fought back. "I'll get that stuff to you right away."

෴

"Mr. Engel, this is Barry Minkow. I got your name off the Internet. My research reveals that when it comes to the Thoroughbred industry, no one knows more about it than you."

"Well, that depends on who you ask," he joked. I knew right then that Don Engel from the Thoroughbred Information Agency in Northern California was the right man for the job.

I needed his expertise to evaluate the TC Enterprises, LLC investment package. I explained the investment opportunity and confessed my absolute inexperience in the Thoroughbred industry. "But investment fraud I know," I said as I launched into an explanation of my past.

Don agreed to evaluate the deal by examining the offering memorandum, reviewing the TC Enterprises official Web site, and making some calls to the company as a potential investor. While he did that, I began my research.

The first item on my list was to meet with Bret Lageson, the national sales and marketing person for TC Enterprises, LLC. We met in my office at the church. I disclosed my past criminal activities at ZZZZ Best but later found out that he attended the same church as Rod Bleakley and knew all about my past. He explained that I could earn 30% to 80% annually by investing between $50,000 and $500,000 in TC Enterprises.

"And if you don't have that kind of cash, use your IRA money," Lageson recommended. "We have all kinds of people investing in our company who are doing so with their retirement funds because they are dissatisfied with the returns they are making on Wall Street."

That reminded me of the Financial Advisory Consultants fraud case, where James P. Lewis had lasted twenty years and perpetrated one of the longest-running Ponzi schemes in American business history by convincing people to invest using their life savings. This solved a lot of problems for Lewis because people could easily put money in, but they could not withdraw it until they were fifty-seven and a half. This meant he only had to show the supposed almost 40% annual profits on paper in monthly statements as opposed to coming up with the actual cash. By using people's retirement, you get the best of both worlds. You obtain people's money and do not have to worry about giving it back for years—and by then there would most certainly be a cure for the crime.

The other advantage to this method was psychological: any investment entity that is allowed to accept IRA money *must* be legitimate. There is an imputed credibility to companies that can accept retirement money, and that fact did not escape Lageson's presentation. Perpetrators exploit any kind of credibility, just as Lewis did for twenty years. The implication is that the IRS "blesses" the authenticity of certain investment products when in reality the IRS only confirms compliance with withdrawals and deposits and does not perform due diligence on the veracity of an investment. But there was no denying this new trend in investment fraud: targeting qualified money.

Lageson went on to tell me that there would always be a demand for horse racing and he likened my investment to the gaming industry by saying, "Hey, people are always going to bet on horses. All you are doing is putting the slot machines in the casinos."

He left me with a list of investors and an investment package. I made the usual calls to the California Department of Corporations, the NASD, and the SEC to see if TC Enterprises was a registered security in Tennessee, where the company had its corporate headquarters, and in California, where it boasted of a San Diego location. There was no registration in either place. Just to make sure that this offering did qualify as a security under the law, I had Mike Jones, our general counsel at Higgs, Fletcher & Mack, examine the prospectus and provide me with his analysis. It took him three hours to concur that it appeared that TC Enterprises was offering a security that was apparently not registered.

I called the investors and learned that one of them owned a yacht and worked out a deal with TC Enterprises whereby they would charter his yacht and tour perspective investors around the San Diego harbor in hopes of impressing them and getting them to invest in TC Enterprises. Apparently, it worked like a charm. Each investor I talked to also confirmed that Tim Disney was related to either Walt or Roy but was definitely a "Disney." In fact one investor told me "right now Tim Disney is on Air Force I in Tennessee with President George Bush."

I hung up the phone and put the pieces together. First, Bret Lageson and other company officials wanted investors to know that Tim Disney was related to the Disney family. Then, they used the imputed credibility of accepting IRA money. Next, they used a yacht chartered especially to impress new investors. And to top it off, Tim Disney, the chairman of TC Enterprises, eats lunch with President George Bush. *These guys will stop at nothing to divert attention from the investment deal to the people involved, the yacht, and any other diversion they can think of,* I thought. *This has to be because the deal itself is weak and inconsistent and could not hold up to strict scrutiny.*

So I called Roy Disney's office in Burbank, California, and talked to his assistant. She told me that she would immediately check the family archives to see if Tim Disney, whom she did not recognize, was related to Walt or Roy. An hour later she e-mailed me and said that Tim Disney was not related to Roy or Walt. I was not surprised. My next call was to Don Engel. He had completed his analysis. The news was not good for those already invested in TC Enterprises.

"To put it simply, Barry, the horses they are selling, the broodmares, are not worth a fraction of what they are selling them for. Additionally, the foals they are projecting to sell for between $100,000 to $150,000 each are materially inflated. In an industry where most breeders struggle to survive, there is no way that this company can generate 30% to 80% annual returns to investors."

I called Karen Patterson at the California Department of Corporations. She is a lawyer in the enforcement division whom I had worked with on several previous cases of companies like MX Factors, Chicago D&P, and Financial Solutions. I was always impressed with Karen's tenacity and depth of knowledge in securities law. She took her job personally and hated when people were ripped off in investment scams and unregistered securities—especially the elderly. She had my complete respect.

It took an hour, but I finally finished explaining the TC Enterprises deal to Karen. I told her about the high returns, the unregistered security, the IRA money, the Tim Disney discrepancy, the yacht in the San Diego harbor, and the alleged Bush luncheon. She took copious notes, asked follow-up questions, and instructed me to overnight her all the materials. While we were on the phone she asked me if I knew that the corporate address for TC Enterprises listed on their Web site was really a Mail Boxes, Etc. P.O. Box.

"No, I did not know that, but I would have figured it out," I lied. She laughed. Over the next few days Karen and I talked at least twenty times. She also interviewed Don Engel.

The next call I made was to Peter Norell, my contact at the FBI in Washington, D.C., to ask him to check out the claim that Disney had lunch with George Bush on Air Force I in Tennessee.

"Hey Barry, great to hear from you," Peter said. "I wanted to tell you how impressed I was with your report on Chicago Development and Planning and on Financial Solutions."

"Thanks, Peter. Now I have a question. Are you my handler at the FBI?" I asked. "Should all my case referrals go through you?"

"No," he replied.

"Why, you don't like me?" I asked.

"No, I like you. But you don't need a handler because you know what you're doing. You're a credible source for the Bureau and submit research and reports that contain independent corroboration that we can confirm," he said. "But if you want to use me for your referrals, please do. And don't forget you've got training to do for us at the end of August."

I told Peter Norell about TC Enterprises, the annual returns, the yacht in the San Diego harbor, and what Don Engel had concluded. I then told him to check out Tim Disney's President Bush lunch meeting. He thanked me for all the information and told me to immediately get him the report on TC Enterprises. Within two days he had my report. I sent Peter an e-mail to see if he had received my report, and I will never forget what he added in his written reply. After thanking me for the report he said, "No one works harder for the Bureau than you, Barry."

First Peter Delgreco and then Peter Norell. Two men from the arena least likely to encourage and believe in me—law enforcement. *God certainly has a sense of humor,* I thought as I read his words.

I also learned that Tim Disney had not met with President Bush for lunch on Air Force One in Tennessee. Surprise, surprise.

⁓

"I'm calling you as a courtesy," Karen Patterson said about two weeks later. "Today the California Department of Corporations is shutting down TC Enterprises and charging them with using fraud to sell an unregistered security," she declared. *Man, that was fast!*

"I also wanted to thank you for all the hard work you put into this case. Your cooperation was invaluable, and I may have to call you as a witness later on."

"But, Karen, I'm an ex-con," I exclaimed. "A defense lawyer would tear me apart on the witness stand!"

"I know all about your background, and I also know that you are more than capable in defending your findings," she said. "Good work, Barry."

And with that the conversation ended. I called Lisa immediately. Working on Financial Solutions and TC Enterprises simultaneously meant I was putting in too many hours. Naturally, the church still needed to be pastored. That meant less time for Lisa and the boys. But Lisa never complained. She was my biggest fan.

"I'm so proud of you, honey. I hope you know that. And there is no doubt in my mind that if Peanut were here, he would be equally as proud." I knew she was right.

THOROUGHBRED INVESTMENT FIRM SKIPS HEARING, DENIES IT'S A SCAM
By Don Thompson, Associated Press
October 7, 2004

SACRAMENTO—Although California regulators shut it down in July after accusing it of bilking investors out of $15 million, a Tennessee company claiming to invest in thoroughbred racehorses is continuing to operate under a different name as its lawyers say company did nothing wrong.

TC Enterprises LLC or Triple Crown Enterprises is still doing business as Thoroughbred Champions Enterprises LLC, but it will no longer sell horses in California to comply with the July desist-and-refrain order by the California Department of Corporations, said attorney Gayle Mayfield-Venieris.

Mayfield-Venieris denied the company's activities are a scam, as the state and some investors claimed, but she wouldn't say if the company is working in other states. Messages left on the firm's answering machine in Tennessee were not returned over two days.

The firm, on its now discontinued Web site, said investors could participate in the "sport of kings" by breeding horses instead of betting on them, earning "a king's ransom" by selling broodmares and their foal. The state says the firm illegally sold unregistered securities and overstated the value of its horses, while investors complain they haven't seen the promised profits.

The state cited claims by San Diego salesman Bret Lageson that the firm collected about $15 million from American investors, 80 percent of whom were in the San Diego area. That included members of a church congregation in Rancho Bernardo who were solicited by fellow churchgoers who had previously invested, in what the department alleged was an example of affinity fraud.

The company's mailing address is a Mail Boxes Etc. drop in Alcoa, Tenn., though Mayfield-Venieris said it also has offices in nearby Maryville, Tenn.; San Diego; and Bangkok, Thailand.

After initially challenging the state's July order, the company dropped its appeal last week. Still, company officers have been falsely telling investors the now-final order isn't significant, said Corporations Department spokeswoman Susie Wong.

Dropping the appeal was a business decision, Mayfield-Venieris said, and the company did nothing wrong.

In a letter to regulators Tuesday, Mayfield-Venieris offered several responses that include:

—Selling horses doesn't count as selling securities, so it shouldn't matter that one of the firm's former salesmen had his securities license revoked. Not so, said Wong: "We've determined that this investment did involve the sale of securities. Our order stands."

—Denying that co-founder and managing partner Tim Disney ever suggested he or the company has ties to the Walt Disney family. Investors and the state say such claims were made repeatedly. Mayfield-Venieris wrote that Disney "was told as a child that he is distantly related to the Walt Disney empire."

—Mayfield-Venieris denied Lageson was ever a member or officer of the company, though she acknowledged company materials identify him as the firm's national sales manager. The state says Lageson and the company promised 25 percent to 50 percent returns on investments. Lageson did not return a telephone message, and Mayfield-Venieris said he's no longer with the firm.

—"Mr. Disney is also very active in the Republican party, as evidenced by his appointment as an Aide-De-Camp of the 21st Legislative District in the Tennessee House of Representatives and his appointment in 2003 as an Honorary Chairman of the Business Advisory Council by Majority Leader U.S. Rep. Tom DeLay."

But any Tennessean can get an aide de camp certificate, suitable for framing, just by filling out a form on the governor's Web site, and aides to Tennessee Gov. Phil Bredesen or 21st District Rep. Russell Johnson said there's no record of such an appointment.

Being called an honorary chairman of the Business Advisory Council is meaningless as anything other than "a fund-raising tool," said Chris Paulitz of the National Republican Congressional Committee, which gives out the titles. Federal campaign finance records show Disney contributed $1,500 last year and $2,500 this year; "he has not had a long history of interacting with the party," Paulitz said.

The state investigation began after disgruntled investors contacted Barry Minkow, a former federal convict turned fraud investigator who turned over his findings to the Department of Corporations. Mayfield-Venieris' letter attacked Minkow, who has helped federal and state agencies uncover several Ponzi schemes over the last year. One, Orange County-based Financial Advisory Consultants, allegedly swindled investors out of more than $814 million.

Investor Mike Uyematsu said he was guaranteed an almost immediate profit of 25 percent to 50 percent on his $22,000 investment in a broodmare and her foal in June 2003. He said he was told this spring he could sell the mare and foal for $10,000 to recoup a portion of his investment.

"Back in June I said, 'Go ahead and sell it and give us our 10 grand.' We're still waiting," Uyematsu said.

Instead he got a letter from Mayfield-Venieris' office recommending he wait until next year to get a better price, and noting there is no profit guarantee in the horses' bill of sale.

Another investor, who spoke on condition he not be named,

said he was refunded his $27,000 investment, partly by Lageson and partly by the company, though what he wanted was the extraordinary profits he had been promised. That investor says he has since talked with the FBI.

California securities regulators also are continuing their investigation, Wong said.

✺

The fallout from the closing of TC Enterprises was dramatic. The perpetrators and the people who went to Rod Bleakley's church who had invested in the company accused me of investigating the fraud so I could make their church look bad which would in turn somehow make my church look better. Others accused me of "seeking headlines" as the reason for investigating TC Enterprises. And instead of blaming the people who profited from their investment and holding them accountable for offering an unregistered security through misrepresentation, the investors went after me. They usually do. But Rod was happy—happy that he had come to me before he invested. Besides, I was used to the reactions by now, and rather than spend a lot of time defending myself, I just carried a book of matches in my pocket as a constant reminder.

✺

It took Peter Delgreco until November 4, 2004, to finally file an injunction and a cease-and-desist order against Financial Solutions. He included my six-page affidavit in his filing. The SEC alleged that Hashimoto had taken in eight million dollars. As for the parole officer who met Juan and me at the investor meeting, I e-mailed him our thorough report on Financial Solutions (it was a fifteen-page, written report that provided law enforcement with a road map to the fraud) *before* he invested. Not only was he thankful, he cooperated with Peter Delgreco and the SEC. "Thanks, Barry," he said after reading our report and speaking to the SEC. "It's hard to believe that an ex-con saved me from investing my life savings in a fraud."

PONZI SCHEME TARGETS BLACKS IN LOS ANGELES, SEC SAYS
By Don Thompson, Associated Press
November 4, 2004

SACRAMENTO—A Southern California investment scheme took at least $8 million mostly from the Los Angeles area's black community, the Securities and Exchange Commission alleged Thursday as it shut down two Riverside-based companies.

The alleged Ponzi scheme targeted black investors since at least July 2003 by offering them what the federal agency says are $150 million worth of fraudulent promissory notes in companies it said had or were in line for lucrative federal defense contracts.

Investors were told the notes paid 10 percent to 20 percent a month and were secured with a $100 million government bond, the SEC said.

Ultimately, investors in several states purchased at least $8 million worth, the SEC said. Some investors were allegedly solicited through some of the Los Angeles area's largest black churches, the SEC said.

But it said the firms may have collected millions of dollars more by soliciting hundreds of mostly African-American investors at "lavish" sales events—including a lobster and prime rib dinner Oct. 22 at the Ritz-Carlton hotel in Marina Del Rey that attracted nearly 500 people.

Those invited to the event were told Mike Tyson, Magic Johnson and other black celebrities would attend. Tyson actually attended as the guest of honor, said Lisa A. Gok, an SEC assistant regional director.

Potential investors at an Oct. 29 event in Chicago were told they would be lending money to a contractor who was going to build "invisible walls" for the FBI, the SEC alleges.

A federal judge on Wednesday granted the SEC's request for a temporary restraining order and asset freeze for Ohana International Inc., Financial Solutions, and 44-year-old Christiano Hashimoto of Riverside, the president of both companies. The judge also appointed a temporary receiver for the two companies, with a decision on permanent sanctions set for Nov. 12.

Hashimoto allegedly told potential investors that they were lending the money to government contractors, including Gentech Fabrication Inc. of Chino, which he said had $13 million in government contracts and was in line for $105 million more.

In fact, Gentech has 19 contracts worth less than $1.4 million, the SEC said. The Air Force canceled one $10.6 million contract in May after aircraft scaffolding built by Gentech proved to be unacceptable, the SEC said.

Investors were paid not in profits from the contracts, but in fees collected from their fellow investors, dozens of whom were paid extra for bringing in new clients, the SEC alleges.

"This is the first time I've seen a legitimate government contractor named in a fraud," said Barry Minkow, a convicted con artist himself who went undercover with a private investigator to help expose the alleged Ponzi scheme. Minkow is co-founder of the for-profit Fraud Discovery Institute in San Diego and has helped break up several alleged scams in the last year.

However, there's no evidence Gentech received any of the money or violated any securities laws, and the company cooperated in the investigation, said Gok.

The telephone at Financial Solutions rang unanswered Thursday. An e-mail to Hashimoto brought no immediate response. The company's corporate attorney, David Michael, did not immediately return a telephone message from The Associated Press.

❧

It is November 2004 as I write these words. I just met with Dr. French, and he told me I should to take a weekly day off. Can you imagine?

Tony Nevarez once told me that in life there are five balls that we juggle in the air. Three are glass balls, and if they drop and break there is no replacing them. Your relationship with God is one of those glass balls, your health is another, and your relationship with you family is the third.

The other two balls are rubber and can be dropped. One is your career and the other is, well, according to Tony Nevarez, it differs from person to person. However, I think that fifth ball is failure in general. You can bounce back from failure. It is everyone's fifth ball. Admittedly, some health failures are irreparable, but no failure-with-God ball is. My experience is that God always lets you bounce back with Him. He did with me.

And as for those who may doubt you in the comeback-from-failure part of your life? Find one person who believes in you, and carry some matches in your pocket.

Oh, and one more thing. Someone has just sent me a proposed business opportunity that is offering them 37.5% annual returns if they invest a hundred thousand dollars or more. I'm looking through it right now, and it is neatly packaged in a high-gloss, four-color dossier.

Wanna invest?

Class
- Video
- Unusual laws
- Introduction
- Background
- The Cart
  - Jurisdiction
- USMC